Beyond Help

A consumers' guide
to psychology

Susan Hansen
Alec McHoul
and Mark Rapley

with Hayley Miller
and Toby Miller

PCCS BOOKS
Ross-on-Wye

First published in 2003

PCCS BOOKS
Llangarron
Ross-on-Wye
Herefordshire
HR9 6PT
United Kingdom
Tel +44 (0)1989 77 07 07
www.pccs-books.co.uk

Beyond Help: A consumers' guide to psychology

ISBN 1 898059 54 3

The cover, designed by Alec McHoul and Denis Postle, is based on a
photograph by Juliana Stein, 'Eyes behind the door', which appeared in
COLORS magazine, issue 47, December 2001/January 2002, page 93. It
shows Simone, aged 19, Hospital Psichiatrico Nossa Senhora da Luz, Curitiba,
Brazil.

Cover Credit: Juliana Stein/COLORS magazine (www.colorsmagazine.com)
Design: Alec McHoul and Denis Postle

Printed by Bookcraft, Midsomer Norton, Somerset, UK

Contents

1. Co-authored with Toby Miller.
2. Co-authored with Hayley Miller.

PCCS Books — publishers of counselling, psychotherapy and critical psychology texts

CRITICAL PSYCHOLOGY DIVISION

Commissioning Editors: Craig Newnes and Guy Holmes

This is Madness:

A Critical Look at Psychiatry and the Future of Mental Health Services

Edited by **Craig Newnes**, **Guy Holmes** and **Cailzie Dunn**

This is Madness Too:

Critical Perspectives on Mental Health Services

Edited by **Craig Newnes**, **Guy Holmes** and **Cailzie Dunn**

Personality as Art:

Artistic approaches in psychology

Peter Chadwick

Spirituality and Psychotherapy

Edited by **Simon King-Spooner** and **Craig Newnes**

The Gene Illusion:

Genetic research in psychiatry and psychology under the microscope

Jay Joseph

Beyond Help:

A consumers' guide to psychology

Susan Hansen, Alec McHoul and **Mark Rapley**

Trading in the self

Once upon a time, in the early part of the twentieth century, there were such things as factory production, time-and-motion studies, the Hawthorne Effect, Taylorism and Fordism, in fact, a whole panoply of techniques for turning workers into mere objects of knowledge, for turning persons into tools of the production process, and so forth. These things are sometimes referred to as scientific management. Today, this scientific management has a bad name. And probably rightly so. Scientific management traded in the self and, in the trading, transformed it into a machine for tending other machines, with precise calculations of its energy outputs and the time it required to generate a given unit of work. But today, so the story goes, we can work at our own pace, from home if we choose; we are autonomous selves beyond the measure of the stopwatch and the clipboard. Today, to continue the story, we are supposedly task-based and object-oriented. No scientific calculation appears to mark the timing of our labour — so long as the appointed task is completed and the nominated object produced.

Plausible as it may be, what this story fails to acknowledge is that the scientific management of *production*, so prevalent in the early days of the twentieth century, has been displaced by a new scientific management of *consumption*. The early twentieth century had no television or other broadcast media, no global advertising, no mass distribution of specialist magazines and Internet sites and, to all intents and purposes, no popular psychology. At the time, the new-fangled domain of psychological help was the preserve of the rich and leisured classes. While factory workers had their every bodily movement measured and calculated, those who derived their wealth from industry could afford sufficient time and money to invest in self-analysis. They had the luxury of being allowed not only to *have* an interiority but also to have it analysed and corrected. But with the move from the positioning of the 'ordinary person' as producer to her respecification as *consumer*, attention shifted from the scientific management of the external body to the scientific management of the internal self, the mind. And the new science of psychology took over as the relevant toolkit for doing this. Today, psychology is the primary discipline on which this new scientific management of the self depends.[1]

Nikolas Rose, who coined the term 'psy-complex' (Rose, 1985) and on whose path-breaking research much of this book depends, marks this change to late modernity as follows:[2]

> television, advertising, magazines, newspapers, shop windows — the signs and images of the good life were inscribed on every surface that could carry their imprint. The new technologies of citizenship formation were to gain their power through subjective commitments and ways of life that were generated by the technique of choice and consumption. (Rose, 1990: 227)

'Choice and consumption', then, are not the mere 'lifestyle' luxuries that they once were for the middle classes who benefitted from early capitalist forms of production. Rather, they are ways of anchoring what Rose calls 'the new technologies of citizenship'. The citizen, nowadays, is she who correctly and properly lays bare her soul to suitably ratified professionals, ensuring supposedly proper mental hygiene throughout the population. The new economy of consumption absolutely requires this. So it is now our civic duty to invite TV ratings polls into our lives; to attend GP check-ups of our emotional, sexual and dietary habits; to fill in magazine quizzes which will tell us the 'true nature' of our sexualities; to be prescribed complex psychotropic drugs such as antidepressants; to log on to the Internet and make our inner feelings known to collectors of psychological data; to call phone help-lines catering to remedies for a panoply of late-modern 'conditions' from child abuse to eating disorders; to read pamphlets from government and voluntary agencies designed to cope with everything from parenting to psychosis; to enter 'competitions' so that marketing companies can register and tabulate our consumer preferences. And so on, through myriad forms of citizenship technologies.

Today, all of this is 'normal'. To refuse is to render oneself beyond official commercial citizenship, beyond help from the new scientific regimes that always appear to be 'for' the individual (you!) but which, at the same time, are the bedrock of the economic formation of post-productionist consumer calculation. In effect, the 'commodity' is no longer something you produce during your working day; rather it is you yourself. The self itself has become commoditised, so that this very self is now the basic traded commodity.

For example, why is it that what you pay for your morning news-

---

1. We use the terms 'psychology', 'psychiatry' and 'psy' interchangeably throughout this book, in the same way as Nikolas Rose (1985) uses the term 'psy-complex' to refer to all of the disciplines that concern themselves with 'mental health'.
2. We are grateful to Danielle Gallegos for unearthing this passage from Rose, and several other aspects of the shift to the late-modern and the consuming self noted in this chapter. See Gallegos (2002).

paper is much less than the actual value of the material paper you are purchasing? Say your Sunday paper costs £1.30, but the sheer volume of paper would, elsewhere, cost you more than £5.00. The reason for this apparently strange economy is this: you are not 'buying' your newspaper. Rather, its owners are selling *you* to their advertisers. The cover price you so willingly pay each morning is no more than a bonus, an occasional windfall for the decreasing pool of global media owners. In short, the consuming self is now the world economy's fundamental commodity. Is this a paradox? Yes and no, but mostly yes — especially from the point of view of the consumer herself. Hence the intervention of a discipline pre-established to both produce and deal with such structurally problematic selves.

So, central to this structural condition is the nexus between the official science of the self, psychology, and marketing. To all intents and purposes, 'applied psychology' *is* mostly marketing. As well as providing expert advice to the producers of game shows and 'reality' TV programmes, applied psy assists in, for example, advertising strategies: attempting to specify the psychological profiles of the various demographics of consumption. But this is only part of the story. At the same time, and because the consuming self is now the dominant version of the self for governmental purposes, psychological techniques of self-assessment, monitoring and surveillance are now important commodities in their own right. In fact, they may be considered *the* meta-commodity par excellence: for the dominant psychological techniques of governing populations at large have now become popular commodities actively sought and purchased by the individuals making up those populations.

This is, no doubt, a fabulous opportunity for suitably qualified professionals — in either for-profit, private practice or in what remains of socialised health care systems such as Britain's NHS — and perhaps explains the increasing popularity of university psychology courses. These new professionals can cash in their expertise, aiding an increasingly anxious clientele and, at the same time, wipe their hands of any calumny, knowing that their services are precisely definitive of what constitutes the official contemporary social 'good'. Much more so if, as in the UK's NHS, no filthy lucre actually changes hands and the practitioner is handsomely paid by the state. Indeed British psy-practitioners may feel that this arrangement relieves them from the odious charge of a vested interest in the suffering of others, of profiting from their pain. But such a belief is merely a self-serving delusion. When mortgages, new cars, foreign holidays, professional (doctoral) status and all the other trappings of a comfortable middle-class lifestyle depend upon sustaining the endless flow of clientele, then a direct pecuniary interest is at stake.[3] And this is to leave the

---

3. UK Department of Health data suggest that the average NHS psychologist's salary is £32,000 a year, with consultant psychologists being paid up to ...

cash benefits of waiting-list initiatives to one side. NHS practitioners may not — yet — engage in the sharp practices of their resolutely commercial American peers that we document later in this book but, after all, they have no need to. Thus while most UK psy-professionals may, on a charitable reading, have only an *indirect* material interest in maximising suffering, in endlessly expanding the forms of misery held to require their assistance, in increasing the numbers of people queuing at their NHS doors, they certainly have little incentive to publicly identify the emperor's state of undress. Thus, although we may be used to hearing popular complaints about, for example, commercial TV stations being licences to print money, few level the same charge against the psy-professions. They appear benign — even beneficent — as they go about the routine business of the new scientific management of trade in the self.

The purpose of this book is to lift the lid on this trade. Chapter two introduces some of the basic facts and figures that characterise the commercial psychological scene today. For example, mental health care has been estimated to be a $70 billion industry in the US alone (Dunaway, 2000). In 1892, the American Psychological Association had 31 members; by the year 2000, this had extended to 83,096 (APA, 2002). Ten million Americans are treated with anti-psychotic drugs every year (*Colors*, 2001/2002: 100). Much the same is true for the UK and Australia. Here, despite the differences in types of provision, in both the British NHS and in Australia's public and private systems, psy-practitioners report overwhelming demand for their wares. So much so that Britain's 3,500 NHS clinical psychologists are seriously contemplating the need for an increase in their number to 17,000. Perhaps in consequence of this flood of need, MIND reported that, between January and March 1999, 2,800 people in the UK received 'about 16,500' administrations of ECT, supposedly a treatment of last resort (MIND, 2002). How has this explosion of need come about? What is so attractive to consumers about their own pathologisation by the psy-professions and the drug companies, as well as a range of allied agencies and trades? We speculate that the motto of this age of psychologisation is, in fact, 'I want, therefore I am' — that there is a new and emergent discourse of the consumption of ourselves *as* our selves.

Chapter three begins by discussing two recent and crucial changes to the regulations by which psychologists are permitted to trade. In *Pax Americana*, these presage that which is to come on a global scale. The ethical changes in question are those ordered by the US Federal Trade Commission (FTC), and the American Psychological Association's (APA) subsequent erasure of the long-standing prohibition against

---

...£64,000. In Australian terms these are astronomic figures, with most public sector psychologists earning in the region of $40–50,000. Our thanks to Craig Newnes for these figures.

providing psychological services outside the context of professional relationships (especially through the media). Briefly: in 1988, the FTC found portions of the APA's 'Ethical Standards of Psychologists' to be illegal restraints of trade. The offending sections restricted the content of advertising and other public statements intended to represent the desirability of services. The APA was ordered to amend its standards on 16 December 1992. The order lifted APA prohibitions against 'truthful advertising' that presented comparisons between services, claims to provide unique services, appeals to emotions or fears, and personal testimonials. In this chapter, we examine excerpts from professional publications and the popular press to provide an historical overview of the professionalisation of psychology and of recent changes to the (permissible) relationships between psy-practitioners, the media and the ordinary consumer.

Our fourth chapter addresses what is sometimes called 'biblio-therapy': the use of manuals and self-help books to promote mental hygiene. Since 1859, with the first publication of Samuel Smiles' *Self-Help*, these manuals have become a multi-billion-dollar indus-try worldwide. What is this burgeoning phenomenon? Part of the secret to the success of the genre is that it counts on psychological help being 'intimate' or 'private'. That is, the last thing readers want, even if they are constantly called upon to do so, is to air their worries and concerns to a broad public and that to do so may count as a disorder in its own right, a kind of psychological hypochondria. As the number of official afflictions ('illnesses', 'syndromes' and 'disor-ders') has grown, particularly since the 1980s, the market for pri-vately finding the self — and, of course, finding the self *wanting* — has expanded accordingly. In this chapter, then, we look at this his-torical connection between 'therapy' and the 'privacy' of reading and examine the discursive means by which such popular 'recognition effects' can be brought off by reference to a transcribed discussion between best-selling self-help book writers.

The first part of chapter five explores the arrival and exponential growth of pop self-help texts in cyberspace. Self-help sites are amongst the most popular destinations on the world wide web (excluding por-nography sites) and are effectively an interactive short form of the paper-based genre. They too offer 'privacy' of reading, but with the possibility of supposedly anonymous interaction with others seeking to 'find themselves'. A number of self-help websites facilitate entry into a virtual 'community' as a form of extra, free, 'assistance' (group therapy with the comfort of limited self-identification) — users who gather either in themed chatrooms (on, for example, 'co-dependency', 'emotional abuse', 'shyness', 'stress', 'parenting' and 'workaholism') or who are linked through asynchronous email discussion lists.

Upwards of 110 million people seek health-related information on the Internet each year. Of this number, the largest group is com-prised of people seeking mental-health-related information. The second part of chapter five therefore attends to three instances of the 'professional' psychological site: information sites providing searchable information on common and emergent 'psychological disorders'; test sites, offering interactive 'psychological' testing services (with automated feedback); and therapy sites furnishing a series of electronically-mediated treatment options (with real-life therapists). Often, such sites are linked in a strategy designed to move users from a new awareness of the possibility that they are 'disordered'; to a series of interactive tests which may confirm their 'diagnosis' (of 'sex addiction' for instance); to an appropriate therapy site, where a range of (on- and off-line) treatment options is presented, most often on a profit-oriented, fee-for-service basis.

Chapter six turns to one official/semi-official and one semi-official/unofficial source of pop psych dissemination and (in some cases) propaganda: the information pamphlet and the popular magazine. We begin by analysing the rhetorical dimensions of 'informational' and other packaging materials in the promotion of a designedly consumer-friendly version of 'mental health'. The focal materials here are information leaflets about 'psychological problems' produced for distribution in GPs' surgeries and pharmacies by the professional and voluntary sectors of the psy-complex. They include texts aimed at broadening lay understandings of 'schizophrenia', 'bipolar disorder', 'depression' and 'anti-psychotic medications' among numerous other topical questions in the domain of (roughly) 'mental health'.

Following this, in the second part of the chapter, we examine the 'problem page' and its recent avatars, standard features of a wide range of popular magazines with target readerships as diverse as those encompassed by *Woman's Own*, *Cleo/Cosmopolitan* and *Reader's Digest*. Here, we address the psychologisation and individualisation of 'problems' in these texts. In particular we focus on the progression in the 'professionalisation' of these pages (via the changes in ascribed status of the putative advice-giving 'respondent') and also on the progressive lowering of the threshold for 'referral' to psychological experts, and the simultaneous broadening of the category of difficulties that are held to 'require' professional assistance. Of specific interest is the relatively recent trend towards graphic depictions of 'sufferers' and their 'conditions' in both reader-solicited and in-house-generated discussions of 'life's problems'.

In chapter seven, and continuing with the graphic-visual theme of chapter six, we look at how the next generation of commercial-psychological practitioners are trained via textbooks which increasingly draw upon popular culture in order to buttress their knowledge claims. Images of a dishevelled and hatchet-wielding Jack Nicholson from *The Shining* feature in pedagogic material on 'schizophrenia'. Pictures of a slightly less dishevelled Jack Nicholson dodging cracks in the pavement from *As Good As It Gets* illustrate 'obsessive compulsive disorder'. And stills of an extraordinarily dishevelled Jack Nicholson (post-ECT) in *One Flew Over The Cuckoo's Nest* appear in instructions for the management of depression. This chapter examines both the increasing use of popular cultural forms such as cinema, and also the appropriation of historical images, in the naturalisation of contemporary psychological stories about misery and madness in these texts.

In our final and concluding chapter, we look at some of the underlying reasons for the popular appeal of mass-mediated psychological help. We suggest that what such consumption goods do is to tap into and repeat a deep-seated, almost commonsensical, view of the 'modern subject', of what it is to be (any sort of) person today. This self is always divided, right from the start, into its sensuous (bodily) and thinking (mental) components, and it is continually urged, via a predominant 'politics of life itself' (Rose, 2001), to seek a resolution of its two 'sides'. Popular psychology embraces this 'model of man' and exploits it for explicitly commercial ends. Effectively it trades in a spurious ideal of human perfection and wholeness. Finally, then, we look at the history of how this peculiar idea of 'being human' came about; how such a limited and limiting story about ourselves became unproblematic and natural. And we beg to suggest possibilities for an alternative ethics and politics of the self that presages the demise of psychologised 'man'.

Our overall aim is, therefore, explicitly political. This is not a balanced book. Rather it is a balancing book, unearthing and also running counter to the massive dissemination and intrusion of psychological techniques into (indeed, *as*) the life of the consuming subject of late modernity. Everywhere today, the consumer-citizen of the global market-state is required to be inspected and to inspect themselves for si(g)ns of imbalance. They are increasingly policed and self-policed in terms of their status (or, more often, lack of it) as 'well-tempered' selves (Miller, 1993) or 'reasonable souls' (Foucault, 1990). This is a fundamental ensemble of techniques that support and bolster what has been called the 'risk society' (Beck, 2000). As Giddens reminds us, the phenomena of risk 'have entered deeply into our everyday lives' (Giddens, 1999: 52). And central to this thematics is the risk of therapy, including the risk of *avoiding* therapy. As Rose says of the late-modern self, it must:

> style its life through acts of choice and, when it cannot conduct its life according to this norm of choice, it is to seek expert assistance. On the territory of the therapeutic, the conduct of everyday existence is recast as a series of manageable problems to be understood and resolved by technical adjustment in relation to the norm of the autonomous self aspiring to self-possession and happiness. (Rose, 1992: 151)

The omnipresent possibility of risk carries the continual possibility of the failure of the self — and very little chance of its harmonic resolution. Anxiety, then, is not merely a default option (something that happens when failure actually raises its ugly head); nor is it merely a surface symptom, condition or 'syndrome'. Policing risk means that anxiety becomes the normal, routine, quotidian backdrop against which every ordinary everyday event is staged. How we drive in traffic, how we shop, which substances we ingest, how and with whom we have sex, which books we read, what clothes we wear ... and the rest of everyday decision-making: all of these are now subject to the calculations of the new psycho-scientific management. Driving, shopping, eating, fucking, reading, dressing: all such consumer activities are now open to diagnosis and therapy by the meta-commodity par excellence: capital-T Therapy. Conditions and syndromes are constantly being specified and respecified to apparently manage such otherwise uneventful events: road rage, co-dependency, shopaholism, sex-addiction, bibliophobia, fashion-victimhood.

In the brave new world of psychological types, no stone is unturned, and no turn is unstoned. You, the reader, cannot not be a consumer. And, insofar as you are a consumer, you are, by definition, an analysable entity. This book begins to scratch at the surface of that deep condition of late-modern being. It is, as the title says, a consumers' guide. But it is also a guide to the at-once simple and complex fact of *being* a consumer as such and (*as* such) being the willing or unwilling subject of the new psycho-scientific management.

References

American Psychological Association (2002) Yearly Membership, American Psychological Association. Retrieved 27 February: (www.apa.org/archives/yearlymembership.html#31)

Beck, Ulrich (2000) *What is Globalization?* Trans. P. Camiller. Cambridge: Polity Press

Colors (2001/2002) Madness/Follia. *Colors, 47* (December/January)

Dunaway, Marian (2000) Assessing the Potential of Online Psychotherapy. *The Psychiatric Times, 10.* Retrieved 15 May (www.psychiatrictimes.com)

Foucault, Michel (1990) *The Care of the Self: The History of Sexuality, vol. 3.* Trans. Robert Hurley. London: Penguin

Gallegos, Danielle (2002) Mapping Ethno-foodscapes in Australia. PhD thesis, Murdoch University, Western Australia

Giddens, Anthony (1999) *Runaway World: How Globalization is Reshaping Our Lives.* New York: Routledge

Miller, Toby (1993) *The Well-Tempered Self: Citizenship, Culture and the Postmodern Subject.* Baltimore: Johns Hopkins University Press

MIND (2002) *Shock Treatment: A Survey of People's Experiences of Electro-Convulsive Therapy (ECT).* London: MIND Publications

Rose, Nikolas (1985) *The Psychological Complex: Psychology, Politics and Society in England 1869–1939.* London: Routledge and Kegan Paul

Rose, Nikolas (1990) *Governing the Soul: The Shaping of the Private Self.*

London: Routledge

Rose, Nikolas (1992) Governing the Enterprising Self. In: P. Heelas and P. Morris (eds) *The Values of the Enterprise Culture: The Moral Debate.* London: Routledge, pp. 141–64

Rose, Nikolas (2001) The Politics of Life Itself. *Theory Culture and Society, 18* (6), 1–30

'That boy needs therapy'

A snapshot of our present

As the new millennium dawned, The Avalanches' 'Frontier Psychiatrist' — with its chorus, 'That boy needs therapy' — was an international smash hit (Avalanches, 2000). In the following year, the *Guardian* reported that Ludwig Wittgenstein, Albert Einstein and Bill Gates all share (or shared) a 'mental disorder' called 'Asperger's Syndrome' (Gold, 2001). In the year 2000, self-help book sales in the USA alone were worth $5.63 billion (Paul, 2001). In Australia, the 2001 league table of expenditure on the government-subsidised Pharmaceutical Benefits Scheme saw Zyprexa, an 'anti-psychotic', come in fifth (at an annual cost of $118 million) and the 'antidepressant' Zoloft at number ten ($64 million) (Kerin and Hickman, 2002: 6). Drug companies in the USA spent more than $2.5 billion on 'direct to the consumer' advertising in 2001 alone (Mintzes, 2002). The helpful 'facts about Zyprexa' offered by manufacturer Eli Lilly on the drug's very own webpage (www.zyprexa.com) states that 'over six million patients in 84 countries worldwide' have been prescribed the drug 'since its market entry in 1996' and that its 'successful implementation' in the UK was honoured by the granting of the Queen's Award for Enterprise in Innovation in 2000 (Eli Lilly, 2000). More recently, Kjaergard and Als-Nielsen (2002) reported a significant positive relationship between the results of so-called randomised controlled drug trials and pharmaceutical company funding of the studies in question.

Elsewhere, in the *Medical Journal of Australia*, Peter Harradine, Sydney Williams and Steven Doherty (2001) describe anti-psychotic-induced Neuroleptic Malignant Syndrome as a routinely missed condition that is a 'major cause of morbidity and mortality' (Harradine et al., 2001: 594). American psychiatrists Eri Kuno and Aileen Rothbart (2002) report that black Americans diagnosed as schizophrenic are nearly twice as likely as non-black citizens to receive depot administration of older and more dangerous 'typical' anti-psychotic medication. In a story headlined 'Death Knell For Recovered Memory', the February 1998 issue of *Psychotherapy in Australia* reports (in the 'Trade Talk' section) that, in 1997 in the US, Patricia Burgus was awarded $10.6 million in an out-of-court settlement after psychiatrist Dr Bennett Braun fraudulently persuaded her that she had 'recovered' memories of satanic child sexual abuse. Likewise, Lynn Carl was awarded $5.8 million after being persuaded by psychiatrists at a Houston hospital that she had 500 personalities and had been abused by satanists after she was admitted for 'depression'.

In Britain the number of prescriptions for antidepressants rose from under ten million per annum in 1991, to a staggering 21 million a year in 2000. The World Health Organisation (2001) estimates that by 2020 depression will be the single largest cause of global morbidity. Every year, the US has 19 million people suffering from 'a depressive disorder' and holds a National Depression Screening Day every October 'in over 3,000 hospitals, schools, retirement homes and doctors' offices across the country'. Prospective depressives are advised to 'complete a short, written test and discover if you have any early symptoms of depression' (*Colors*, 2001/2002: 98).

Writing in the *Lancet*, a worried Dr Alexander B. Nicolescu III calls for prophylactic treatment with SSRIs of *all* people admitted to hospital, for any reason, in case they could become depressed (Nicolescu, 2000). In the BBC report 'Modern Mums Suffer from Sleep Deprivation', 56 per cent of women said their sleeplessness led them to 'a state of despair' (BBC, 2002a). And the companion piece, 'Sleepless Mums "Like Drink Drivers"' warns that this should not be confused with 'post-natal depression' — in which case a doctor should be consulted (BBC, 2002b). Deborah Hope (2002) reports in the *Australian* that the study of 'suicidal' Israeli sand rats offers a new understanding of human 'genetic depression', and the consequent hope expressed by Ian Hickie, the chief executive of Australia's national depression initiative, that this will lead to a new class of antidepressant drugs.

This is truly 'the Antidepressant Era' (Healy, 1997). Recent estimates suggest that nearly 20 per cent of male Britons are diagnosable with a 'mental disorder' in any given week (Double, 2002). And in Australia, psychiatrists estimate that their GP colleagues are 'failing to recognise' the presence of 'mental disorders' in upwards of 56 per cent of the cases they see (Hickie et al., 2001). Richard Reeves, in the *Guardian* (2002), notes that 40 per cent of Britons think life is worse now than it was five years ago and asks why 'we feel so bad'. SANE Australia (corporate slogan — 'Meeting the Challenge of Mental Illness') issues a 'Factsheet' which claims that 'mental illness is common'. It continues: 'twenty in every hundred people will experience some form of mental health problem at some time in their lives' (SANE, 2000) and publicly reprimands Unilever Australasia for its Sunsilk shampoo commercial which SANE's 'StigmaWatch' campaign claims stigmatises the 'depressed'. Unilever withdrew the ad (Gauntlett, 2002).[1]

---

1. For more details, go to (www.sane.org) and follow StigmaWatch's electronic equivalent of book burning, thought censorship and lingua-fascism.

The *New Scientist* (2000: 3) editorialises that 'the human condition is now so thoroughly medicalised that few people can claim to be normal'. Double (2002) tells us that the number of psychiatrists employed in Britain's NHS has climbed to nearly 3,000, a doubling in 22 years. The global explosion of 'mental disorder' — and this consequent 'need' for more and more psy-professionals — can perhaps be gauged by the exponential growth of the American Psychiatric Association's *Diagnostic and Statistical Manual of Mental Disorders*, the DSM-IV (APA, 1994), which now contains no fewer than 357 different 'mental disorders', compared to the modest 106 forms of known madness in the first edition. Shyness — which is, along with smoking, now a psychiatric condition — is 'the third most common psychiatric disorder in the United States, after major depression and alcohol dependence. Lifetime prevalence has been estimated at 13.3%' (Double, 2002: 901–2). Shyness is not now simply a matter of difficulty with interpersonal relationships. Instead 'social anxiety disorder' (or 'social phobia') is an officially recognised 'mental disorder' with its own celebrity endorsement — Moynihan (2002) reports that 'US professional football sensation Ricky Williams' was being paid by GlaxoSmithKline to promote Paxil® (paroxetine).

Similarly, being a child can now be a form of psychopathology 'with estimates that between three and four million [American] children and teenagers have been diagnosed with attention deficit hyperactivity disorder (ADHD) and prescribed amphetamines' (Baldwin, 2000: 453), and prescription rates in Britain increasing by a factor of 15 in the three years between 1994 and 1997. In the US, the number of children between the ages of two and four using antidepressants doubled between 1991 and 1995 despite such chemicals not being approved for use on children under six (*Colors*, 2001/2002: 102). In Western Australia, it is estimated that three-quarters of all school classrooms contain children taking psychostimulants, with a survey of Australian doctors indicating that eight per cent have prescribed psychostimulants, and ten per cent have given sedatives, to children under the age of three (Hewitt, 2002: 8). The 19 February, 2001 edition of Australian *Woman's Day* features regular health 'expert' Dr David Worth answering readers' questions about asthma, the pill, and dentistry for those with heart murmurs. The health page also contains two 'factfiles', 'Nosebleeds — What can be done about them?' and 'What is ADHD?' Dr Worth tells his readers:

ADHD stands for Attention Deficit Hyperactivity Disorder, a condition found in children where they're inattentive, mischievous and slow learners. Once other causes, such as hearing or eyesight deficiency, have been eliminated the ADHD diagnosis must be accepted and treated. It is caused by a genetic lack of chemical activity in the part of the brain involved in concentration and retaining information .... Amphetamine and Ritalin stimulate

affected parts of the brain to allow the learning process to proceed .... Frequent dosing is essential and the dose required var-
ies. Psychological treatment and family support are important
in the management of this condition. (Worth, 2001: 45)

Being 'inattentive, mischievous and slow', it would seem, is now a
factual matter of brain biochemistry for the medical profession (not to
mention a handy 'factfile' to be offered to concerned readers of *Woman's
Day*). Likewise, the pharmaceutical industry describes going bald as a
'medical condition' (Moynihan et al., 2002) and advertises solutions
via 'www.seeyourdoctor.com.au' posters on suburban buses.
'Healthcare e-commerce', according to market researchers, will be worth
$370 billion by 2004 (Paul, 2001). Supporting and promoting
'healthcare e-commerce' is accomplished by a range of clever marketing schemes on the web, as well as on the buses. Type 'www.luvox.com'
into a web browser and you are redirected to a site called
'www.ocdresource.com', and a very helpful webpage providing two
options — 'The Resource Centre [general info]' and 'Club OCD [young
people]'. 'Club OCD' — a fun webpage for kids — fails to mention the
connection between taking Luvox and serious disturbances in young
people (Breggin, 2002) but reassures the young surfer that 'blaming
yourself for Obsessive Compulsive Disorder is like blaming yourself
for the colour of your eyes'. Another handy hyperlink (via the brand
name Luvox®) takes us to a page which suggests:

> Obsessive Compulsive Disorder comes in many forms, any of
> which can overpower someone's life. But LUVOX® Tablets have
> proven effective in reducing symptoms of OCD, and are widely
> prescribed for the condition. (www.ocdresource.com)

In June 2002, eminent psychiatrist Professor Norman Sartorius
editorialised that the 'stigma of mental illness begins' not with the
uninformed and ordinary malice of the public but with the 'behaviour
and attitudes of medical professionals' (Sartorius, 2002: 1470). In
March of the same year, Pfizer was publicly reprimanded by the
British Pharmaceutical Industry Association for breaching the industry code of conduct by trying to persuade GPs to prescribe
Ziprasidone, an unlicensed 'anti-psychotic' drug. Psychotropic medication was also at the centre of the 7 February 2002 story 'Pet-
owner Resemblance Evidenced in Science' shown on the Australian
Broadcasting Corporation flagship current affairs program, *The 7.30
Report*. The story described the breakthrough understanding of
human misery afforded by the administration of SSRIs to 'Noah the
Dog'. The story features both 'Noah the Dog' and Professor Judith
Blackshaw — 'an animal behaviourist on a quest to solve human
misery' — who told viewers that:

Depression and anxiety are terrible states of mind and unfortunately a lot of people suffer from them .... The big thing we're trying to achieve is to show people that the species of animals are very similar. A depressed person — and, of course, there's a lot of depression in the world — and a depressed animal are very similar. For example, I had a cat who died from depression. (ABC, 2002)

This putative inter-species continuity in misery is cemented by the next segment of the story. One Cam Day, described simply as a 'veterinarian', explains how 'depressed' dogs can be helped — and presumably this is intended to offer some reassurance to their identically afflicted owners:

Well we're giving Noah a medication called a selective serotonin uptake [sic] inhibitor, which is one of the new vogue anti-anxiety medications that we use on dogs and cats to solve a variety of behavioural disorders that they can experience. So these medications are good for these dogs. It leaves them normal. They're not tranquillisers, they're not sedatives, they're just medications designed to tip out that anxiety in their behavioural profile and make them feel so much more calm and at ease with normal everyday life. (ABC, 2002)

This is madness. And there's the rub. Not feeling 'calm and at ease with normal everyday life' is precisely the problem of the present, and not just for cats and dogs. As *New Woman* has it in April 2002: 'part of the change in the way that we move through life comes from the pressure to "live". No longer can we simply "exist"' (Tait, 2002: 75). And to 'live', to have a *'lifestyle'* rather than merely a life, we must consume.

Indigeo ergo sum — I want, therefore I am

As a snapshot of our present this presents an amazing portrait. Serious TV current affairs programs unironically (and completely uncritically) screen stories suggesting that because 'depressed' dogs do well on SSRIs, then people will do likewise. The pharmaceutical industry produces a (dangerous) pill for every ill, and record numbers of people apparently swallow them. Popular magazines inform their readers that fictitious 'disorders' of myriad shapes afflict them and their children, and that the answer is — a pill with its own webpage and 'Club OCD'. Self-help books fly off the shelves and yet, despite this, misery and madness are inexorably increasing. The ranks of the psy-professions continue to swell, and the numbers of 'chemically imbalanced' citizens soar. The 'helping' professions abuse the trust (and the brains) of their 'clients', and with every passing day another aspect of life becomes accepted as a 'medical problem'. Science is, we are told, a story of progress; but our greatest scientists and philosophers are retrospectively diagnosed as 'mentally disordered'. Our politicians declare a 'war on drugs', and the psy-professions prescribe (in many cases identical) drugs in record quantities. And, with a few exceptions — the beginnings of a *samizdat* literature is evident — there is little political protest.[2] A paradox. How on earth has this come to be?

The answer to this question is immensely complex, and here we can do little other than sketch some of the outlines. One part of the answer lies in the failure of counter-politics in so-called liberal democracies, and another lies in the self-conscious efforts of the psy-professions to precisely this end. That is, the production and marketing of the idea that the inevitable alienation, dispossession and injustice inherent in consumer capitalism is an individual and personal — rather than a political and economic — problem is, and has been from the beginning, a central self-assumed task of the psy-formations. As David Smail (1999) has put it:

> Our disillusion with and widespread rejection of what passes for politics these days — that is, for the most part, the acquisition and manipulation of power by large interest-groups — leave us exposed to ideologies at least as dangerous as those *recognized* as political. For the marketed ideology of interiority, the world of 'third ways' where public opposition is supposed to be at an end and the interests of all can be reconciled, where exhortations to 'personal responsibility', 'naming and shaming' and other forms of sanctimonious moralizing take the place of government, all these take us in to a realm of make-believe where there is only an illusion of control, and where the real, material principles of social reality threaten to run riot. (Smail, 1999; our emphasis)

The consequences of inhabiting this world of make-believe are all around us. In the West we inhabit a world saturated with advertisements, expert pronouncements and Agony Aunts all singing from the same song sheet.

Choice is always possible. We can 'just do it'. We are 'worth it'. We must internalise our happiness. We must dump our emotional baggage. The presidency of the USA is within the grasp of the lowliest in the land. If we just work hard, we can have whatever we want. The

---

2. See Newnes, Holmes and Dunn (1999; 2001), Bracken and Thomas (2001), Boyle (2002a) and Double (2002) for excellent contributions to this literature. Anti- (or Post-) psy has yet to seize an international agenda in the same way as, for example, the S11 anti-globalisation protests. This is clearly needed.

class system doesn't apply any more in Cool Britannia. In Australia we must aspire to being 'relaxed and comfortable'. À la Michael Jackson, if we are dissatisfied with even the most fundamental aspects of ourselves, they are changeable at whim. While being ubiquitously present, misery and madness are not an acceptable part of being human. There is a technical solution for every problem with which we are confronted. Material circumstances determine our happiness and nowadays celebrity is 'normality'. Look at Posh and Becks — ordinary everyday folk (even those from dodgy backgrounds) can acquire more money, possessions and property than they know what to do with. We can all have our 15 minutes of fame, and not wanting it is probably an illness. Success can be anyone's and failure is 'no fault'. Consuming will make us whole. Poverty, violence, discrimination, unemployment, racism and abuse have no contribution to make to madness and despair; 'it' (whatever 'disease' it happens to be) is 'a chemical imbalance in the brain'. Our parents have no influence on the way we turn out in the world. Driving in an inconsiderate manner, fidgeting in class and feeling sad are medical problems just like diabetes, cancer and nosebleeds. Psychologists understand unhappiness and they can help. If we just adopt some 'Good Thinking®' (Australian Psychological Society, 2002), she'll be right mate. If we buy the cleverly 'marketed ideology of interiority', the world will be fair, just and equitable and we will be happy (ever after). Misery and madness are not *moral* problems, but rather biological conditions. That boy needs therapy. And all the time the material principles of a market-based social reality no longer merely 'threaten to run riot'.

In his 'case study' of the 1980s Smail (2002) suggested that:

> Consumerism is, of course, not just a phenomenon of the eighties, but the necessary ideology of an economic system which depends for its survival on limitless expansion of the market .... The most important social function of the vast majority of the population of a country such as Britain is to consume. It is true, of course, that so far our lives as social beings are ordered, perhaps even fundamentally, by public 'forms' of morality which arise more from our common humanity than from the dictates of consumerism, but such 'forms' have become tacit, unofficial, and survive only as the embodied practice of a collectivity of individuals who no longer have access to any coherent, clearly articulated, statement of them. The only values which are made manifest to someone living an everyday life are Business values ... The ultimate Business logic is, then, to reduce the average member of the consuming class to an addict of the mass market, locked by the nervous system into an optimally cycled process of consumption, rendered immune to unprofitable distractions, dissociated from any form of solidarity which might offer resistance to the function of enjoyment.

And sustaining our incomprehension of this is a task assiduously, enthusiastically and tirelessly tended to by psy. Every day, in every way, we are found — find ourselves — wanting. For, as we will see later in this book, psychology has largely abandoned any pretence it might once have had to stand for social justice or the rights of the poor, the miserable and the dispossessed. Instead it has become, nakedly, a business. Where, once, on a romantic reading, psy may have been concerned to understand and to help 'patients', now the disciplines concern themselves with 'trade talk', 'market share' and 'consumers'.

In the Preface to *The Order of Things* Michel Foucault (1970: xv), via Jorge Luis Borges, describes a mythical and outlandish categorisation scheme contained in a 'certain Chinese encyclopaedia' for the animals of the world — those that belong to the Emperor, those that are embalmed, those that have just broken the water pitcher, those that, from a long way off, look like flies, and so on — and reflects upon the 'stark impossibility', for us, of thinking *that*. Here we would like to follow the example he, and writers like Nikolas Rose (1999) and David Smail (1999; 1993), offer and suggest that the way that we have come to think ourselves in the present is *also* an outlandish — if unacknowledged — marketed mythology. How has the evidently widely shared subscription to our current myth of our-selves been achieved? In the rest of this book, we examine the means of production, distribution and exchange of the ultimate consumer product, the 'illusion of control' that psy insists is the final solution to what it means to be human. *Indigeo ergo sum.*

On method

Since the consumption of popular psy-type 'goods' is the main theme of this book, we depend to a considerable extent on media texts of various sorts: on the net, on TV and radio, in magazines and news-papers, and via the book and pamphlet publishing industries. Clearly, the media is a prolific source of popular access to psy-based ideas. For example, according to Diefenbach (1997) audience reception stud-ies by the Daniel Yanklovich Group, Inc. in the US suggested that 87% of respondents cited television programs, including the news, as their source of information about 'mental illness', with 76% citing newspapers, 75% radio news, and 74% popular magazines. By con-trast, family and friends were cited as information sources by just over half. One study even found that stories currently in the news 'can have a significant impact' on the contents of hallucinations ex-perienced by patients in intensive care units, apparently a common post-heart-attack complication (Skirrow et al., 2002: 87). It would seem that the popular media are a crucial candidate technology for the installation of a 'psy-shaped space' (Rose, 1999: 282) at the heart of each and every consumer. This is not to say that media texts — pace SANE's StigmaWatch — have direct and unmediated effects on popular ideas and values through a kind of 'hypodermic' action on people's 'minds'. However, today, they do at least provide the main *resource* for the formation of popular understandings of, for example, 'mental illness' and proper 'mental hygiene'.

In this book, then, we examine key technological sites in the contemporary production of our selves. The way we do this is, emphatically, *not* the way in which the psy-complex routinely goes about (or at least claims to go about) creating knowledge. What Michel Foucault has called the 'positivity' of the 'knowledges' promulgated by the psy-disciplines — their incredibly rapid popular uptake and dissemination, and the power wielded by that knowledge — is in direct proportion to the strength of discipline's claim to truth. And the psy-shaped truth which we have come to tell ourselves about our selves over the last couple of hundred years is predicated on a *double* truth claim.[3] Psy claims adherence to a code of quasi-medical 'ethics' and hence claims to tell *moral* truths: the adoption (or at least the proclamation) of the use of scientific method lays claim to *epistemic* truth. Hence the pervasiveness, powerfulness and apparently commonsensical quality of what David Smail, as we have seen, called this 'realm of make-believe'. But these claims to truth are, sadly, bogus. As we will see, the profession, by the psy-disciplines, of an ethical code is a sham and the use of scientific method is little more than a rhetorical gambit. So here, in our analysis of psychology, we will not be using the methods of psy: there are no appeals to statistical significance, no randomised stratified sampling, no questionnaires, no attitude scales, no diagnostic tools. Although now completely taken for granted, the use of such methods makes the fundamental error of assuming that to be human is to be no different from being a rock, a capybara or an amœba.[4] That is, these approaches depend and rely upon a false assumption about the nature of culture.

As an alternative view, here we conceive of culture not as an atomised, and aggregable, collection of inherently meaningless phenomena which require sophisticated statistical abstraction and manipulation in order for truth to be revealed, but rather see culture as being something which Harvey Sacks (1992) described as showing 'order at all points'. That is, if we want to know about the way that, say, psychology textbooks draw upon Hollywood to reinforce conten-

---

3. The Editorial introducing the very first issue of the *British Journal of Psychology* in 1904 states that 'psychology ... has now at length achieved the position of a positive science .... "Ideas" in the philosophical sense do not fall within its scope; its enquiries are *restricted entirely to facts*' (BPS, 1904: 1; our emphasis). Of course no self-respecting modern psychologist would describe themselves as anything other than a 'scientist-practitioner'.
4. See McHoul and Rapley (2001; 2000) for a more detailed account of this position and its implications for psychology.

tious claims about madness, or how 'mental health information' sites on the world wide web persuade us that 'that boy needs therapy', it doesn't matter much at which, or at how many, one looks. If Sacks is right, any one instance of such a cultural object will reveal the shape of the culture as a whole. And as Ludwig Wittgenstein (1958) remarked: 'here is the whole: if you complete it, you falsify it'. Thus we examine — using an analytic approach often known as discourse analysis — the smoke and mirrors (Boyle, 2002b) with which the psy-disciplines (particularly via popular media forms) train us to *want to* install and to maintain, at the heart of what we have come to believe is our 'being', our very own psy-shaped space.

References

American Psychiatric Association (1994) *Diagnostic and Statistical Manual of Mental Disorders.* 4th edition. Washington: APA

Australian Broadcasting Corporation (2002) Pet-owner Resemblance Evidenced in Science. *The 7.30 Report* (7 February). Sydney: ABC

Australian Psychological Society (2002) APS Psychologists: Good Thinking. Retrieved 5 April 2002: (www.psychsociety.com.au/servicing/fr_servicing.htm)

Avalanches, The (2000) Frontier Psychiatrist. On: *Since I Left You.* Melbourne: Modular Records. MODCD009

Baldwin, Steve (2000) Living in Britalin: Why Are So Many Amphetamines Prescribed To Infants, Children and Teenagers in The UK? *Critical Public Health, 10*(4), 453–562

Boyle, Mary (2002a) *Schizophrenia: A Scientific Delusion?* 2nd edition. London: Routledge

Boyle, Mary (2002b) It's All Done With Smoke and Mirrors: Or How to Create the Illusion of a Schizophrenic Brain Disease. *Clinical Psychology, 12* (April), 9–16

Bracken, Pat and Thomas, Phil (2001) Postpsychiatry: A New Direction for Mental Health. *British Medical Journal, 322* (24 March), 724–7

Breggin, Peter R. (2002) Eric Harris Was Taking Luvox (A Prozac-like Drug) at the Time of the Littleton Murders. Retrieved 8 April: (www.breggin.com/luvox.html)

British Broadcasting Corporation (2002a) Modern Mums Suffer Sleep Deprivation. Retrieved 3 April 2002: <news.bbc.co.uk/hi/english/health/newsid_1067000/1067188.stm>

British Broadcasting Corporation (2002b) Sleepless Mums 'Like Drink Drivers'. Retrieved 3 April 2002: <news.bbc.co.uk/hi/english/health/newsid_1067000/1067188.stm>

British Psychological Society (1904) Editorial. *British Journal of Psychology, 1*(1) 1

Colors (2001/2002) Madness/Follia. *Colors, 47* (December/January)

Diefenbach, Donald L. (1997) The Portrayal of Mental Illness on Prime-Time Television. *Journal of Community Psychology, 25*(3), 289–302

Double, Duncan (2002) The Limits of Psychiatry. *British Medical Journal 324* (13 April), 900–4

Eli Lilly (2000) Facts About Zyprexa· (Olanzapine). Retrieved 27 May: (www.zyprexa.com/sch/html/Zy_facts.shtml>

Foucault, Michel (1970) *The Order of Things: An Archaeology of the Human Sciences*. No translator named. London: Tavistock

Gauntlett, Kate (2002) Media Often Insulting To Mentally Ill: Report. *The West Australian* (22 May), 14

Gold, Karen (2001) High-Flying Obsessives With Limited Social Skills. *The Guardian Weekly* (28 December–3 January), 18

Harradine, Peter; Williams, Sydney and Doherty, Steven (2001) Neuroleptic Malignant Syndrome: An Underdiagnosed Condition. *Medical Journal of Australia, 174* (June), 593–4

Healy, David (1997) *The Antidepressant Era*. Cambridge: Harvard University Press

Hewitt, Susan (2002) Child Drug Use Soars. *The West Australian* (7 May), 8

Hickie, Ian B.; Davenport, Tracey A.; Scott, Elizabeth M.; Hadzi-Pavlovic, Dusan ; Naismith, Sharon L. and Koschera, Annette (2001) Unmet Need for Recognition of Common Mental Disorders in Australian General Practice. *Medical Journal of Australia: Supplement, 175* (July), S18–24

Hope, Deborah (2002) Suicidal Rats Help Tackle the Black Dog. *The Australian* (6 June), 5

Kerin, John and Hickman, Belinda (2002) PM Orders Inquiry After Drugs Blowout. *The Weekend Australian* (13–14 April), 6

Kjaergard, Lise and Als-Nielsen, Bodil (2002) Association between Competing Interests and Authors' Conclusions: Epidemiological Study of Randomised Clinical Trials Published in the *BMJ. British Medical Journal, 325* (3 August), 249–52

Kuno, Eri and Rothbart, Aileen (2002) Racial Disparities in Antipsychotic Prescription Patterns for Patients with Schizophrenia. *American Journal of Psychiatry, 159*, 567–72

McHoul, Alec and Rapley, Mark (2000) Sacks and Clinical Psychology. *Clinical Psychology Forum, 142*, 3–11

McHoul, Alec and Rapley, Mark (2001) 'Ghost: Do not forget; this visitation/ Is but to whet thy almost blunted purpose': Culture, Psychology and 'Being Human'. *Culture and Psychology, 7*(4), 433–51

Mintzes, Barbara (2002) Direct To Consumer Advertising is Medicalising Normal Human Experience. *British Medical Journal, 324* (13 April), 908–9

Moynihan, Ray (2002) Celebrity Selling: Part Two. *British Medical Journal, 325* (3 August), 286

Moynihan, Ray; Heath, Iona and Henry, David (2002) Selling Sickness: The Pharmaceutical Industry and Disease Mongering. *British Medical Journal, 324* (13 April) 886–90

Newnes, Craig; Holmes, Guy and Dunn, Cailzie (1999) *This is Madness: A Critical Look at Psychiatry and the Future of Mental Health Services*. Ross-on-Wye: PCCS Books

Newnes, Craig; Holmes, Guy and Dunn, Cailzie (2001) *This is Madness Too*. Ross-on-Wye: PCCS Books

New Scientist (2000) 'An End to this Madness' (17 November), 3

Nicolescu, Alexander B. III. (2000) Prophylactic Antidepressant Treatment Before Patients Are Admitted [Letter to the Editor]. *The Lancet, 355* (29 January), 406

Paul, Annie Murphy (2001) Self-help: Shattering the Myths. *Psychology Today, 34* (March), 60

Psychotherapy in Australia (1998) 'Death Knell for Recovered Memory' (February), 6

Reeves, Richard (2002) Life's Good: Why Do We Feel So Bad? *The Guardian* (18 May). Available at: (www.observer.co.uk)

Rose, Nikolas (1999) *Governing the Soul: The Shaping of the Private Self.* 2nd edition. London: Free Association Books

Sacks, Harvey (1992) *Lectures on Conversation.* (ed.) Gail Jefferson. Oxford: Blackwell

SANE Australia (2000) Mental Illness: The Facts (Pamphlet). Melbourne: SANE

Sartorius, Norman (2002) Iatrogenic Stigma of Mental Illness. *British Medical Journal, 324* (22 June), 1470–1

Skirrow, Paul; Jones, Christina; Griffiths, Richard D. and Kaney, Sue (2002) The Impact of Current Media Events on Hallucinatory Content: The Experience of the Intensive Care Unit (ICU) Patient. *British Journal of Clinical Psychology, 41*, 87–91

Smail, David (1993) *The Origins of Unhappiness: A New Understanding of Personal Distress.* London: Harper Collins

Smail, David (1999) Psychotherapy, Society and the Individual. Paper presented to the 'Ways with Words' Festival of Literature. Dartington, 12 July. Available at: (www.nottm.freeserve.co.uk/talk99.htm)

Smail, David (2002) *The Origins of Unhappiness* (Chapter four. Case Study: The 1980s). [Edited web version] Retrieved 27 May 2002.(www.nottm.freeserve.co.uk/chapter4.htm)

Tait, Allison (2002) Why Thirty is the New Twenty. *New Woman,* (April), 74–6

Wittgenstein, Ludwig (1958) *Philosophical Investigations.* Oxford: Blackwell

World Health Organisation (2001) *World Health Report.* Geneva: WHO

Worth, David (2001) What is ADHD? *Woman's Day* (19 February), 45

Psychomercials

A young profession trying to establish itself may often be tempted
to oversell itself and its competencies. (Sanford, 1951: 670)

One waits in vain for psychologists to state the limit of their
knowledge. (Chomsky cited in Dineen, 1998: 6)

How has psychology come to be recognised as a scientific discipline
and as a profession; to achieve near universal acceptance for its claims
to truth; and an incessant and overwhelming level of popular demand for its products and services? How has the new and ethically
precarious genre of 'psychological television' — *Big Brother* (in 2000),
the BBC's *The Experiment* (in 2001) and *The National IQ Test* (in 2002)
— come to out-rate even the most popular soaps? How is it that an
academic discipline has become so much at home in the marketplace and the media that we can accept, as good for us, the recent
intervention of the American Federal Trade Commission (FTC) into
the ethics of professional psychologists?[1] How have ordinary people
come to be trusting and loyal consumers of psychology's wares? How
is it that professional psychological associations can now earnestly
describe themselves as 'consumer advocacy groups'? (APA, 2002).
How has a Bill of Rights for consumers come to supplant a Code of
Ethics for practitioners? How have consumers come to (want to) exert
such an influence in determining the 'quality' of professional psychological products and services? How has competition for customers
come to overwrite a professional commitment to social responsibility
and service to society? And how did all this become such an apparently natural state of affairs?

In this chapter we examine the commercialisation of professional
psychology, and the ways in which we have been encouraged to become part of this trade, as 'empowered consumers' of psychological

---

1. The FTC is an independent agency of the US government which regulates
trade. It has two main branches: The Bureau of Competition, which is concerned with antitrust issues, and the Bureau of Consumer Protection, which
deals with charges of false or deceptive advertising.

products and services. In keeping with our attention to the globalisation of psy-consumerism, and because much of what happens in the USA today will affect the rest of the world tomorrow, we take a close look at two recent changes to the regulations by which American psychologists are permitted to trade: the ethical changes ordered by the FTC in the affairs of the American Psychological Association (APA); and the erasure of the long-standing prohibition against providing psychological services outside the context of professional relationships (for example, and especially, through the media). We ask how professional associations, once concerned with social responsibility and the welfare of their patients, have reshaped themselves to become pro-consumer advocacy groups. And we'll see how these changes fit with the shifting aspirations and anxieties of the profession. By way of addressing these questions, we turn to look at the American Psychological Association, and specifically at one of its oldest and one of its newest regulatory documents, and their function in serving the profession, society, and the ordinary consumer. We inspect two documents, The *Ethical Principles of Psychologists* (1952–2002), and the *Bill of Rights* for consumers (1996-2002). Extracts from the professional and popular press provide a historical backdrop to the professionalisation of psy-commerce, and of consequent changes to the (permissible) relationships between practitioners, the media and the rest of us.

The professional project

Psychology is a (somewhat precocious) adolescent amongst the professions. It has existed, as such, only since the end of World War II, since which time it has grappled with the difficult task of becoming an autonomous, self-governing profession that is recognisably distinct both from allied professions and also from charlatans and quacks. As a new business, psychology faced a number of challenges. There was the immediate and pressing problem of brand recognition, as psychology sought to claim a distinctive and authoritative place amongst the professions. Beyond this product recognition, consumer trust in, and demand for, the expertise of psy-professionals also had to be established. This was facilitated by promoting psychology as a profession concerned foremost with both human welfare and with the maximisation of the efficiency of the state — indeed, as a public service. This double-headed project is still with us, even though, in the USA at least, it is the protection of the consumer *from* the state which is now the official mission of the profession. Psychology's helping credentials also acquired legitimacy by association with the scientific basis of psychological knowledge and practice. Pilgrim and Treacher (1990), for example, illustrate the manner in which the goals of professional aggrandisement, capital and the state coalesced prior to World

War II in the production of docile workers:

> Industrial psychology in Great Britain between the wars ...
> legitimised the individualisation of social and economic rela-
> tions by working within a (scientific) psychological framework.
> Political dynamics (like inherent conflicts of interests between
> owners and workers) became reframed as problems between
> individuals to be managed using psychological technologies.
> Accordingly, applied psychology was offering a technical 'fix'
> for political tensions and the experience of alienated labour
> was rendered a problem of stress, neurosis or adjustment.
> (Pilgrim and Treacher, 1990: 30)

During the early years of the project, professional associations were
extremely cautious about how the rendering of, for example, class
conflict into psychoneurosis might reflect on the public reputation of
scientific psychology, and stressed the ethical obligation to protect
the profession from scientific discredit. Then, as now, the denial of
any nakedly political alignment with capital meant that public education in the apolitical and objectively scientific status of the discipline was considered vital to the survival and collective social mobil-
ity of the profession. Such concerns resonate in the present: Wigdor
and Garner (1982) for example go to pains to stress that scientific
psychology cannot be held responsible for the consequences of the
progress of science; it is just happenstance that developments in
psychological techniques are pressed into service by psychologists in
the interests of capital.[2] They state of psychological tests that, 'because they are visible instruments of the process of allocating economic opportunity, tests are seen as creating winners and losers.
What is not readily appreciated, perhaps, is the inevitability of making choices: whether by tests or some other mechanism, selection
must take place' (1982: 205). That, via such doublespeak, psychological testing offers nothing more than a veneer of scientificity to the
supposedly 'inevitable' inequity of distribution of economic opportunity in western societies, and thus disguises the central role of the
psy-professions in the creation of 'winners and losers', may not be
readily appreciated if we are to take at face value the self-proclaimed
adherence of the psy-professions to social welfare, or — more commonly nowadays — to the rights of the consumer. But others are not
so shy. For example, in the *Medical Journal of Australia*, Pete Ellis,
Don Smith and John Bushnell (2001: 8) are unabashed about the
value to capital of the psy-professions' identification of winners and
losers: 'detection and effective treatment of common mental illnesses

---

2. Responsibility for the social consequence of progress in genuine sciences is
often explicitly accepted. Oppenheimer and the Manhattan Project come to
mind.

will help our society reap the social and economic rewards of a mentally healthier society'.

Many of these challenges continue to preoccupy the contemporary professional project. The profession remains fiercely protective of the scientific basis of psychological claims to truth. However, professional psychology is now confronted with the prospect of competition from a range of its professional progeny over the right to the expert administration of psychological assessments.[3] The proliferation of, and public demand for, forms of psy-expertise has led to the creeping deprofessionalisation of many once-exclusively psychological techniques. The chair of the Queensland Branch of the Australian Psychological Society is particularly candid about this worrying trend:

> Today, nurses want to be counsellors. Physiotherapists want to do stress management at work. Occupational therapists want to assess patients for neuropsychological problems. Teachers want access to psychological tests. Doctors want to be family counsellors. Social workers want to do critical incidence [sic] debriefing. Trainers want to be able to categorise the personality of managers and staff. Psychiatrists are discovering the benefits of cognitive behavioural therapy. (Cooke, 2000: 238)

Like much of the rest of everyday neo-liberal life, professional psychology is now resolutely consumer-oriented. Along with the former passengers who are now 'customers' of railway companies, the academics who have become 'content providers' and the patients who have metamorphosed into 'clients', so too the APA has begun to describe itself as a 'consumer advocacy organisation' (helping.apa.org/spreadtheword/access.html). It has developed both a 'Consumer Help Centre' and a 'Bill of Rights' for consumers. The APA's code of ethics no longer contains any reference to 'human welfare' or 'social responsibility', and has, indeed, been redesigned to protect psychologists from dissatisfied customers. The advent of commodified health care (in the US, 'Managed Care') is argued to pose a 'significant threat' to the autonomy of the profession (APA, 2002). Coupled with the more relaxed stance toward advertising encouraged by government agencies, this makes the highly aggressive direct marketing campaigns and media appearances of contemporary psychologists, the healthy side-industry in marketing techniques for busy professionals, and the insistent public education campaigns of the professional associations, themselves, not only (suddenly) ethical, but also *necessary* for the future of the profession.

---

3. The 'democratisation of psy-techniques' and psychology's claims to exclusive rights over scientific practice are covered elsewhere in this volume. See chapters four, five and six for more on the former, and chapter seven for more on the latter.

Captivating the consumer

> Of all the sciences it was the youngest and least scientific which
> most captivated the general public .... [O]ne had only to read
> the newspapers to be told with complete assurance that psy-
> chology held the key to the problems of waywardness, divorce,
> and crime. (Allen, 1931: 165)

While professional psychology as we know it today can only be said
to have been in existence since the mid-1940s, this is not to say that
its direct progenitors were any more reticent about the scope of the
psychological project or the magical claims made under its rubric.
Thus the mental hygiene movement marked an early — and crucial
— bridgehead into popular culture for the future profession of psychology. Until the 1940s, the only official mental illnesses to receive
professional attention — usually in the form of interminable incar-
ceration — were considered to be organic and incurable (Rose, 1999).
The mental hygiene movement drew on the growing body of scientific
psychological knowledge to lobby for the importance of more trivial
— and *treatable* — forms of mental disorder as a key to understanding (or respecifying as personal) perturbing *social* problems: from
delinquency to divorce, to inefficiency in the workplace. These ideas
altered the ways that people understood the role, and relevance, of
psychology in their everyday lives. The current plagues of social phobia, ADHD and shopping addiction are, then, nothing other than
contemporary manifestations of this politics of experience. All that
has changed is the currency in which the claims are cashed: we have
merely moved from scientific assertions of the causal role of heredi-
tary degeneracy and vice to MRI scans, Positron Emission Tomogra-
phy and genome mapping, as the scientific warrant for psychology's
claims to hold the key to our problems.

The new idea of mental health was essential to accomplishing this
shift. Mental health was something that required *both* expert guidance
and the cooperative efforts of ordinary people. Mental health could be
promoted and maintained by adjusting various aspects of one's work
and home life. Poor mental hygiene could lead to (newly psychological)
problems such as antisocial conduct, unhappiness, inefficiency at work,
and so on. Thus popular psychological paperbacks of the 1930s (such
as Montgomery, 1938; Weatherhead, 1934) stressed their duty to inform readers of the importance of mental health and hygiene:

> The time has come today when we may safely disseminate facts
> about mental and psychological hygiene. We shall not make
> the majority morbid. We shall save many from pitfalls and help
> others climb out of them. I think we can show them how essen-
> tial to the mastery of the art of living is a grasp of simple, psy-
> chological truths. (Weatherhead, 1934: 6).

Psychology and Life: Sound Psychology Made Vivid and Practical, by Dr Leslie Weatherhead, a 'recognised authority' in the field of pastoral psychology, for those 'busy people who have little time for reading' (1934: 5) is, then, explicit that it is only by accepting psychological truths that a 'mastery of the art of living' will be guaranteed. According to the cover blurb, the author provides 'an exposition for thoughtful but non-technical readers of the modern outlook and method of psychology in relation to conduct'. Intriguingly anticipating other influential early twentieth-century figures like Eysenck, Weatherhead is also unambiguous when it comes to psychotherapy. He writes: 'my advice to people is to think of it [psychotherapy] as one thinks of a major abdominal operation. Avoid it if you can' (1934: 7). Montgomery is similarly sceptical of the value of *professionalised* assistance. In *Can Psychology Help*? she offers a qualified 'yes'. That is, achieving good mental health (which, on pages 41–2, she likens, Bunty-esque, to 'a certain kind of elasticity within us like the bounce of a good tennis ball') is a matter of *self-directed* application of the 'directions' offered by psychological knowledge.

> Psychology is that branch of knowledge which shows us how mental growth may become possible for us if we are sufficiently concerned about the quality of our living to make voluntary efforts to improve it; but neither psychology nor any other kind of knowledge can relieve us of the necessity to give its directions practical application if we are to derive the benefits they confer. (Montgomery, 1938: 2)

She concludes that mental health, or the qualities of 'wholeness, independence, self-direction ... can be attained only as we accept personal responsibility for our behaviour' (1938: 83). Of course, this emphasis on the personal responsibility of the self for efforts to improve 'its' mental health has remained a constant trope in the public education efforts of the psy-professions ever since. What has changed, as we chart in the remainder of this chapter, is the relationship of the self to therapy encouraged in these texts, accompanied by the increasingly shrill insistence that individual consumers, in their pursuit of 'improvement', have the right — if not the obligation — to seek professional assistance.

But this is to get ahead of ourselves. In the earlier part of the twentieth century, for the survival of the profession, it was necessary for ordinary people to believe that 'simple psychological truths' were indeed 'essential' and 'practical' tools for the 'mastery of the art of living', and that 'mental hygiene' was something to which we all had a responsibility to contribute. Having acquired a 'reputable', and scientific, status as the purveyor of such truths, it was, according to these early professionals, now 'safe' for psychology to begin to market these helpful facts, and to somehow convince people of their utility vis-à-vis the problems of their everyday lives.

In the academic psychological literature of the 1940s, similar hopes were held out for the future development of psychology as an indispensable part of everyday life. In his reflections on 'some unfinished business' for psychology in 1944, Remmers observed that:

> The life and vigour of ... psychology is directly dependent on the extent to which it grows out of human problems .... This need not mean merely 'giving the customer what he wants'. It does mean *capitalising maximally upon available motivation*. This motivation, in general is ... wanting the answers to the questions: How to care for bodies, rear children, work and live together, play, and to learn the ends to be lived for .... Psychology must ally itself more actively with departments and agencies that play an important part in culture control — such as journalism, radio, and in the near future, television, to the end that the 'social lag' between science and its technological consequences may be kept at a minimum. (Remmers, 1944: 714–15; our emphasis)

Here, the then Executive Secretary of the APA does not assume (as perhaps do the pop-psychs of the 1930s) that it will be simply a matter of the *dissemination* of psychological truths, and the *demonstration* of their necessity for mastering the arts of everyday living. Rather, psychology — as some form of parasite or (more charitably) symbiont — must take root in, feed on, grow out of, overwhelmingly *mundane* human problems, and not just address itself to those things that people might already feel require expert assistance. That is, in order to ensure the 'life and vigour of psychology', the customer should 'not merely get what he wants', or what he might have come to expect psychology to offer. The task of psychology, as a professional project, is to 'capitalise upon available motivation';[4] and to build upon prior *moral* and/or *existential* questions (how to care for bodies, how to rear children, how to work and live together, how to play, all the way through to identifying 'the ends to be lived for') by reframing them as *existing wants*. That is, it had to sell itself as having *the* answers to the practical questions that people tend to ask about their lives; questions that must be respecified as *psychological* rather than as ordinary *practical-moral* matters or problems. The self-consciously despotic undercurrent of this project is evident in the explicitly Orwellian recognition that psychology 'must ally itself more actively with departments and agencies that play an important part in *culture control*' — a theme to which we will return shortly.

---

4. 'Motivation', as we will see, is yet another term re-invented by psychology in order to market its knowledge to those industries (including the self-improvement industry) interested in influencing human behaviour.

By the 1950s, the popular appetite for psychological solutions had been firmly established. Via early efforts at 'culture control', people had indeed come to problematise their lives in psychological terms, and to recognise the authoritative expertise of psy-professionals as the source of correct and useful answers to such mundane questions. In his 1952 paper, 'Psychology and the Newspaper Man', science journalist Alton Blakeslee wrote that:

> People want to know — why they feel like they do, act like they do, how to rear children, how to get more fun out of their jobs, how to solve many of their problems, how to live more fully up to their capabilities .... The public has a right to know. It is a fundamental right and strength of democracy. (Blakeslee, 1952: 91)

Published in the *American Psychologist*, Blakeslee's article advised psychologists on how to 'pitch' their work to the media. By now, it seems, psychological knowledge had become something of which it could sensibly be said that the public had come to feel they had a 'right' — if not an obligation — to know about. Psychological truths were then, by the early 1950s, well on their way to achieving their contemporary commonsensical status as essential to our understanding of ourselves and to the ways in which we conduct our daily lives.

People, then, are now described as having the 'right to know' the (psychological) solutions to their everyday problems. Again, the numbingly mundane nature of the problems — 'why they feel like they do, act like they do, how to rear children, how to get more fun out of their jobs' — upon which psychological experts are democratically bound to pronounce is striking. But, in addition, according to the Executive Secretary of the APA in 1951, the people also have a strong and conscious *need* for professional psychological services. Anticipating Foucault's notion of the 'positivity' (immediate and local applicability) of psychological knowledges Sanford observed that:

> Our society appears particularly willing to adopt psychological ways of thinking and to accept the results of psychological research .... People seem to have a strong and conscious need for the sorts of professional services psychologists are ... equipped to give .... The age of the psychological man is upon us, and ... psychologists must accept responsibility not only for having spread the arrival of this age, but for guiding its future course. Whether we like it or not, our society is tending more and more to think in terms of the concepts and methods spawned and nurtured by psychologists. And whether we like it or not, psychologists will continue to be a consequential factor in the making of social decisions and in the structuring of our culture. (Sanford, 1951: 74)

Here, people are described as particularly willing (or motivated) to adopt 'psychological ways of thinking'. It is also suggested, quite unproblematically, that people just happen to have — by some quirk of evolution perhaps — 'a strong and conscious need for the sorts of professional services psychologists are ... equipped to give'. How people can more effectively be persuaded to want, or to feel that they are in need of, professional psychological assistance is a question that continues to preoccupy the professional associations — and the techniques by which this creation of need is accomplished is the central topic of this book.

The notion of 'need', of course, has an interesting history in the human services, where everyday human wants, desires or requisites get routinely repackaged in terms of 'needs' for the services which professionals can or want to provide. So used are we to hearing things like 'Freddy needs speech therapy', 'Jane has special educational needs' or 'Hugo needs a residential service' that we often forget that no one *needs* speech therapy, 'special' schooling or a place in a group home *per se*. Rather, people may *want* assistance with communicating, would *like* more help with their maths, literacy, etc., or *prefer* to live somewhere other than they do right now. Everyone may need to eat, but no one *needs* a Big Mac.

However, while the announcement of the dawn of the 'age of the psychological man' may now seem incredibly arrogant and self-aggrandising, this brave new world is characterised as an *inevitable* state of affairs. 'Whether we/they like it or not', professional psychologists have an obligation to recognise the growing demand for, and market penetration of, 'concepts and methods spawned and nurtured' by psychology, and to take responsibility for 'guiding its future course'. With a prescient confidence in psychology 'continuing to be a consequential factor in the making of social decisions and in the structuring of our culture', Sanford notes that the psy-professions 'have a *down-to-earth investment* in [the] future [of] the first *deliberately designed profession* in history' (Sanford, 1951: 75; our emphasis).

Psychology's close involvement in 'the structuring of our culture' was such that, as early as the late 1960s, eminent American psychologists were claiming that the public demand (or need) for psychological services outstripped the available supply of psy-professionals. In his Presidential Address to the APA in 1969, George Miller stressed that the role of psychology should not be restricted to the provision of expert services, but rather, because of prevailing personnel restrictions, 'people at large will have to be their own psychologists':

> We are not physicians; the secrets of our trade need not be reserved for highly trained specialists. Psychological facts should be passed out freely to all who need and can use them .... Our

scientific results will have to be instilled in public consciousness in a practical and useable form so that what we know can
be applied by ordinary people. There simply are not enough
psychologists ... to meet the need for psychological services.
   The people at large will have to be their own psychologists ....
Our responsibility is less to assume the role of experts and try
to apply psychology ourselves than to give it away to the people
who really need it — and that includes everyone. (Miller, 1969:
1067–71)

Psychology's ethical commitment to 'human welfare', and the resolution of 'social problems', suggests Miller, demands that we give psychology away to 'the people who really need it — and that includes
everyone'. And yet this is a carefully nuanced beneficence. Yes, we will
give our secrets away. Yes, people will tend to their psychological selves
— having had the right 'scientific results instilled' into them. But at
the same time as avowing a communitarian generosity, Miller is careful to note that 'ordinary people' will not be able to apply psychology's
'scientific results' in their pure form. Rather, the 'secrets of the trade'
should be translated into a suitably practical set of techniques of the
self in order that we can be sure that ordinary people will (want to)
adopt them. In what remains a ubiquitous device, psychology appears
to give with one hand while taking with the other. It publishes its
'secrets', but retains copyright. As we will see, the late 1960s was a
period of critical expansion for the professional project and hence these
calls to 'give psychology away' also acknowledge the consumer's burgeoning 'need' for self-determination, and 'right' to information — as
well as a growing social antagonism toward the professions.
   In 1967, the first issue of the popular periodical *Psychology Today* appeared; and, in 1969, *Time* magazine launched its 'Behavior'
department. Psychology's promises — by way of its techniques and
topics, problems and solutions, personnel and clientele — have since
then increasingly filled the pages of our newspapers, magazines and
pulp fiction and are also increasingly to be found in the broadcast
media, in our cinemas, and more recently, on the Internet. Agony
Aunts — who have existed, in some form, since the late seventeenth
century — were, by the 1980s, more likely to be psy-professionals
than concerned elderly spinsters.[5] By 1975, the first 'psych-jockeys'
hit the radio airwaves. This latter development was initially met with
some concern by the APA and an official investigation was launched

---

5. Hendley (1977–1978) argues that the first 'advice columnist' was one John
Dunton, an English bookseller who, in the late seventeenth century, produced
and distributed a newsletter containing answers to the various everyday problems submitted by his readers. Uniquely, to our knowledge, on the Australian
edition of *Cosmopolitan*'s problem page, the strap line once took the trouble to
reassure its readers that Agony Aunt, Tracey Cox, held a BA in Psychology.

into the ethics of professional psychologists providing services via the media. Intriguingly, barely two years later, the 'psych-jockey' in question, Dr Toni Grant, received an award for her services to the profession (Avery, 1990). 'Media Psychology' was officially adopted as an area for 'research and practice', in 1982, by a conference of (American) talk-back psychologists. And, by 1986, the APA created a Division of Media Psychology — the stated purpose of which is to redeem Blakeslee's promise — to 'assist psychologists to use the media more effectively for informing the public about the science and profession of psychology' (www.apa.org/divisions/div46). By 2002, the routine appearance of psychologists as consultants to TV game shows raised scarcely a ripple of comment.

However, in the face of the *de facto* growing media presence of psychology and psychologists, the ethical codes of the professional associations continued — at least for a time — to prohibit, *de jure*, 'the use of psychology for the purposes of entertainment'; the provision of advice or professional services outside of a professional relationship (that is, via the media); and the direct advertisement of psychological services. These prohibitions were soon lifted — but not without the assistance of government agencies acting on behalf of American consumers.

So it seems that, despite the expressed anxiety of contemporary professional psychological associations about the perils of the 'deprofessionalisation' and 'democratisation' of psychology, successful psy-commerce *demands* that 'psychology be practised by nonpsychologists'. Indeed, psychology's vocabulary and methods of (self) assessment have become indispensable and ubiquitous in our everyday lives. However, notwithstanding the (newly ethical) concerted marketing campaigns of the psy-professions, and much to the chagrin of the professional associations, it remains the case that just less than half of the US population seek the direct services of psychologists or psychiatrists; even though the proportion of people that do choose to enter into a formal 'therapeutic contract' is rising.[6] Also on the rise is the number of registered professionals per capita in America, Australia and Britain — where the British Psychological Society's Division of Clinical Psychology has recently held a conference to explore the implications of having some 17,000 clinical psychologists by 2012. Although the number of psychologists in the US is generally considered to be the highest in the world, in Australia and Britain the growth of psychology has, in fact, exceeded that of the American industry (Cooke, 2000: 221). Across these countries, per capita, there is approximately one licensed psychologist per 4,000 citizens. However, if the numbers of allied

6. According to Dineen (1998) in the 1960s, 14%; by the 1970s, 26%; by 1990, 33%; and in 1995, 46% of the (US) population had seen, or were seeing, a psychologist.

psy-professionals (family therapists, social workers, crisis workers and so on) are also counted, the ratio of professionals to ordinary people closes to an astonishing figure somewhere in the region of 1/250 (Dineen, 1998).[7]

Psychology and psychologists are now everywhere, and not always where you might expect. A recent survey of the occupational status of (Australian) psychology graduates suggests that psychologists may be found working in:

> Businesses; Career Services; Centres for the developmentally disabled; Community Agencies; Consulting Firms; Correctional facilities and prisons; Defence Forces; Family and Health Services; Government organisations; Hospitals; Law courts; Market Research Companies; Mental Health organisations; Non-Profit organisations; Police Force; Professional Associations; Private clinics; Recruitment Agencies; Rehabilitation Agencies; Research Institutions; Schools; Social welfare services; Substance abuse services; Test development corporations; Training and Development Services; Universities; Youth Services. (UNSW, 2002)

As in Britain, in Australia clinical psychologists in private practice were a rarity until the 1970s. Indeed, 'private practice' was not even available as a category in most surveys until this time (Leahey, 1997; McCallum, 1977). However, since the birth of this category, private practice has remained the most significant area of growth for Australian psychology, with 100 per cent growth predicted over the next decade (Francis and Cameron, 1997). In the UK too, increasing numbers of practitioners supplement their NHS salaries with private practice, consultancy and the provision of workshops for other NHS staff and government. Just like private practitioners, who are understandably very much invested in the application of ever more direct and effective ways of encouraging ordinary people to seek professional help, these entrepreneurs of state-based psy are ardent exponents of, and lobbyists for, the expansion of the profession into ever-widening areas of newly-identified concern: hence such schemes as 'assertive outreach', early intervention for psychosis, and the proposed new Mental Health Act.

As we continue to explore the commercialisation of professional psychology, we should remember that this remains only (the most obvious) part of the story. As Nikolas Rose has noted, the installation of a 'psy-shaped space at the heart of each and every consumer' (1999: 282) has not been a simple exercise of professional domination:

---

7. That this level of provision has no necessary bearing on the wellbeing of such well-served populations may be gauged from the work of Warner and de Girolamo (1995) and Warner (2000) which clearly shows that both the likelihood and the speed of recovery from 'schizophrenia' are much higher in countries such as Botswana — which are not noted for their high ratio of psy-professionals.

> Our contemporary regime of subjectification cannot simply be understood in terms of the proliferation of an 'expert discourse' — a science of the soul together with its accredited scientists. The relation between the psy saturation of 'popular culture' and 'everyday experience' is more complex .... The profession-als of psy are characterised by their generosity — they are happy to give away their vocabulary, their grammars of conduct, their styles of judgment to others .... A whole raft of professionals — lawyers, doctors, architects, financial consultants, priests — and quasi-professionals, policemen, probation officers, man-agement consultants, beauty therapists — have come to operate a quasi-psychological ethics. (Rose, 1999: 264)

Thus today, we are as likely to find ourselves engaged in some form of psy-commerce in the beauty salon, the bedroom or the super-market, as in the workplace, the classroom or the therapy session. However, while more than happy to proliferate the vocabulary of psy-discourse to these sites, the generosity of psy-professionals does not extend to (willingly) allowing others to claim 'special competence', or psychological expertise — or to administer and interpret official psychological instruments. To this end, the professional associations have sought to regulate the profession (and, in some cases, to seek regulation from the state) in order to protect the market for psycho-logical expertise.

Regulating the profession

> The time for ethical codes, charters and professional standards is clearly upon us. (Smith cited in Cooke, 2000: 93)

In American and Australia (but not in Britain), psychologists are required to be registered — or in some way certified by the state. Attempts by the British Psychological Society to secure such state recognition have been routinely unsuccessful and the BPS-spon-sored voluntary alternative, 'chartered status', is seen by many as a crude bid for the professional standing — or bourgeois preten-sions — of chartered engineers, accountants and the rest. As else-where, however, the motivation for securing licensing has been, since the early days of the profession, the containment of compe-tition, from both 'charlatans' and from allied professionals, which then posed (as they still do) a significant problem for psychology. In Australia, calls for the registration of psychologists began in the 1940s, when compulsory registration was suggested in order to curtail the claims of 'pseudo-psychologists'. The saturation of the market by fringe practitioners was a matter of some concern for the Victorian Branch of the APS which, in the 1960s, created a list of 'pseudo-psychological' practices. These included vocational guidance, marriage guidance, hypnotherapy, and certain forms of psychotherapy (Cooke, 2000). Notably, all of these practices are nowadays normatively performed by state-registered (mainstream) psychologists. Formal state regulation was not pursued as an issue until the 1960s, when the Standing Committee on the Profession of Psychology drafted a Registration Bill. This prohibited the unregistered practitioner from using the epithets 'psychologist', 'psychological consultant', and so on, and from using any psychological test, technique, or instrument of measurement (Cooke, 2000). These efforts to protect the professional psychologist's claims to special competence made it unethical, if not illegal, to treat psychological products such as assessment instruments as separable from their producer, once sold. The 'special competence', or professional expertise, of the psychologist is (ideally) inseparable from the consumption of such materials (Danziger, 1990).[8]

That registration is not a requirement for British psychologists indicates that, although 'certification is one of the major ways in which unrecognised or underrecognised professions achieve parity and recognition' (Dineen, 1998: 2), state regulation is not a necessary requirement for the growth of the profession — British psychology is currently debating the desirability of an unsolicited offer of greater powers from the state, with many in favour of such a move. As yet, the British Psychological Society remains officially opposed to this radical extension of psychologists' powers of coercion and compulsion (Kinderman and Cooke, 2000). Professional lobbying on such issues may — or may not — be effective: the first Act requiring Australian psychologists to be registered came to pass by accident rather than design. In 1965, The Victorian Psychological Practices Act was created as one of the recommendations of a Board of Inquiry into Scientology which found that a variety of pseudo-psychological practices — of which Scientology was an exemplar — were a moral threat to the community. The Inquiry recommended that these 'fringe practices' should be controlled by regulating psychology (Cooke, 2000).

Regardless of the legal status of psychology, one of the things that the national professional associations do have in common is some system of internal regulation — a code of ethics, governing the conduct of professional psychologists. In the following section, we examine one of the founding documents of professional psychology. The APA's *Ethical Standards for Psychologists* has existed, in one form or

---

8. Though this ethical prohibition is still evident in the professional code of ethics of the APA (and APS and BPS), minor breaches are seldom pursued. Various popular forms of psychological tests are available for the general public for self-completion, scoring, and contemplation. Of course, the results of such tests may well indicate the need to engage the services of a licensed professional.

another, for over 60 years.[9] During this time a number of substantial revisions have taken place. Despite early hopes for a timeless code of ethics (Holzman, 1960), many contemporary routine professional practices are, according to the standards of previous ethical codes, clearly unethical. Here, we briefly examine these shifting prescriptions, with particular attention paid to the (permissible) relationships between practitioners, the media, and the ordinary consumer.

A formal code of ethics is a defining feature of the modern profession. Today, it seems unethical for professionals to be without some formal and binding 'code of conduct'. It seems obvious that such regulatory documents are necessary to assure 'consumer protection' from professional misconduct, and to ensure the consistent quality — and accountability — of the professionals and their services. However, in the early part of the twentieth century, psychology was still primarily an academic discipline — and psychologists had 'little need' for their own code of ethics:

> In the early years of the American Psychological Association, the problems of ethics were relatively simple. We were essentially an organization of college teachers. The only ethical problems which seemed to present themselves were those of plagiarism and of academic freedom. (Rich, 1952: 440)

The development of a formal code of ethics was, however, recognised as a useful instrumental tactic in the professionalisation of psychology. As Hobbs argued in the *American Psychologist* in 1948: 'A formalized code of ethical practice would be of ponderable significance on furthering acceptance of psychologists as a group with professional status' (Hobbs, 1948: 81). The self-evident necessity of a formal code of ethics for psychologists had yet to become obvious, however, and there was considerable debate amongst American psychologists in the 1950s about the wisdom of adopting a formal code:

> If it is necessary to have a device by which the most flagrant miscreants can be ejected from the APA, I would suggest a simple statement on the application blank to this effect: 'As a psychologist, I agree to conduct myself professionally according to the common rules of decency, with the understanding that if a jury of my peers decides that I have violated these rules, I may be expelled from the Association'. Since every mature person knows in his heart what the common rules of decency are, it is not necessary to spell them out. (Hall, 1952: 431)

---

9. This document has changed names several times over the past 50 years. To avoid confusion, we will refer to all versions, hereafter, as 'the code of ethics', or 'the Code'.

Similarly, the negative consequences of the public acknowledgment of the possibility of violations of the 'rules of decency' were noted.

> If we, as an organisation, feel that we must specifically proscribe such gross and simple-minded misconduct in our professional code, the uninitiated but critical reader may conclude that the APA is unduly afflicted with human frailty and psychologists may not be trustworthy. Such a reader may be inclined to ... suspect that if psychologists have to be told not to do such things, it may do no good to tell them. (Hunt, 1952: 432)

Here, the 'common rules of decency' are argued to be more than sufficient for ensuring the ethical conduct of all members of society, including psychologists. Why, indeed, should psychologists adhere to a different set of rules? The second critic raises the possibility that a formal code of ethics may, in practice, be detrimental to the professional reputation of psychology, even suggesting that 'psychologists may not be trustworthy'. Both of these critics argue for the utility, and decency, of a form of ethics that does not have to be 'spelled out', and that is part of the 'common rules' that are recognisable by 'any mature person'. These (prescient) critical psychologists argued that a code of ethics would encourage 'crooks' to take advantage of the 'loopholes' that any formal code would be bound to create.

Despite these calls for retaining 'the common rules of decency', the American Psychological Association went on to develop an official Code of Ethics for Psychologists. After three years, and nine drafts, the 1959 version was adopted for use on a trial basis (APA, 1959). Though redrafted every decade or so, this document remains central to the regulation of the conduct of American psychologists.[10] Hopes were high for the timeless utility of the new code:

> The Committee on Ethical Standards hopes that these major principles stated in general form will weather considerable growth of psychology without drastic alteration. (Holzman, 1960: 247)

Less than 50 years later, although the Code still exists (albeit under a different name), it bears only a passing family resemblance to the document launched so enthusiastically by the APA. The first edition was primarily concerned with the conduct of psychologists as this reflected on the discipline's scientific authority, professional status, and its regard for human welfare.

---

10. In 1949 the APS — known, at that time, as the Australian Branch of the BPS — produced a code of ethics. Although the BPS showed interest in the 'Code of Professional Ethics' adopted by the Australian branch, they decided, on balance, not to follow suit, and indeed, did not adopt a formal code until 1985.

So what is ethics for?

> Ethics evolve to protect people from harm. In the case of psy-
> chological ethics, the harm stems from two sources: (a) poten-
> tial harm to consumers of our services and (b) *potential harm to
> the field as a whole if we say things that, in the eyes of the public,
> denigrate the field and make it appear as less of a science*. (Klonoff,
> 1983: 853; our emphasis)

This is a particularly candid account of the purpose of psychological
ethics. The considerable revisions to the Code are glossed as the
'evolution' of ethics, to 'protect people from harm'. The ethical obligations of modern psychologists are now no longer centred on such
outmoded notions as 'human welfare', or 'social responsibility'. However, vestiges of these now defunct responsibilities were evident until
the most recent revision (APA, 2001), from which the following para-
graph (existing in several forms since 1953) has been deleted:

> Psychologists are aware of their professional and scientific re-
> sponsibilities to the community and the society in which they
> work and live. They apply and make public their knowledge of
> psychology in order to contribute to human welfare. Psycholo-
> gists are concerned about and work to mitigate the causes of
> human suffering. When undertaking research, they strive to
> advance human welfare and the science of psychology. (APA,
> 1992: (Principle F: 'Social Responsibility'))

'Social responsibility' is, ironically, one of four 'Criteria for a Good
Profession', according to the consensus document produced by the
APA's 1951 Committee on 'Relations with the Medical Profession'
and reported to the membership by APA Executive Secretary Fillmore
Sanford who declared that 'a good profession is one that is motivated
by a sense of social responsibility' (Sanford, 1951: 668). So, what
does the deletion of this clause imply? Sadly, but perhaps
unsurprisingly, not the recognition that the statement is such a self-
evident account of the rules of decency dear to Hunt and Hall that it
does not need stating. Rather, in a substantial restructuring of the
existing Code, the most recent version has dispensed with a number
of similarly obsolete obligations and commitments.[11] The preamble
has been removed altogether, along with its 'unenforceable goals'.
Older versions of the Code, with their unhealthy reliance on
'aspirational principles', were described by the review committee as
'difficult to enforce' and as 'vulnerable to legal challenges for behavioral vagueness, which *deprived psychologists of their right to practice*'

11. A redline comparison of the 1992 and 2001 Codes can be accessed via the
APA's ethics website: (www.apa.org/ethics)

(Fisher and Younggren, 1997: 584; our emphasis).

Vasquez (1994: 323) explains that 'principle-based decisions [by ethics committees] are highly vulnerable to overturn on appeal because the complainees can argue that they had no forewarning that specific behaviours were ethical violations and the extent to which a specific behaviour is in violation of a general principle is open to interpretation'. Despite these noble concerns about the enforcement of the Code, the 1992 revision included, for the first time, a number of new qualifiers — phrases such as 'reasonable precautions', 'wherever feasible' and 'attempt to' — which in and of themselves introduce a raft of behavioural vaguenesses. The appearance of these terms, which now pervade many of the principles and standards contained in the Code, was explained by the APA as providing a means to 'guard against a rigid set of rules that would not be applicable across the broad range of activities conducted by psychologists, would be quickly outdated, and would preclude opportunities for moral growth within the field itself' (www.division42.org/MembersArea/APA2001/EthicsCode/42Response_intro.html).

What kind of moral growth could this be? Surely the insertion of qualifying terms can only make the code *less* enforceable (at least from the point of view of complainants). Rather than being concerned with 'potential harm to consumers', then, these editorial changes would appear to be designed to protect psychologists by placing their 'reasonable' and 'professional' conduct beyond the reach of (less reasonable?) consumer-complainants. Indeed, the qualification of the Code probably reflects the legal counsel — three attorneys with experience in the defence of psychologists on legal and ethical matters — solicited by the APA to advise the review committee.

The Code of Ethics no longer serves to remind psychologists of the powers and obligations derived from their common membership in a collective professional body. Rather, the psychologist is now addressed as a professional free to selectively interpret those ethical standards that may — reasonably — apply, in order to provide competitive services in the name of the consumer, and in the service of the profession. Should misconduct occur, instead of being rigidly bound to publicly espoused forms of conduct imposed through a formal and binding code of ethics, and the ever-present possibility of peer intervention, today's psychologist is faced with a selection of 'appropriate standards' for ethical conduct. He or she is also protected from dissatisfied consumers by a code of ethics that once appeared more concerned about 'social responsibility' than 'risk management'. The new professional is enjoined to assert their 'right to practice', which older versions of the code of ethics — as a collectively imposed regimen — threatened to thwart.

To make the newly-freed practitioner's judicious selection of ethical standards easier, the APA Insurance Trust is currently promoting — to both future and current psychologists — the use of an interactive CD-ROM designed to train professionals in what are now apparently the conjoined arts of 'ethics and risk management'. A recent article in the APA's member magazine the *Monitor* delivers the pitch: not only can you protect your practice — you can earn Professional Development points too!

> 'Ethics and Risk Management', a new CD-ROM instructional series from the APA Insurance Trust is a comprehensive risk-management education in eight CD-ROM modules. The set offers 24 hours of continuing-education course credits .... These are lessons for any psychologist ... because, explains project director Patricia M. Bricklin, PhD (professor of ethics in psychology), 'people are tempted to do a lot of things on the basis that they feel they are doing good without thinking about all sides of the situation' .... Ensuring that future psychologists understand their legal and ethical liabilities was one of the Trust's foremost objectives in developing this instructional series. 'Ethics and Risk Management' will also be made available to psychologists outside university programs .... They can ... take it home, put it in their computer and get risk-management information with continuing-education credits. (O'Connor, 2001: np)[12]

It seems that professional education on ethical matters need no longer include any actual discussion of ethical matters. This trend is not peculiar to psychology. Today, professional ethics committees are more likely to convene to discuss legal liabilities than to reflect on ethical issues as such (Longstaff, 2002).

Consorting with the media

The vexing problem of demarcating professional psychological terrain from that of 'popular psychology' and other 'pseudo-scientific' enterprises is a defining feature of the first draft of the APA's code of ethics. Indeed, these issues continue to vex the professional associations, and are of particular contemporary relevance to the BPS. Perhaps not surprisingly, then, the very first Standard ('Public Responsibility') of the first draft of the APA's code of ethics contains a section on 'Pseudo-psychology and the popularisation of psychology'. This section addresses the 'serious professional problem' posed by the (on the face of it impossible) need 'to make psychology popular without popularising it' (APA, 1952: 647). To this end: 'Exaggeration,

---

12. The requirement for professional psychologists to accrue 'continuing education credits' is received, by many professionals, as an insult to their professional competence. On this, see ongoing discussions in the e-journal of the Academy of the Psychoanalytic Arts: (www.academyanalyticarts.org).

sensationalism, superficiality and other kinds of misrepresentation must be avoided, since these may mislead the public and discredit the profession' (APA, 1952: pr1.44–1).[13]

This particular prohibition survived until the 1981 revision (briefly resurfacing in 1989 (see APA, 1990)) — but *all* versions from 1992 onwards contain no reference to the dangers of 'sensationalism' and 'misrepresentation', or the need to refrain from misleading exaggeration or superficiality. Since the intervention of the FTC in the 1980s, and the subsequent revision of the Code, American psychology has become a more 'consumer friendly' — that is, commercial — profession. It is no longer regarded as unethical to 'apply commercial, rather than professional, standards in the advertisement of psychological services' (APA, 1953: pr1.42). Neither is it currently unethical to 'employ psychological techniques for the purpose of entertainment' (APA, 1953: pr2.62–2).

However, consorting with the media was, until recently, considered an unambiguously unethical practice. Though no such prohibition is evident in the British Psychological Society's (2002b) code of ethics, a formal complaint lodged by a *sociologist*, David Miller, about the involvement of British psychologists in the production of reality TV programs such as *Big Brother* and *The Experiment* has seen the formation of a BPS working party on 'Psychologists, Ethics and the Media' (White, 2002). Here, our analysis of the changes to the APA's code of ethics with respect to these matters is intended as a worked example, or preview, of the kinds of 'ethical developments' that have allowed American psychologists to engage, on a nakedly commercial basis, with the media industries. In keeping with our attention to the globalisation of psy-consumerism, and as the BPS is currently examining these issues, we offer a detailed account of the successive revisions of the APA's code of ethics. The APA Code used to state that:

> psychological services and products for the purpose of diagnosis, treating, or giving personal advice to particular individuals are provided only in the context of a professional relationship and are not given by means of public lectures or demonstrations, newspaper or magazine articles, radio or television programs, mail or similar media. (APA, 1959–1981: pr4)

As we have seen, early versions of the Code emphasised the 'welfare of the consumer' as the proper focus for psychologists. Psychologists were not permitted to 'participate for personal gain in commercial announcements', and were reminded to adhere to professional, rather than commercial, standards in the presentation of public announcements or advertisements, and to ensure that any statements made were 'scientifically acceptable' (APA, 1959–1981: pr4). Notably, the ethi-

---

13. Principles and standards of the various versions of the Code are referenced as 'pr' and the relevant number.

cal obligations of psychologists once, but no longer, included the duty
to 'correct others' found to be acting in breach of the Code.

In 1981, the Code was amended to read, '*when* personal advice is
given by means of ... radio or television programs ... the psychologist
utilises the most current relevant data and exercises the highest level
of professional judgment' (APA, 1981: pr4). Principle 4 of the Code
(1959–1992) stated that therapy and diagnosis should be reserved for
professional psychologist relationships. Until the most recent revision
of the Code (where 'online therapy' is permissible), providing psychological services (and particularly, therapy) via the media was regarded
as a serious ethical violation. However, since the 1981 revision, providing 'advice' via the media has been considered an acceptable part of
professional practice. This revision was not entirely inconsistent with
those sections of earlier versions of the Code concerned with 'public
education'. The notion of 'advice', as educational rather than prescriptive, is also congruent with the practices of modern behavioural — or
'skills-based' — therapies, where the consumer can expect to acquire
a set of practical skills for overcoming particular problems, or 'work
with' a 'life-coach' to fine-tune their skills at living.

The revised 1992 and 2001 guidelines provide psychologists with
further details about their ethical obligations and this newly respect-
able aspect of professional practice. In 1992 American psychologists
were advised that:

> When psychologists provide advice or comment by means of
> public lectures, demonstrations, radio, or television programs,
> prerecorded tapes, printed articles, mailed material, or other
> media, they take reasonable precautions to ensure that (1) the
> statements are *based on appropriate psychological literature and
> practice*, (2) the statements are otherwise consistent with this
> Ethics Code, and (3) the recipients of the information are not
> encouraged to infer that a relationship has been established
> with them personally. (APA, 1992: 1604, pr3.04; our emphasis)

A mere nine years later ethically sound media practice was described
somewhat differently:

> When psychologists provide public advice or comment via print,
> internet, or other electronic transmission, they take precautions
> to ensure that (1) the statements are *based on their professional
> knowledge, training, or experience in accord with appropriate psy-
> chological literature and practice*, (2) the statements are otherwise
> consistent with this Ethics Code, and (3) the statements do not
> indicate that a professional relationship has been established
> with the recipient. (APA, 2001: pr5.04; our emphasis)

Although these revisions appear very similar, they mark some subtle shifts in the ways that the permissible relationship between the professional psychologist and the media-consumer is described: 'Personal advice' (1981) has become 'advice or comment' (1992), and finally 'public advice or comment' (2001). The duty to ground this (once forbidden) advice in 'appropriate psychological literature and practice' has been overwritten by the duty to base media-borne advice on 'professional knowledge, training or experience' in accord with appropriate literature. The long-held intention of the Code, to enhance the credibility of professional psychologists by promoting the findings of 'scientific psychology' has, it appears, been somewhat diluted. Finally, it seems, the knowledge and expertise of the professional — obtained simply by virtue of being one — is considered sufficient grounds for the public advertisement of psychological services. After all, the Code still insists that 'psychologists are guided by the primary obligation to aid the public in developing informed judgements, opinions and choices' (APA, 1981: pr4–g).

A final telling standard excised from the latest (October 2001) revision of the Code is that describing 'Professional and Scientific Relationships' (formerly pr1.03). This stated that: 'Psychologists provide diagnostic, therapeutic, teaching, research, supervisory, consultative, or other psychological services *only* in the context of a defined professional or scientific relationship or role'. With the increasing acceptance of psychology as entertainment, and with the practitioner's reach legitimately extended to the targeted solicitation of potential consumers, this finite list of services and permissible scientific and professional relationships threatened to deprive modern psychologists of their 'right to free trade'.

Selling psychological services: advertising and psychology

> Psychology must search its motives carefully before engaging in lobbying or in aggressive public relations. As a profession we must not become so interested in improving our status that we ever forget the welfare of the client. (Sanford, 1951: 668)

As we have seen, an early — and continuing — tactic in the advancement of psychology's professional project was the self-conscious emulation of the established medical and 'allied' professions. In the 1950s, the APA promoted the guidelines adhered to by medical practitioners as those most suitable for appropriation by their neophyte practitioners. Thus, the newly drafted Code of Ethics forbade the advertisement of psychological services, and the direct solicitation of clients. Rather, psychologists were enjoined to follow the practices of doctors and 'to describe [their] services with accuracy and dignity, adhering to professional rather than to commercial standards' (APA, 1953: pr1.42–1). Calling cards and, when necessary, restrained public announcements of availability, were permissible, as were understated individual listings in local telephone directories.

The APA's 'Guidelines for Telephone Directory Listings' (APA, 1969) recommends that psychologists list only their name, highest relevant degree and — perhaps — some indication of specialisation. Reciting multiple specialisations was considered 'a form of self-aggrandizement and ... unwarranted' (1969: 70). Bold, irregular or italic typeface was frowned upon. Listings of irregular size, or of overt prominence were also proscribed, as were entries in directories outside one's immediate geographical area. Here, it seems, psychology was taking its own conclusions seriously. According to early studies of the 'psychological impact' of typography:

> In the arrangement and choice of type many psychological mistakes are made in displayed advertisements .... Excessive elaboration makes us feel there is an insincere straining after effect. Ponderous type that 'shouts' is associated in our minds with a case that is so weak that it needs bolstering up by every possible means; but unfortunately that effort to bolster produces the contrary effect. Italic is often a reflection on the reader's intelligence — the impression given is one of desperately strained emphasis. (Higham, 1925: 52)

Subsequent changes to the advertisements permissible to American psychologists have been so radical as to make the above restrictions appear somewhat quaint, not to mention outmoded and restrictive. However, Australian and British psychologists remain notionally bound by codes of professional conduct that adhere to an austere 'calling card' model, whereby active efforts to attract clients are still regarded as unethical and unprofessional (see APS, 1995; BPS, 2002a). The APS, unlike the BPS, has, however, adopted an 'American-style' logo and marketing strategy, complete with the slogan: 'APS Psychologists: Good Thinking!' (APS, 2002). The BPS, though lacking an overt marketing wing or slogan, enables direct marketing to its members, and has a searchable database of chartered professionals on its website. The professional associations themselves now devote considerable resources to the direct and targeted 'selling of psychology'.

A conservative position on the advertisement of services was a defining characteristic of the American professions until the 1970s, when government intervention (in the name of the marketplace) helped to ensure a more modern, 'consumer-oriented' professional ethics. In the 1960s and 1970s, a series of highly public class-action lawsuits were filed against major corporations (Klein, 2000). This new era of 'consumer activism' — or 'client revolt' (Haug and Sussman, 1969) — attracted the scrutiny of the US FTC, under the direction of the Attorney General, to the ways that professional associations attempted to regulate the conduct of their members.

The FTC vs. the APA[14]

In the early 1970s, the FTC contacted a number of professional organisations with concerns about regulations and practices that prevented consumers from accessing useful information through advertisements. Complaints were lodged against a variety of professional associations, including the American Institute of Architects, the American Institute of Certified Public Accountants, and the National Society of Professional Engineers (Koocher, 1994a). The FTC was specifically concerned with professional ethical codes that prohibited (a) soliciting business by advertising or otherwise, (b) engaging in price competition and (c) otherwise engaging in competitive practices (Koocher, 1994b). Medical societies were informed that their existing medical ethics code was creating *de facto* price interference, and frustrating the consumer's right to choose services in an 'unrestrained fashion' (Koocher, 1977).

In 1976, the APA Ethics Committee raised these issues at its annual convention. Consumer advocate Ralph Nader delivered an invited address entitled 'Bringing Psychology into the Consumer Movement'. The same year, the Ethics Committee declined to take any action on any advertising complaints brought to its attention (Koocher, 1994b). As we have seen, between 1977 and 1981, a number of adjustments were made to the APA's code of ethics. The revised version (APA, 1981) was the first to indicate that advertising in general would be acceptable, so long as certain basic tenets (such as avoiding misleading claims, testimonials, and anxiety-inducing advertisements) were adhered to.

When bills were introduced into Congress during the Reagan administration to exempt the professions (including psychology) from the scrutiny of the FTC, they were actively opposed by organised psychology (Association for the Advancement of Psychology, 1982).[15] The opposition of professional psychology to exemption on the grounds of its status as a profession was widely praised in the consumer protection literature as setting an example for the more reluctant professions: 'American psychology was proactively striving to be a good citizen and proconsumer' (Koocher, 1994b: 358). These actions mark the start of a more general shift in the APA towards its current — self-proclaimed — status as a 'consumer advocacy organisation'. In 1988, the FTC found portions of the APA's code of ethics to be illegal restraints of trade. The offending sections restricted the content of ad-

---

14. For a more detailed account of the APA's 'adventures' with the FTC, see Koocher (1994a; 1994b).

15. Naomi Klein (2000) notes that, under the Reagan administration, the FTC pursued 'uncompetitive' — and uncooperative — professional associations with a vengeance. During this same era, the FTC lost half of its staff. Billion-dollar mergers opposed by Reagan's own government passed unopposed.

vertising and other public statements intended to represent the desirability of services. The APA was ordered to amend its standards on 16 December 1992. The order lifted APA prohibitions against advertising that presented comparisons of services, claims of unique services, appeals to emotions or fears, and personal testimonials. (FTC, 1992).

The more 'relaxed' standards for advertising psychological services encouraged by the FTC, and the advent of commodified health care more generally, have seen the development of a side industry in 'marketing techniques' for psy-professionals. Professional magazines such as *Psychotherapy Finances* explain that 'practice success stories have in common the identification of a practice niche, effective marketing, and a mainly self-pay client base' (www.psyfin.com). Other advisers note that the 'direct advertising' of psychological services must be delicately handled. Targeted 'information' campaigns should, apparently, be sent separately from any announcement of specific services. Paradoxically, *helpyourselftherapy.com* tells its readers: 'the more direct the advertising, the less likely there is to be ongoing appreciation for this free service [the provision of 'useful psychological information'] and the caring behind it. We learned that announcements of specific activities should be sent separately'.

Amongst the other marketing strategies recommended for the enterprising practitioner are so-called consumer-information newsletters. *Helpyourselftherapy.com* offers a newsletter service, whereby psychologists are told they can 'Build Your Practice, Enhance Your Reputation, And Simultaneously Demonstrate Your Competence With Each Mailing'. The newsletter contains short articles on a range of common psychological problems and solutions. For a fee, practitioners can have their name and contact details reproduced on the front page, and can disseminate their new promotional product as their own. According to the vendor:

> The newsletters work because you are doing what potential clients expect a therapist to do: you are helping and you are giving. You are subtly selling your skills, and you are not embarrassing yourself in the process. You are demonstrating knowledge, skill, competence, and confidence.
> (www.helpyourselftherapy.com)

For all this, *helpyourselftherapy.com* doesn't specify quite what the therapist is 'demonstrating knowledge, skill, competence, and confidence' in.

Other recommended marketing strategies include using 'drop-in' social therapy groups. These appear to work in much the same manner as your friendly local chemist will offer you half-price toilet paper to win your ongoing trade. As *Psychotherapy Finances* explains:

Group therapy usually means one clinician and eight to ten participants. A therapist in the Midwest decided to expand the idea. So he set up a drop-in group for singles who want to deal with relationship issues. Soon he had 40 people dropping in every Friday night at $5 a head. He then added a monthly communications group for couples, also with a $5 fee. Of course he's not offering intensive group therapy, but 'sort of guides the conversation and sees that things don't get out of hand'. The main payoff: about $3,000 a month in billings from group members who come to him for individual therapy. (Psychotherapy Finances, 2002)

Here we see the self-conscious promotion of personal problems as a cash-generating activity. It doesn't even seem to take much valuable professional time or skill; 'guid[ing] the conversation and see[ing] that things don't get out of hand' is, arguably, an equally accurate description of, for example, the activities of bouncers at nightclub doorways.

As is abundantly clear from these examples of the new promotional tactics available to American psychologists, the upshot of the APA's misadventures with the FTC, and the concomitant commodification of mental health care, is that it is now 'ethical' — and an economic imperative — for American psychologists to directly solicit targeted groups (such as parents of difficult adolescents; couples with relationship concerns; single people, the recently bereaved, and so forth) and to appeal to people's fears in order to motivate them to enter into a 'therapeutic contract'. It is also now 'ethical' for psychologists to claim that they offer unique services (which may be patented, as proof of such) and to solicit and publish testimonials from 'satisfied consumers'.

The American Psychological Association is not alone in (once) considering unethical advertising that appeals to fear if services are not obtained. Indeed, in an earlier incarnation, the FTC once adhered to a similar position and, until recently, deemed advertising that promises the reduction of fear or anxiety to be 'unfair' (Shimp, 1983). What has occurred in the meantime has been a spate of 'information campaigns', in the public interest, which can legitimately claim an ethical *obligation* to excite the anxiety of the ordinary consumer. In his review of the APA's encounter with the FTC, Koocher notes that a number of 'highly successful advertisements appeal to fear at some level' (1994a: 327). He goes on to provide a series of examples drawn from public health campaigns — e.g., fear of injury or death if you ride in a car without seatbelts; fear of AIDS if a condom is not used during intercourse; fear of tooth decay if you don't brush your teeth.

Such campaigns have helped to make ordinary people into ever-vigilant assessors of personal risk. For those purveying health or psychological services, anxious consumers are attentive consumers

(Rose, 1998). Here, psychology continues to enjoy the fruits of its concerted association with the medical professions. 'Mental health' and 'mental health promotion' have entered the lexicon of the 'new public health', and global (psychological) wellbeing now features as a goal of the World Health Organisation, and of governments around the (developed) world. The conflation of physical and mental health has led to 'depression' being touted as the leading cause of disability globally (World Health Organisation, 2001). That is, the toxic sadness which some would argue is itself a direct product of the inevitably dissatisfying consumerism encouraged by globalised capital has supplanted cancer, cardiovascular disease and diabetes as the world's most disabling 'health problem'. If arousing anxiety is ethically justifiable in encouraging people to seek medical advice, and to take responsibility for managing the 'lifestyle' factors associated with these 'real' diseases, then surely it is in the public interest for consumers to enter into similarly prophylactic relationships with psy-professionals, and to devote similarly vigilant attention to everyday risks to our mental health.

Engineering consumers: psychology and advertising

Any examination of the commercialisation of professional psychology would be incomplete without examining one of the earliest ventures of applied psychology — the field of advertising, itself.[16] Psychology — ever generous with its vocabulary and methods — was instrumental in professionalising the industry of sales and selling. By the 1920s, advertising professionals were coming to see that 'nearly all the problems connected with advertising are psychological problems. It is only as they are solved in the light of the data this young science has recorded that advertising becomes scientific and verifiable' (Higham, 1925: 43). The newly professional advertising industry, imbued with psychological expertise, assisted in the shift to mass production and mass consumption. Prior to the professionalisation of selling, advertising was more commonly described as a public service (and of course, still is by those with investments in 'public education'). E.T. Guidlach's (1931) *Facts and Fetishes in Advertising* describes advertising as being of great service to civil society, by promoting a 'revolution in literacy' — i.e. by making newspapers available to millions of ordinary people. Guidlach was suspicious of the intrusion of psychology into the salesman's terrain, and sceptical of psychology's claim that 'advertising gives birth to specific relations within individual brain cells' (Guidlach, 1931: 314).

---

16. The first recorded lecture on the psychology of advertising was delivered in 1901 by Walter Dill Scott, Director of the Psychological Laboratory at Northwestern University, Chicago.

The techniques best suited to fostering the development of 'specific relations within individual brain cells' were detailed in the advertising literature of the 1920s and 1930s in such titles as *The Mind of the Buyer* (Kitson, 1929); *The Psychology of Selling and Advertising* (Strong, 1925); *A Theory of Consumption* (Kyrk, 1923); and *Consumer Engineering* (Sheldon and Egmond, 1932). The latter pitched the practical expertise of the applied psychologist as a 'consumption engineer', responsible, through the application of specialist psychological knowledge, for the manufacture of consumers — the psychologist as necessary complement to the 'production engineer'. Notions of 'stimulus and response' from behavioural theory were mapped onto the economists' rhetoric of supply and demand, and applied psychological research was designed to demonstrate the construction of new 'wants' in potential consumers (Strong and Loveless, 1926). Whilst the lay vocabulary of intentionality — 'want' and 'need', 'desire', and so on — was acceptable, even necessary, for the popular appeal of the 'psychology of selling', academic psychologists proclaimed their research interest in the 'superordinate' topic of the 'psychology of motivation' (e.g. Perrin, 1923).[17] This topic was designed to appeal more broadly to a range of industries interested in influencing human behaviour (education, factory administration, the self-improvement industry, etc.). All behaviour was now describable as 'motivated', and the task of the psychologist now lay in discovering 'scientific' ways to shape people's actions (Danziger, 1997).

Another staple of applied psychology, the opinion poll, has been an integral part of market research since the 1920s (Danziger, 1990). It has long ceased to be strange to be asked, as consumers, to indicate the degree of our agreement or disagreement with a list of statements read to us by a complete stranger. Indeed, we often feel obliged, if not slightly flattered, when asked to participate in such polls. In the 1950s the post-war consumer boom, and rise in available goods and services, saw advertising firms becoming social science research companies engaged in the collection of overwhelming amounts of data on consumers. Applied psychology followed a similar trajectory, and devoted corresponding resources to survey research. The APA created a Consumer Psychology division in 1960.

Applied psychologists of the 1960s primarily described advertising as 'educational'; as providing 'instruction on what to anticipate and aspire to as consumers' (Boyd and Levy, 1967: 49). They also assisted in defining 'consuming as a way to express a way of thinking or living ... how people create a lifestyle that is meaningful and coherent' (Boyd and Levy, 1967: 34–8). Again, psychological methods promised the means to motivate, and to manufacture, particular kinds of consumer. Psychology continues to lend authority and legitimacy to the 'science' of modern advertising, and to offer its vocabulary and

---

17. For more on the history of the psychology of motivation, see Danziger (1997).

assessment methods in 'engineering' the modern consumer. Consumers are currently assumed to be more active, complex, and sophisticated creatures than early models would allow. Indeed, late-modern consumers are *obliged* to be such:

> The ... processes involved in shaping the 'commercial domain' in the mid-twentieth century ... were not a matter of the unscrupulous manipulation of passive consumers: technologies of consumption depended on fabricating delicate affiliations between the active choices of potential consumers, and the qualities, pleasures and satisfactions represented in the product, organised in part through the practices of advertising and marketing, and always undertaken in the light of particular beliefs about the nature of human subjectivity. (Miller and Rose, 1997: 31)

As we have noted, the modern consumer has become a commodity in their own right. Whilst our motivation, as *enterprising* selves, tends to be assumed (self-actualisation, self-determination, empowerment, participation, responsible autonomy, the right to choice), the intricacies of our habits, interests, attitudes, opinions, impressions, intentions, likes and dislikes, hobbies, 'personalities' (and so on) are pervasively relevant, in everyday transactions, to the new economy of consumption.

The empowered consumer

> The future of health care is the consumer. (Keith, 2001: 16)

The rhetoric of 'freedom of choice', 'empowerment' and the 'right to participation' has come to dominate both the psy-professions and the realm of health care more generally. As good consumers, we are compelled to seek out and evaluate psychological information, to maintain vigilance over new risks to ourselves, to be aware of the conditions under which relevant experts should be consulted, and to be 'empowered' to assert our right to therapeutic attention, and appropriate medication or psychological treatment:

> The consumer's increased role in ensuring his or her own health and welfare ... requires both greater freedom — in this case, freedom to receive information — and greater responsibility. (Calfee, 2001: 11)

In whose interests, we might ask, are consumers 'empowered'? The following extract from *Economic Realities in Health Care Policy* (produced by Pfizer) gives some indication of the (commercial) benefits of 'fostering increasingly empowered consumers':

It will be our challenge to respond to, but also, to foster, increasingly empowered consumers .... Equipping patients with
more information, and probably more questions, may encourage a more active dialogue ... which in turn can nurture the
growing health care competence of the individual patient .... It
can also promote adherence to the prescribed therapeutic regimen (How much better is patient 'adherence' to an agreed-
upon regimen than patient 'compliance' with a paternalistically
imposed regimen!) (Calfee, 2001: 15)

The 'health care competence' of the new 'consumer' has become a
desired characteristic of the formerly compliant patient. Consumers — even at their most vulnerable — are obliged to become more
responsible, more actively involved, and more committed to the
project of maintaining their health and wellbeing. So-called 'expert
patients' are even now being recruited by the UK Department of
Health to assist others develop their expertise. These new responsibilities are the corollary of the new 'freedom' of the empowered consumer which, it seems, boil down to the 'right to information' and/
or to be subjected to a panoply of 'motivational' (and motivated)
educational campaigns, courtesy of the psy, health and pharmaceutical professions:

Advertising seems to serve an educational role, the benefits of
which accrue first and foremost to patients ... brand promotion often provides basic information that consumers need to
know, but that no one has an incentive to provide to consumers unless the missing information is promoted with a branded
product. (Calfee, 2001: 15)

Armed with information, consumers are empowered to make responsible and autonomous choices about the products and services that
best meet their needs — though the veridicality of this information
may well be questionable. Indeed, the consuming citizen has become an integral and active agent in the regulation of professional
expertise, and in the maintenance of 'quality' and competitive services. Various consumer activist groups have, since the late 1960s,
sought to intervene in the once private affairs of the professions. In a
neat symmetry, pharmaceutical companies now admit to 'fostering'
so-called 'consumer activist groups' as front organisations to lobby
the same professions to prescribe more of their branded products
(Moynihan, 2002). As we have seen, a number of highly publicised
and successful lawsuits attracted the attention of the state to the
(de)regulation of professional matters, and other efforts to ensure
the 'consumer-orientation' of professional ethics — culminating, for
the APA, with the recent intervention of the FTC on behalf of America's
consumer-citizens.

The psy-professions are now unabashedly consumer-centred. The APA currently boasts an online 'Consumer Help Center' and has proclaimed a 'Bill of Rights' for consumers. Key to these changes is the wider shift from a 'welfare' based model of governmentality, to the current, 'neo-liberal' order:

> In place of the themes of collective provision and social solidarity, with the rational planning of welfare and its administration through bureaucracies, are proposed notions of security provided through the private purchase of insurance schemes, health care purchased by individuals and provided by the health industry ... efficiency secured not through selfless dedication and commitment of professionals but through the discipline of competition for consumers. (Rose, 1999: 230)

In the next section, we examine these new developments, in the light of the parallel development of commodified health care (or 'managed care').

Public education — 'Good Thinking!'

As we have seen, the need for 'public education' has long preoccupied professional psychological associations. The most recent 'public education' campaigns of the major professional psychological associations are — transparently and self-consciously — marketing exercises. According to research on the 'effects of advertising on psychology', such 'collective' advertisements present the profession in a more positive light than do the self-advertisements of individual professionals who may vary in their adherence to ethical conventions (Frisch and Rebert, 1991). The American Psychological Association is not the only national association actively promoting psychology via the kind of advertising campaigns that might once have been considered unethical. Indeed, the Australian Psychological Society, despite a continuing ethical prohibition (for individual professionals) on all self-promotion save the restrained 'calling card' model of advertising, has developed over 20 years an increasingly 'American-style' marketing campaign of its own.

The inception of APS brand marketing of psychology began in the late 1980s, with the first part of the campaign seeing the Australian Psychological Society itself becoming an Agony Aunt for the Melbourne *Age* newspaper. In the 'Consulting Room' column, the APS advised readers on such matters as 'the balance between work and leisure'; a 'balanced married life' (*Age*, 1987a); and 'the stresses of modern living', under the heading 'More time to have fun, but we are still unhappy' (*Age*, 1987b). The current 'Good Thinking!' campaign has produced and disseminated 'consumer information' in the form of a 'brochure' which is also readily accessible via the APS's website. This is (as we will see in chapter seven) regularly recommended in the health and problem pages of popular Australian magazines:

APS Psychologists: 'Good Thinking!'
'Good Thinking', Wellbeing and Psychologists
Everyday life problems such as workplace stress, family and relationship matters or coping with illness can seriously affect your quality of life. At these times it is important that people do not neglect their health and relationships with others. Seeking a consultation with an APS psychologist is 'Good Thinking'. APS psychologists equip their clients with the skills and the 'Good Thinking' that they need to function better in their life and to prevent ill-health and other problems developing. People often think psychologists only provide therapies for mental health problems. While some psychologists do specialise in this area, most psychologists assist mentally healthy people to find ways of functioning better ....
For help with — Marital, family and relationship problems; Stress, migraines, or pain; Fears, phobias, anxiety and panic attacks; Depression and unresolved grief; Sexual difficulties; Sleeping difficulties; Eating and weight control problems; Children's learning, behaviour and management problems; Addictions; Making good relationships better; Becoming better parents and teachers; Personal growth; Career planning; Making better workplaces; Improving sports performance; Training and developing staff; Improving employment selection; Reviewing organisational structure and practices; Improving industrial relations and occupational health and safety; Studying consumer needs — see an APS psychologist.
(www.psychsociety.com.au/servicing/fr_servicing.htm.)

This officially-produced marketing brochure works to 'captivate' the consumer, in the ways we noted earlier: everyday problems can affect not only your own 'quality of life', but that of your nearest and dearest. Thus, you have an obligation to look after your mental health, in order to prevent problems from surfacing, and to find ways of becoming ever more functional. You have a concomitant obligation to remain vigilant about the mental health of your children, lovers, relatives and workmates. 'Good Thinking!' is thus not directed primarily to people experiencing 'psychological problems' — but to the ordinary 'healthy' person, who may wish to invest in the preventative maintenance and enhancement of their mental health, as part of the process of responsible self-actualisation.[18]

---

18. Advertisements from individual practitioners follow a similar trend. One psychologist describes himself as: 'similar to a personal trainer, and psychotherapy as analogous to working out at a health club. One need not be ...

The exhaustive list of problems for which APS psychologists are available to help offers the consumer considerable choice, and certainly appears to contain 'something for everyone'. Strangely absent is any mention of the sorts of difficulties that the public might associate with madness or mental illness. As we will see in chapter five, the online information pages of professional psychologists follow a similar logic.

> It might ... happen that you simply feel vaguely dissatisfied with your life, but you can't get a clear sense of what the problem is. In this case you might consult a psychologist to help define the problem. (Richmond, 2002)

'Talk to someone who can help'

The stated aim of the American Psychological Association's public education campaign, 'Talk to Someone Who Can Help', is to 'help people understand when it is appropriate to seek psychological services and how a psychologist can help with everyday life problems' (helping.apa.org/spreadtheword/index.html). The APA's online 'Consumer Help Center' is the public face of the campaign. Much of the Center is devoted to instruction on the issues posed by managed care plans and insurance coverage.[19] 'You can learn about how the current health care system limits consumer's access to quality mental health services and how to change the system'. One of the things that appeals to 'consumer rights' is the legitimate use of other terms from the language of various progressive social movements (feminism; environmentalism; gay, lesbian and transgender rights, etc.). So, as in the instruction above, issues of 'access' and the imperative to 'change the system' are invoked. 'Empowerment', 'participation' and 'equity' are, of course, also part of this 'progressive' arsenal.

... morbidly obese to benefit from a work-out, nor do you need to be psychotic to benefit from therapy' ('Dr Larry Gard', 2002).

19. According to U'Ren (1997: 1), managed health care divides service providers into 'competing economic units .... There are two basic strategies for commodifying health care. In the first, an entity called a health maintenance organization (HMO) manages all aspects of care: selection of psychiatrists and other physicians who agree to accept a discounted fee; prior authorisation of all treatment by either the patient's primary physician or the plan's administrative physician; and standard protocols of treatment that favour less-expensive therapies: medication instead of psychotherapy, short-term therapy instead of long-term therapy. The second method is called capitation. An HMO offers to pay a group of psychiatrists (or other clinicians) a fixed fee per person (per head = capitation) to assume responsibility for a cohort of patients for a certain period of time. Responsibility for holding down costs is shifted to the treating psychiatrist, who makes money if patient needs are low and loses money if patient needs are high'.

The public education campaigns of the professional associations appear greatly concerned with the serious problem posed by the reticence of the public to seek professional 'help'. Or, as plaintively posed in the APA's 'Help Center', 'why don't people seek the help they should?' After citing a study by the National Institute of Mental Health, which reports that a 'significant number' of people in need of mental health care do not seek help, the APA speculates on the reasons for this reluctance: people may 'mistakenly believe their symptoms are of their own doing, and that they can overcome their problems by themselves', or may avoid seeking professional help for fear of being stigmatised by their family or community. Apparently, 'some people don't realise they even have a problem, thinking the condition is normal .... People may also think that their symptoms are physical in origin, when actually their complaints stem from psychological factors' (www.apa.org/practice/paper). This last impediment to appropriate mental health care consumption is somewhat paradoxical in the light of the assiduous efforts made by psychology textbook writers to convince undergraduate psychologists that nearly all 'mental disorders' are, actually, the result of 'chemical imbalances in the brain'. (See chapter eight.)

However, according to the 'Help Center', the 'major obstacle to seeking help' is not patient resistance to therapy *per se*, but rather the restrictive limits placed on access by mental health insurance coverage. Apparently, many insurance plans limit mental health hospitalisation to 30–60 days per year. The APA also expresses considerable outrage that 'some insurers do not place restrictive limits on cancer treatments, but they do limit treatment for mental health[!]'

It is unfortunate that many people who could benefit from treatment do not seek help, because they are unsure about where to seek help, have limited mental health insurance coverage, or do not have any mental health insurance coverage. This situation will hold true, although to a lesser extent, even when the new Mental Health Parity Act goes into effect in January 1998. (www.apa.org/practice/paper)

In the section of the 'Help Center' devoted to 'Accessing Quality Care', we are informed that, 'for many Americans, quality mental health services are no longer accessible in the new health care marketplace. *The APA and other consumer advocacy organizations* have begun to challenge the status quo in the legal and legislative arenas' (helping.apa.org/spreadtheword/access.html; our emphasis). The American Psychological Association appears to have achieved a rather dramatic shift in focus — from a professional association concerned with the scientific integrity of the discipline, to a campaigning consumer advocacy organisation. The 'Quality Care' section provides consumers with links to press releases, proposals and news relevant to 'efforts to secure quality psychological services for all'. It seems we now have a democratic right not just to learn about useful psychological facts, but also to access 'quality' psychological services.

It is these 'rights' that the APA is keen to champion. Further information is provided by way of an exposition of the relevance, to consumers, of the 1996 Mental Health Parity Act. In 'Consumers to benefit from historic parity legislation' the APA explains that this Act 'heralds an historic step toward ending discrimination against individuals in need of mental health services' (helping.apa.org/spreadtheword/parity.html). The legislation in question, passed by Congress in 1997, prevents the imposition of annual and lifetime limits on mental health services. The executive director of the APA Practice Directorate, Russ Newman, characterises the Act as 'an important victory for consumers. The law will expand patients' access to appropriate mental health services by allowing necessary treatment to continue without the risk of an arbitrary dollar limit stopping it ... 69% of Americans acknowledge the importance of seeking professional help for problems they cannot resolve themselves' (helping.apa.org/spreadtheword/parity.html).

The APA's 'Consumer Help Center' also contains a handy set of 'Questions to Ask Your Employer's Benefits Manager'. These are centred on the right of the consumer to 'shop' for a therapist and to select, from the market of expertise, a psy-professional of choice. The homepages of private practitioners also remind consumers of their right to 'informed choice', and to 'shop around':

> Remember: You Are HIRING The Therapist! YOU decide if they are right for you, and you have every right to 'shop around' ....
> Therapists Are The Experts On Therapy. But YOU Are Always The Best Expert On YOU!
> Remember that as a consumer you have the right to interview the psychologist thoroughly. Select at least two candidates who seem favourable ... make it clear that you are 'shopping around' .... And remember that this interview process, however long it takes, is really part of the process of getting help. You will learn many things about yourself just in this initial selection process. (secure4.hostmysite.com/helpyourselftherapy/topics/considth.html)

Such 'shopping expeditions' are described as valuable 'learning experiences', and as an necessary part of the process of 'getting help' — though, by this description, they appear to bear more of a resemblance to a job interview than to a therapy session, as traditionally conducted. The resemblance ends at the point where the empowered consumer is asked to pay for the consultation.

The 'Bill of Rights'

Mental Health Bill of Rights Announcement: Leaders of nine organizations representing more than 600,000 mental health professionals have issued a 'Bill of Rights' to protect individuals seeking treatment for mental illness and psychological and substance abuse disorders.
(helping.apa.org/spreadtheword/apanews.html)

The APA argues that restrictive insurance plans deprive consumers of their right to 'shop for a therapist' — thus consumers are enjoined to lobby their benefits manager (or insurance company) with such questions as:

Which mental health professionals are covered by your plan? Does the plan cover a full range of mental health professionals? What is their training and experience? Are they licensed or certified? What kinds of treatments are available? What treatments are excluded? Are you able to choose any licensed/certified professional for your mental health care services?
(helping.apa.org/spreadtheword/seven.html)

These questions are the short form of the APA-sponsored 'Bill of Rights' for the 'protection' of consumers seeking psychological assistance. The 'Bill of Rights' is a joint production of a novel coalition of the major American psy-professional organisations which brings together the American Association for Marriage and Family Therapy (membership: 25,000); the American Counselling Association (membership: 56,000); the American Family Therapy Academy (membership: 1,000); the American Nurses Association (membership: 180,000); the American Psychological Association (membership: 151,000); the American Psychiatric Association (membership: 42,000); the American Psychiatric Nurses Association (membership: 3,000); the National Association of Social Workers (membership: 155,000); and the National Federation of Societies for Clinical Social Work (membership: 11,000). In sum, a 'consumer-friendly' group made up of over 600,000 psy-professionals, with the support of the National Mental Health Association, the National Depressive and Manic-Depressive Association, the American Group Psychotherapy Association, the American Psychoanalytic Association, and the National Association of Drug and Alcohol Abuse Counsellors.

The Bill of Rights, drafted by professionals concerned to protect the rights of consumers to access their services, comes with endorsements from both the President of the American Psychological Association, and the President of the other APA — the American Psychiatric Association. Harold Eist, President of this other APA notes that it is the *responsibility* of consumers to 'demand and receive the care they need'. The Bill of Rights has been designed to empower consumers to assert these rights:

> As mental health professionals, we have dedicated ourselves to the welfare of our patients. Yet every day in our offices, we see the harm caused to our patients who frequently are denied the care they need by managed care or insurance plan representatives who have never seen them .... We hope that people will use the principles embodied in this Bill of Rights to demand and receive the care that they need.
> (helping.apa.org/spreadtheword/apanews.html)

Dorothy Carter, President of the American Psychological Association, is hopeful that the Bill — which reflects the rights of consumers *as imagined by professionals* — will be supported by patient advocacy groups:

> The present obsession of today's health care system on controlling costs is compromising the rights of individuals to competent and quality care. The principles embodied in this Bill of Rights reflect what we as professionals believe individuals are entitled to when they select a health plan and when they seek treatment. We are pleased that the major national patient advocacy groups agree, and have given us their moral support.
> (helping.apa.org/spreadtheword/apanews.html)

Gratifyingly, Laurie Flynn, Executive Director of the National Alliance for the Mentally Ill (an advocacy group and grateful recipient of massive funding from pharmaceutical companies), was so impressed with the Bill that she composed an official letter to Dr Eist:

> There has never been such a consensus document; it is a breakthrough. It is healthy for consumers and providers to speak in closer harmony in opposition to health system provisions that impede access, or reduce quality and consumer satisfaction.
> (helping.apa.org/spreadtheword/apanews.html)

So, what does this new Bill of Rights for consumers contain? The preamble asserts the commitment of the psy-professions to provide their services to everyone — even if they happen to be from a minority social group:

> Our commitment is to provide quality mental health care to all individuals, without regard to race, color, religion, national origin, gender, age, sexual orientation, or disabilities.
> (helping.apa.org/spreadtheword/rights.html)

Fourteen 'Principles for the Provision of Mental Health Services' are given. The Bill is concerned with such principles as the right of access to detailed information about the expertise (knowledge, skills, experience, credentials) of psy-professionals, and to information on the range of available treatment options (including risks, benefits and 'cost implications'). Further, 'Individuals have the right to choose any duly licensed/certified professional for mental health services' (helping.apa.org/spreadtheword/rights.html). The only principle vaguely concerned on the face of it with issues of social justice and responsibility — 'Discrimination' — turns out to be about avoiding 'penalisation' when seeking health insurance. Indeed, the entire document is centred on the ideal interaction between psy-consumers, providers, and the American health care system. Issues of liability dominate all but three of the 14 principles.

As we have seen, the public education campaigns of the professional associations have a traditional focus on the perplexing reticence of the public to seek professional 'help' — despite being avid consumers of popular psychological products and services, including books. In its address to these 'reluctant' consumers, the APA (as consumer advocacy organisation) seeks to reassure us of our centrality to the profession. The APA's 'Consumer Help Center' and 'Bill of Rights' work to inform us, as consumers, of our right to seek professional psychological services, of the threats that insurance plans may pose to these rights, and of the appropriate strategies for asserting these rights. As consumers, we are enjoined to exercise our right to informed choice, to seek out the professional service that's right for us — in the new consumer-friendly marketplace of psy-expertise.

References

Age, The (1987a) The Consulting Room. *The Melbourne Age*, (16 September)
Age, The (1987b) The Consulting Room. *The Melbourne Age*, (20 September)
Allen, F.L. (1931) *Only Yesterday: An Informal History of the 1920s.* New York: Harper and Row
American Psychological Association (1952) Ethical Standards for Psychology. *American Psychologist, 6*, 626–61
American Psychological Association (1953) *Ethical Standards of Psychologists.* Washington: APA
American Psychological Association (1959) Ethical Standards of Psychologists. *American Psychologist, 14*, 279–82
American Psychological Association (1969) Guidelines for Telephone Directory Listings. *American Psychologist, 24*, 70–1
American Psychological Association (1981) Ethical Principles of Psychologists. *American Psychologist, 36*, 633–8
American Psychological Association (1990) Ethical Principles of Psychologists (Amended 2 June 1989). *American Psychologist, 45*, 390–5
American Psychological Association (1992) Ethical Principles of Psychologists and Code of Conduct. *American Psychologist, 47*, 1597–604

American Psychological Association (2001) Ethical Principles of Psychologists. (Draft 6 October 2001). Retrieved 15 March 2002: <anastasi.apa.org/draftethicscode>

American Psychological Association (2002) Consumer Help Center. Retrieved 20 March 2002: <helping.apa.org>

Association for the Advancement of Psychology (1982) FTC's Jurisdiction over Professions Threatened. *Advance, 8,* 5

Australian Psychological Society (1995) *Code of Professional Conduct.* Carlton: APS

Australian Psychological Society (2002) APS Psychologists: Good Thinking! Retrieved 5 April 2002: (www.psychsociety.com.au/servicing/fr_servicing.htm)

Avery, Robert (1990) Talk Radio: The Private-Public Catharsis. In: Gary Gumpert and Sandra Fish (eds) *Talking to Strangers: Mediated Therapeutic Communication.* New Jersey: Ablex, 87–97

Blakeslee, Alton (1952) Psychology and the Newspaper Man. *American Psychologist 6,* 91–4

Boyd, Harper W. and Levy, Sidney J. (1967) *Promotion: A Behavioral View.* Englewood Cliffs, NJ: Prentice-Hall

British Psychological Society (2002a) Advertising Through the BPS. Retrieved 10 April 2002: (www.bps.org.uk/about/advertising.cfm)

British Psychological Society (2002b) Code of Conduct, Ethical Principles and Guidelines. Retrieved 6 April 2002: (www.bps.org.uk/about/rules5.cfm)

Calfee, John (2001) What the FDA Survey Showed about Direct-to-consumer Prescription Drug Advertising. *Economic Realities in Health Care Policy, 2*(1), 10–15

Cooke, Simon (2000) *A Meeting of Minds: The Australian Psychological Society and Australian Psychologists, 1944–1994.* Brisbane: APS

Danziger, Kurt (1990) *Constructing the Subject: Historical Origins of Psychological Research.* Cambridge: Cambridge University Press

Danziger, Kurt (1997) *Naming the Mind: How Psychology Found its Language.* London: Sage

Dineen, Tana (1998) Psychologists and Section 15 (Custody Evaluation) Reports: Illusions of Expertise, Ethics and Objectivity. Address to the Vancouver Family Law Sections, Canadian Bar Association, 6 May

'Dr Larry Gard' (2002) Untitled. Retrieved 10 May 2002: (www.drlarrygard.com)

Ellis, Pete; Smith, Don and Bushnell, John (2001) Treating Depression: Making It Better. *Medical Journal of Australia 175* (Supplement), S8–9

Federal Trade Commission (1992) FTC File No. 861 0082 (15 October)

Fisher, Celia and Younggren, Jeffrey (1997) The Value and Utility of the APA Ethics Code. *Professional Psychology: Research and Practice, 28*(6), 582–92

Francis, Ronald and Cameron, Colin (1997) *The Professional Psychology Handbook.* Melbourne: MacMillan

Frisch, G.R. and Rebert, D. (1991) Effects of Advertising on Psychology. *Canadian Journal of Psychology, 32,* 176–80

Guidlach, E.T. (1931) *Facts and Fetishes in Advertising.* Chicago: Consolidated Book Publishing

Hall, Calvin, S. (1952) Crooks, Code and Cant. *American Psychologist, 7,* 430

Haug, Marie and Sussman, Marvin (1969) Professional Autonomy and the Revolt of the Client. *Social Problems, 17*(2), 153–61

Help Yourself Therapy (2002) Untitled. Retrieved 10 May 2002: (www.helpyourselftherapy.com)

Hendley, W.C. (1977–1978) Dear Abby, Miss Lonelyhearts, and the Eighteenth Century: The Origins of the Newspaper Advice Column. *Journal of Popular Culture, 11*, 345–52

Higham, Charles (1925) *Advertising: Its Use and Abuse*. London: Williams and Norgate

Hobbs, Nicholas (1948) The Development of a Code of Ethical Standards for Psychology. *American Psychologist, 3*, 80–4

Holzman, W. H. (1960) Some Problems of Defining Ethical Behavior. *American Psychologist, 15*, 247–50

Hunt, Howard, F. (1952) On the Applications of the Proposed Code of Ethical Standards for Psychology. *American Psychologist, 7*, 431–2

Keith, Alison (2001) Information Matters: The Consumer as the Integrated Health Care System. *Economic Realities in Health Care Policy, 2*(1), 15–20

Kinderman, Peter and Cooke, Anne (2000) *Recent Advances in Understanding Mental Illness and Psychotic Experiences*. East Leicester: The British Psychological Society, Division of Clinical Psychology

Kitson, Harry Dexter (1929) *The Mind of the Buyer: A Psychology of Selling*. New York: MacMillan

Klein, Naomi (2000) *No Logo*. London: Flamingo

Klonoff, Elizabeth (1983) A Star is Born: Psychologists and the Media. *Professional Psychology, Research and Practice, 14*(6), 847–54

Koocher, Gerald, P. (1977) Advertising from Psychologists: Pride and Prejudice or Sense and Sensibility? *Professional Psychology, 8*, 149–60

Koocher, Gerald, P. (1994a) APA and the FTC: New Adventures in Consumer Protection. *American Psychologist, 49*, 322–8

Koocher, Gerald, P. (1994b) The commerce of professional psychology and the new ethics code. *Professional Psychology: Research and Practice, 25*(4), 355–61

Kyrk, Hazel (1923) *A Theory of Consumption*. London: Pitman and Sons

Leahey, Thomas Hardy (1997) *A History of Psychology: Main Currents in Psychological Thought. Fourth Edition*. Engelwood Cliffs, NJ: Prentice-Hall

Longstaff, Simon (2002) Interview on Professional Standards. *The Law Report*. ABC Radio National, broadcast 23 April

McCallum, James (1977) Private Practice of Clinical and Counselling Psychology. In: Mary Nixon and Ronald Taft (eds) *Psychology in Australia: Achievements and Prospects*. Adelaide: Pergamon Press, 229–42

Miller, George (1969) Psychology as a Means of Promoting Human Welfare. *American Psychologist, 24*, 1063–75

Miller, Peter and Rose, Nikolas (1997) Mobilizing the Consumer: Assembling the Subject of Consumption. *Theory, Culture and Society, 14*(1), 1–36

Montgomery, Eleanor (1938) *Can Psychology Help?* London: Rich and Cowan

Moynihan, Ray (2002) Drug Firms Hype Disease as Sales Ploy, Industry Chief Claims. *British Medical Journal, 324* (13 April), 867

O'Connor, Eileen (2001) Real-world Risk Management . *Monitor on Psychology, 32*(4). Retrieved 21 March 2002: (www.apa.org/monitor/apr01/risk.html)

Perrin, Fleming Allan Clay (1923) The Psychology of Motivation. *Psychological Review, 30*, 176–91

Pilgrim, David and Treacher, Andy (1990) *Clinical Psychology Observed*. London: Routledge

Psychotherapy Finances (2002) Untitled. Retrieved 10 May 2002: (www.psyfin.com)

Remmers, Hermann (1944) Psychology: Some Unfinished Business. *American Psychologist, 1*, 713–24

Rich, G. J. (1952) A New Code of Ethics is Needed. *American Psychologist, 7*, 440–1

Richmond, Raymond (2002) A Guide to Psychology and its Practice: Reasons to Consult a Psychologist. Retrieved 10 May 2002:<members.aol.com/ avpsyrich/reasons.htm>

Rose, Nikolas (1998) Governing Risky Individuals: The Role of Psychiatry in New Regimes of Control. *Psychiatry, Psychology and Law, 3*(2), 177–96

Rose, Nikolas (1999) *Governing the Soul. The Shaping of the Private Self.* 2nd edition. London, Free Association Books

Sanford, Fillmore (1951) Across the Secretary's Desk: Notes on the Future of Psychology as a Profession. *American Psychologist, 6*, 74–6

Sheldon, Roy and Egmont, Arens (1932) *Consumer Engineering: A New Technique for Prosperity.* New York: Harper and Brothers

Shimp, Terence (1983) Evaluative Verbal Content and Deception in Advertising: A Review and Critical Analysis. In: Richard Harris (ed.) *Information Processing Research and Advertising.* Mahwah, NJ: Lawrence Erlbaum, 195–216

Strong, E.K. (1925) *The Psychology of Selling and Advertising.* New York: McGraw Hill

Strong, E.K. and Loveless, J.E. (1926) 'Want' and 'Solution' Advertisements. *Journal of Applied Psychology, 10*, 346–66

UNSW (2002) Psychology: Courses and Careers. Retrieved 10 May 2002: (www.psy.unsw.edu.au/study/careers)

U'Ren, Richard (1997) Psychiatry and Capitalism. *The Journal of Mind and Behaviour, 18*(1), 1–12

Vasquez, Melba (1994) Implications of the 1992 Ethics Code for the Practice of Individual Psychotherapy. *Professional Psychology: Research and Practice, 25*(4), 321–8

Warner, Richard (2000) *Recovery from Schizophrenia: Psychiatry and Political Economy.* 2nd edition. London: Routledge

Warner, David and de Girolamo, G. (1995) *Epidemiology of Mental Disorders and Psychosocial Problems: Schizophrenia.* Geneva: World Health Organisation

Weatherhead, Leslie (1934) *Psychology and Life: Sound Psychology Made Vivid and Practical.* London: Hodder and Stoughton

White, Stephen (2002) Re: Working Party on Psychologists, Ethics and the Media. Personal Email, 28 August 2002

Wigdor, A.K. and Garner, W.R. (eds) (1982) *Ability Testing; Uses, Consequences, and Controversies.* (Committee on Ability Testing, Assembly of Behavioral and Social Sciences.) Washington: National Academy Press

World Health Organisation (2001) *World Health Report, 2000.* Geneva: World Health Organisation

Self-help, etc.

Within you, without you

The title of this chapter is identical to that of the first chapter of what is possibly the first self-help book written in the English language: Samuel Smiles' *Self-Help: With Illustrations of Character and Conduct*, first published in 1859, the same year as Darwin's *On the Origin of Species*. Of course, what Smiles wanted to help selves towards at first sight appears quite different from what we now think of as the goals of the self-help manual. For us, the $5 billion-plus per annum self-help market includes such forms of self-concern as biofeedback, brain enhancement, dating, death and grieving, Feng Shui, massage, positive parenting, self-esteem, time-management. And the list could continue through categories too numerous and too temporally fleeting to mention. By contrast, Smiles, using historical progress as a model of individual development, wanted to help his reader to become as close to perfection, and as self-made a British professional 'hero', as possible. So much so, in fact, that such a well-known aspiring British gentleman as V.S. Naipaul's (1969) Mr Biswas refers to Smiles with reverence as his ultimate training manual.

The case of Smiles and Mr Biswas is illuminating, especially with respect to the 'romanticism' of Smiles' 'practical' advice — here, on how to become an inventor — and to the manual-addiction it leads to:

> [Mr Biswas] stayed in the back trace and read Samuel Smiles. He had bought one of his books in the belief that it was a novel, and had become an addict. Samuel Smiles was as romantic as any novelist, and Mr Biswas saw himself in many Samuel Smiles heroes: he was young, he was poor, and he fancied he was struggling. (1969: 78)

So far, so good, then. But habitus produces different selves, and the one being 'helped' here, Mr Biswas, was a formation of cultural and economic conditions that put him, according to the model, beyond help:

... there always came a point when resemblance ceased. The heroes had rigid ambitions and lived in countries where ambitions could be pursued and had a meaning. He had no ambition, and in this hot land, apart from opening a shop or buying a motorbus, what could he do? (1969: 78–9)

At this point, then, the manual user is driven to improvise, largely via the overtly technical practices suggested by still more manuals:

He bought elementary manuals of science and read them; nothing happened; he only became addicted to elementary manuals of science. He bought the seven expensive volumes of *Hawkins' Electrical Guide*, made rudimentary compasses, buzzers and doorbells, and learned to wind an armature. Beyond that he could not go. Experiments became more complex, and he didn't know where in Trinidad he could find the equipment mentioned so casually by Hawkins. His interest in electrical matters died, and he contented himself with reading about the Samuel Smiles heroes in their magic land. (1969: 79)

We will see this opposition between the romantic (interior, imaginary, subjective, cognitive) and the practical (exterior, concrete, objective, behavioural) emerging throughout our discussion of the self-help book as a technology of the self. Naipaul's enduring insight is to show how, in the actual practice of using such books, the self-help book's dual aspect as half novel and half technical manual — as both romantic and practical — instantiates its assumptions about the modern subject's irreconcilably double aspect.

Smiles' technique, then, was little different from the self-helpers we can read today. His separations of the person into, for example, body and mind, behaviour and cognition, flesh and spirit, still have cogency today — and so does his solution to these differences: a wonderful and ecstatic (re)union of the two: a healthy mind in a healthy body. Take, for example, this passage from his manual:

The success even of professional men depends in no slight degree on their organic stamina and cultivated physical strength. Thus a well-developed thorax is considered almost as indispensable to the successful lawyer or politician as a well-cultured intellect. The thorough aëration of the blood by free exposure to a large breathing surface in the lungs, is necessary to maintain that full vital power on which the vigorous working of the brain in so large a measure depends. (1859: 279–80)

The emphasis here is, no doubt, upon the body: the blood, the lungs, the thorax and all large stations in between. But all of this is considered the co-equal of the 'well-cultured intellect', and equally necessary to it for the well-balanced life.

What are we seeing here? Probably two things. The first is a division of the human being into two kinds of subject, one material and the other a spirit or ghost haunting that materiality. The second is the possibility of an harmonious balance, conciliation or homeostasis between them. In secular times we have become, albeit awkwardly, both the ghost *in*-the-machine and the ghost-*containing* machine. We make selves just as we make working compasses, buzzers and doorbells.

From Smiles' times to the present (and, we would guess, well into the future), this has been the purpose of the self-help book: to find a denouement for this narrative; to find a ghost-machine and a machine-ghost such that each adequates the other — eternally. That would give us the perfect (finished, complete) human being. That is the point of every self-help book — and the impossibility of any such perfectibility is always its downfall.

Smiles recognised this from the start when he wrote, on the first page of the first English self-help book: 'Help from without is often enfeebling in its effects, but help from within invariably invigorates' (1859: 15). And, as he knew, any book — his book — was always 'help from without'. From the very start of the self-help book industry then, there are two paradoxes. The first is a paradoxical subject of help: eternally fragmented but ever in pursuit of wholeness. The second is a paradoxical technique of help: an insistence on the achievement of auto-completion via the book itself, as always 'from without'. To put these into mottos: you may desire completeness, but your basic self-constitution makes this impossible; you can only help yourself, books won't do it for you, but buy them anyway in order that your self-doubt can be explained.

The self-help industry's practices, then, make a person 'subject to someone else by control and dependence; and tied to their own identity by a conscience or self-knowledge' (Foucault, 1982: 781). Such practices derive from the human sciences, the psy-disciplines in particular, which divide the subject and then attempt to reconcile those divisions. The human sciences pronounce on speech, material production, and bodily mechanics; certain practices divide the subject within itself and from others in terms of health and conduct; and the subject identifies as such.

These practices typically accompany three modes of subjectification: the speaking subject (defined as such by linguistics); the working subject (from economics); and the living subject (of the natural sciences, especially biology). Practices that define subjects as internally riven or separated from others nominate the sane versus the mad, the criminal versus the well-behaved, and the healthy versus the sick. These categories are produced through the administrative decisions and apparatuses of institutions driven by forms of scientific knowledge. And self-directed techniques turn a person into a subject: gay versus straight, private versus public, and learned versus learning. Struggles for power take place over:

> the status of the individual: on the one hand, they assert the right to be different, and they underline everything which makes individuals truly individual. On the other hand, they attack everything which separates the individual, breaks his links with others, splits up community life, forces the individual back on himself and ties him to his own identity in a constraining way. (Foucault, 1982: 777–8)

The raw stuff of human beings, then, is *not* individuality: people *become* individuals through discourses and institutions. Take, for example, rites of passage from traditional societies, such as circumcision. They are increasingly displaced, supplemented, or made purely symbolic by scientific accounts of personhood: status and ancestry join measurement and confession, as ritualistic shame meets inner guilt and state authority. Epistemology shifts, with facts and interpretations deriving from experimentation rather than individual authority. But even as this looser model of power appears, so too do hospitals and psychologists — Foucault calls them 'professionals of discipline, normality and subjection' (1979: 193). They use the new forms of knowledge to multiply and intensify the expression of power over bodies. For example, adults who lack the ability to narrate their feelings and struggles to the satisfaction of psychologists can be incarcerated for failing the duty of disclosure that is the corollary of Enlightenment freedoms (Foucault, 1987: 23; Albee, 1977: 152). However, this has not always been so: emotions, as we will see below, have a tendency to be historically relative.

Historical shifts in the discourses of 'feeling'[1]

We can begin with an exemplary instance from another of our psy-commerce genres: US women's-magazine articles on marriage in the 1960s. Here we see a shift towards sexual pleasure and high romance — though not necessarily in combination — and away from earlier themes of self-sacrifice and loyalty. But such shifts bring their own disciplines and loyalties, their grammars and vocabularies of consent and orthodoxy. Far from being Pollyanna-ish accounts of domestic bliss, the magazines of the 1940s and '50s had depicted the household as a site of struggle where happiness and intellect (positive interior values) were awkwardly exchanged for physical-material stability and conformism; perhaps a more realistic version

---

1. This section and the next are redrafted and updated versions of the discussion of self-help and therapy history in Miller and McHoul (1998: 90–133).

of the heterosexual contract than today's mantra, 'you can have it all'. Women read in detail about incredible drudgery, not fantasies of professional *or* romantic fulfilment (see Cancian, 1987: 163; Cancian and Gordon, 1988; Moskowitz, 1996).

Feelings are often held to exist in a state of grace. They seem to be eternal and true rather than being institutionalised forms of understanding how we really are. But emotions are known and spoken. They are part of signification and, as such, are subject to historical, spatial, economic, and cultural forces, just like aeroplanes or cable companies. As Foucault puts it: 'We believe that feelings are immutable, but every sentiment, particularly the noblest and most disinterested, has a history' (1977: 153). Feelings are historical and discursive constructs, determined by certain conditions of definition and response: sympathy and pity shift in meaning in accordance with changes in a given era's view of 'victimhood, poverty, and the social contract'. English-speakers in the Middle Ages, for example, experienced a feeling called 'accidie', now gone. Where English today has over 2,000 emotion-words, with tiny shades of meaning, and Dutch has 1,500, Malay has 230, Taiwanese Chinese 750, and Chewong just seven, while the Yoruba do not have words for depression (Russell and Sato, 1995: 384–5). Translation and back-translation analysis suggests that even seemingly equivalent terms actually describe quite distinct states. Bedouin Arabs, for example, do not inquire about feelings or request line-by-line retellings of conversational exchange (Abu-Lughod, 1990: 24–5). Are we to regard such languages and nations as more repressed than the English?

While some recent ways of thinking about feelings tend to associate them with femininity, this has not always been the case. German Romanticism of the 1800s enshrined Friedrich Schlegel's 'tender manhood', which conceived of men as sensuous, emotional creatures, unlike his ideal of 'independent femininity' (Schlegel in Trepp, 1994: 132). The Enlightenment era of rationality had its double in *Empfindsamkeit*, or spiritual sensitivity amongst intellectuals of both sexes. It called for the expression of feelings and attention to the passions. Men were encouraged to record their emotions in diaries and discuss the results with others. In short, they textualised and voiced what was required in a way that was historically and geographically specific. Closer to our own time, we might consider changes in the management of the American infant. Between the 1940s and 1960s, manuals on domestic pædiatrics moved from describing the child as a machine that should be handled only when broken, to endorsements of spontaneous physical affection as sources of bonding and development for babies and parents. Anthony Synnott (1993: 161) references the alternately contradictory, separate, and isomorphic influences on such developments of 'Freudian theory, psychotherapy, primate research and anthropology ... the Hippy movement, sensitivity training, somatopsychic theory, existentialist philosophy and, especially, the women's movement'.

The history of loss and grief in the United States is also illuminating. After the Second World War, public discourse over grief was muted. It encouraged overcoming the strong, potentially disabling emotions associated with the death of others. This was quite different from the reaction after the First World War, when there was much noise about the appropriate means of responding to such powerful experiences. Death was not discussed as often, especially when compared to the Victorian love of intense melancholy. Mourning was disrespectful to the dead in war, who had lost their lives so others could move on. Grief was to be transcended as part of accepting the many moments of separation that characterise life. Today, by contrast, we find intense therapeutic investments in the generation of new identities amongst the bereaved, enabling them to display full adjustment to new circumstances (Stearns, 1994: 158–9).

Similarly, there wasn't much empathy around the United States before the turn of the century: the word didn't exist in English until psychologists coined it in the 1920s to describe a technical response to emotion. Within a few years, it had come to signify a form of æsthetic response to works of art, but only in the 1950s was it transformed into everyday language to identify with the feelings of others. Today, psychologists struggle to identify and understand the mechanisms of empathy, even as commonsensical norms suggest it is a natural part of life. Empathy developed as a concept at the same time as psychotherapy developed as a profession, endowing an historical event with timelessness (Duan and Hill, 1996: 261–2). There is a similar history to agoraphobia. It was invented to deal with new forms of public life and morality in the late nineteenth century. As European restrictions on women's freedoms were loosened by urbanisation, the means of coping with this innovation in gender relations provoked new anxieties (de Swaan, 1990: 146–7).

Early North American Puritanism stands alongside the frontier as a defining characteristic of the New World via control of the self, moderation of appetites, and calibration of the correct means of conduct, all achieved through devotion to a higher being who transcended base human desires. Mortals who wrestled with their hungers and drives might attain a life-world of the *spiritual* through proper *behaviour* which, in turn, would compensate for the disappointments they might experience in material life. Individuals might even feel liberated by establishing and maintaining an alternative universe to the secular. Puritanism also connotes collectivity, of course, and a decidedly secular domain of law and community. The earthly universe expressed the divine universe. But the notion of a collective good was equally experienced as authoritarian oligarchy and plutocracy by those at the bottom of the social order. Puritanism's ethical technology takes on a deeply pre- and pro-scriptive form that ramifies and intensifies secular law with a duty to obey God's (heavily interpreted) word. This code rarely made sense in terms of an improved everyday life for those subject to it, but appeared to be imposed from above. Lastly, Puritanism became a monetary technology, an index and guide to thrift and self-actualisation via utilitarian calculation (Susman, 1984: 41-45).

This decidedly material mode of salvation stressed the propensity to work, save, and invest rather than consume goods. It supported the formation of capital and the disciplining of the workforce.[2] In the hands of apologists for and heralds of US nineteenth-century capitalism, dominant Puritanism endorsed labour and savings as the keys to building an earthly heaven and ordering individuals through the material rule of law and the interpersonal rule of belief. But from the late 1880s to 1940, Puritanism was held responsible for the personal and social alienation experienced by intellectuals. Writers began to wonder about other forms of self-expression than those mandated by the narrow corridors of the Puritan home. Freudian discourse made desire an inevitable and valuable corrective to the anal retentiveness of prevailing ideology. Æsthetic discourse contributed to notions of expressive totality and sensuous response rather than tightly-buttoned shirts. Temperance and censorship were seen to favour particular categories of person over others. Secondly, a middle class was forming between 1870 and 1910, comprised of folk who were neither property owners nor proletarians. An intellectual class with managerial and scientific knowledge appeared. Science defined corporate health via the discovery of truths that could be tested rather than magically revealed from hermeneutic readings of great books. The corollary to this intense rationalism was a notion of human quintessences that should emerge in art: desires were to be expressed, not denied or displaced. Since the Second World War, Puritanism has enjoyed a revived status, perhaps as a reaction against corporate life and permissiveness, with excessive personal behaviour obsessively chronicled and decried (Susman, 1984: 41–8).

During the nineteenth century, with the rise of capital privileging labour, the economy, and men (all in search, as was Smiles, of transcendence from the social relations produced by birth), self-help ideas emphasised love, family, and women. But within the more recent versions of this Protestant work ethic, the transcendence comes instead from social-movement politics rather than ecclesiastical bonds, as stockbrokers and parsons are supplemented by 'emotional investment counselors'. The 'ascetic self-discipline which the early capitalist applied to his bank account, the late twentieth-century woman applies to her appetite, her body, her love' (Hochschild, 1994: 1–2, 13).

Many writers, from both left and right, are critical of self-help and therapeutic cultures (perhaps forgetting that the greatest number of these groups are devoted to coping physically with disabilities, not learning how to feel). Each revels in denouncing the solip-

---

2. No wonder, then, that Mr Biswas eventually gives up on Smiles and 'the Samuel Smiles depression' (Naipaul, 1969: 159).

sistic absorption and selfish individualism of those derided by Bill Clinton as 'the worried well'. For radicals, the taste for therapy and personal growth is a *bourgeois* phenomenon, a luxury of commercial interiorisation unavailable to those preoccupied with subsistence living, which manifests middle-class guilt at the ravages of capitalism (though North American polls show growth-group members are three times more likely to describe themselves as conservative than liberal). It is also a reminder of the 'Red Scare' of 1919, when the US government was assured that psychotherapy could defuse the appeal of Marxism to the urban poor, and the later rise of behaviourism, a model of person-as-machine that promised to manage individual conduct. Youth-culture critics argue that the pathologisation of young people is part of the way social order and disorder are psychologised. Feminist critics object to the discourse of self-help for encouraging women to adjust to domestic care-giving. (Radical feminists occupied the offices of the *Ladies Home Journal* in the 1970s in protest.)

For conservatives, therapeutic culture represents the decline in spiritualism and the rise of secular selfishness, an elevation of self over service. According to this view, monumental self-absorption over-runs obligations and responsibilities. Alternatively, self-help can be a badge of qualification for high office: the 1992 Presidential election found both Clinton and Al Gore sharing with the electorate their group-therapy encounters and past triumphs over familial alcohol, gambling, and cocaine use. Bush Snr declined to participate in this confessional ritual. (He also lost the election.) Serious supporters of self-help link it to the mutual-aid societies of the eighteenth century, including trade unions, that provided citizens with buffer zones (self-selected ones at that) between church, state, and capital. Four out of ten Americans today belong to groups that are autonomous from their employment (church, sport, local improvement, group-grope and so on), again something taken as a sign of the strength of civil society by its proponents. These included Bush, whose administration sought to push back the work of government in educating, housing, medicating, and assisting poorer citizens onto 'the community' (see Mäkelä et al., 1996: 13; Irvine, 1995: 150; Moskowitz, 1996: 66; Wuthnow, 1994: 4, 71, 336; Musto, 1995; Stenson, 1993: 43; Prilleltensky, 1989: 795, 798; Forbes, 1994: 249–50; Riessman and Carroll, 1995: 12, 176).

Christopher Lasch (1979) claims that the failure of radical popular politics in the 1960s is evident from a retreat to the personal: 'psychic self-improvement' displaced faith in popular democracy and collective endeavour and reward. Health food, recovery groups, learning the discourse of feelings, thumping drums, believing in Jung, not 'beating myself up' and 'having difficulty valuing you at the moment' may be perfectly reasonable activities — until they are 'elevated to a program and wrapped in the rhetoric of authenticity and awareness'. At that point they 'signify a retreat from politics and a repudiation of the recent past' as the New Left's struggles through youth culture and the horrors of Vietnam get displaced onto 'growth'. History is foregone: not merely the collaborative American past, but any sense of participating in the making of history. Unlike the returns to spirituality that characterise American religious cycles, this era lacks a sense of its own origins or the drive towards collective renewal. Confessing to large groups of people, be they readers, group members, cyber-pals, or therapists, suggests a self that depends on the attention and approval of others. Far from the 'rugged individualist' destined to build culture, this narcissistic subject relies on informal institutions for validation. Concerns about economic and social inequality are displaced by the therapeutic apparatus onto individual emotions and psychological histories (Lasch, 1979: 29–32, 38, 43, 63).

Jane Shattuc (1997), conversely, defends this move to the personal as a new form of politics. Two-thirds of daytime talk television focuses on psychological questions. In addition to the testimony of the public and the mediation of presenters, the genre makes significant use of social workers, therapists, self-help writers, and psychologists. The terms of trade vary between discourses of Freudian repression and unconscious drives and twelve-step recovery programs (for which see more below). Free association, vital to the project of psychoanalysis, is off the menu, however; the unconscious must express itself directly in order to fit the TV format: a set number of segments, commercial breaks, and studio apparatus. And the psychologisation of social problems has itself been brought into doubt by Phil Donahue's regular ironised intervention: 'All she needs is to go into therapy and everything will be nice?' (in Shattuc, 1997: 115). That is, populist appeals to experience may debunk some of the very authority figures called upon to explicate topics of the day. This is not to claim a comprehensive opposition, but a negotiation. The cognitive strand of US therapising is well-represented via lists of how to behave: Oprah Winfrey's patent guide to gender-sensitive schooling is a renowned instance, as rational emotive therapy is deployed to detect and treat hidden failings. Shattuc maintains these programs are 'an arena of collective feminine experience' that promises 'a utopian vision of female equality', connecting women to one another and immunising them from 'the stultifying nihilism of Foucaultian skepticism' (Shattuc, 1997: 111–13, 116–17, 120, 122). We'll encounter these tensions as we make our way through other such genres.

Etiquette, sex, lifestyle

There are three forms of self-help manual: general etiquette, sex and parenting education, and lifestyle. General etiquette books advise on everyday living, specifically politeness and how to be popular. Sex-education books use medical discourse to describe people's bodies, moving between primers on manners and more technical treatises. Less æsthetic, such texts are alternately technicist and emotive. Lifestyle books reject grand divisions of art from science in favour of a holistic approach, seeking 'holes' in the person in order to reinte-grate them into a 'whole' person. It presents all problems as arising from internalised social expectations.

Publishers Weekly has charted the best-selling American non-fiction titles since 1917. We have taken a sample from each decade, and annually since 1990. In addition to war books, the inaugural list is dominated by biographies and autobiographies. The same is true ten years later, although history emerges along with *Why We Behave Like Human Beings*, at number nine. Since that time, these genres plus cookery, self-help, humour, and diet books have remained on the list. By 1937, self-help is a regular. Dale Carnegie's *How To Win Friends and Influence People* is in first place (sixth the following year) and his *How to Stop Worrying and Start Living* is popular after the War. A decade on finds *Peace of Mind* at number one, whilst in 1957 Norman Vincent Peale's *Stay Alive All Your Life* is in third spot, con-tinuing a string of best-sellers since 1948, including *A Guide to Con-fident Living* and his massively successful *The Power of Positive Think-ing*. *Games People Play* by Eric Berne, MD is third for 1967 (the third year in a row), while 1977 has *Looking Out for #1* at number two and Dr Wayne W. Dyer's *Your Erroneous Zones* fourth. Erma Bombeck's *Family: The Ties That Bind ... and Gag* is third for 1987, by which time one out of every three Americans has bought a self-help tome. Ge-neric twelve-stepper John Bradshaw's *Homecoming: Reclaiming and Championing Your Inner Child* is sixth in 1990 (a year in which he gave two hundred speeches at a $5,000 per day rate); *More Wealth Without Risk* and *Financial Self-Defense* (both Charles J. Givens) are seventh and tenth in 1991; 1992 sees *How To Satisfy a Woman Every Time* by Naura Hayden at three and Gail Sheehy's *Silent Passage* at number nine; in 1993, Deepak Chopra's *Ageless Body, Timeless Mind* is at five, *Women Who Run With the Wolves* by Clarissa Pinkola Estes is seven, and *Men Are from Mars, Women Are from Venus* (John Gray, PhD) ninth. Gray moves up to second for 1994 and to number one the following year, as well as having *Mars and Venus in the Bedroom* at seven, while Chopra reappears at number four with *The Seven Spiritual Laws of Success*. In January 1997, the hardback edition of *Men Are from Mars* had been on the best-seller list 196 weeks in a row, and *The Seven Spiritual Laws* for 39 weeks. Gray's first book had sold ten million copies. In paperback, Stephen R. Covey's *7 Hab-its of Highly Effective People* celebrated its 308th week on the hit parade early in 1997. By 1994, over 300 US bookstores were exclu-sively devoted to 'recovery' prose (*People Weekly*, 1996: 308–24; Hochschild, 1994: 20; Maryles, 1997: 47; 'Paperback Bestsellers',

1997; Weber, 1997: 29; 'Hardcover Bestsellers', 1997; Mäkelä et al., 1996: 223; Wuthnow, 1994: 118).

This vast process encapsulates the 'commercialization of the individual' (Gerhards, 1989: 740). It is also a *technologisation* of the individual; for just as books are sold and group gropes exchanged, the persons within them learn new forms of conduct under the sign and tutelage of multiple institutions and discourses. Gray, for instance, turned his best-seller into a successful Broadway question-and-answer show in 1997, when his *œuvre* comprised 5 books, 12 videotapes, 22 counselling centres, 30 weekend seminars per year, and 2 websites. Oprah Winfrey-exposure catapulted to fame Ellen Fein and Sherrie Schneider's *The Rules: Time-Tested Secrets to Capturing the Heart of Mr Right*, a 'retro husband-snagging guide'. It recommended women hold out on sex, never telephone men for a date, and refuse to go out on a Saturday night if requested later than Tuesday of that week. Eight hundred thousand copies were on sale in the last months of 1996 and film rights had been bought by Paramount. A similar movie deal was done by Tristar for rights to an unwritten answer, *The Code*, which was announced as offering men 'time-tested secrets for getting what you want from women — without marrying them'. The entertainment audiovisual industries were synchronised for the first time with the interpersonal manual! Lest we view this as an exclusively 'New World' or 'New Age' phenomenon, it should be noted that Germany saw the number of self-help groups double to 60,000 across the 1980s, while the ten best-selling non-fiction books in South Korea for 1996 included three titles on sexual relationships for the young, and three on defeating adversity to study at university. This references another key to the genre: directing workers to some mixture of toil, entrepreneurship, manipulation, and displacement of success onto leisure (Quinn, 1996; 'Congratulations John Gray!', 1997; Mäkelä et al., 1996: 25; 'What the World is Reading', 1997; Biggart, 1983).

The etiquette genre of publishing is often said to begin with Erasmus' *De Civilitate Morum Puerilium*, or *On Civility in Children*, in 1530. Translations followed into English, German, Czech, and French. The book was adopted as a set text in schools and reprinted 30 times over the next few years. By the close of the eighteenth century, it had run to 130 editions. The subject matter of *De Civilitate* is proper conduct: how to look at others, present and maintain clean nostrils, dispose of spittle, and eat. Overt staring at other people becomes a key monitorial manœuvre: sight is now the principal measure of character, with speech carefully subordinated and subjected to formal turn-taking rules. The same period ushers in auto-invigilation, a requirement to evaluate one's own actions and appearances. In the late eighteenth century, the genre is named: 'etiquette' is a neologism standing for *une petite éthique* or mini-ethics. This mini-ethics is a shift from the manners model of earlier. What began as a guide to courtiers became a more widespread model of new class societies: Reinhart von Knigge's 1788 work on courtesy is a break in the literature because it addresses the bourgeoisie as well as the aristocracy (Elias, 1978a: 53–6; 1978b: 78, 82; Arditi, 1996: 421; Wouters, 1995: 120). This process gathers pace across Europe, most spectacularly in the nineteenth century, via 'new fields of social management in which culture is figured forth as both the *object* and the *instrument* of government: its object insofar as the term refers to the morals, manners, and ways of life of subordinate social strata' (Bennett, 1992: 26).

In the US, the etiquette book began during the Republic, with extensive church involvement and direction. It developed into a combination of technically 'correct' instruction and a more utilitarian form of advice that was about making an impression in order to advance one's material prospects. Cas Wouters' (1995) longitudinal study of the US and Western Europe indicates that etiquette literature plays down differences in expected conduct between classes with the advent of welfare societies in the mid-twentieth century. Rules become rules for all, rather than markers of elevated position. Nineteenth-century etiquette manuals empowered women by declaring domestic conduct a key social grace. Authorially, the genre underwent a major change. Up to the 1890s, men had been the dominant givers of written advice, whereas women emerged as equal players from the turn of the century. By 1923, Emily Post's *Etiquette* was the top-selling non-fiction book, and Frances Benton's volume of the same title was fourth in 1956 (Lichterman, 1992: 421; Arditi, 1996: 417; *People Weekly*, 1996: 309, 316).

Many etiquette books explain spatial and occupational differences: the announcement in the mid-1970s that the Germans and Dutch would henceforth accept 'social kissing'; how to behave as a tourist; how to give and not give offence; how to be an anthropologist; how to drive; how to drink alcohol in a restrained manner; how to act in court or congress; how to avoid sexual harassment, and how to recognise it. Consider the experience of retiring for the night on the second evening of a visit to someone's home and finding on the bedside table a copy of an etiquette book, with the page dog-eared at the chapter 'On Staying the Night at Another Person's House' — what a useful pointer to how you are getting along with people, as one of the authors of the chapter you are reading found out some years ago! Alternatively, these works may be directly applied to economic advantage: social psychology claims that waiters who draw a smile on the back of their customers' bills receive a larger tip than otherwise if they are female, a smaller one if male, which rapidly attains institutionalisation in the lore of employees (Rind and Bordia, 1996). Such advice can be more than guides — sometimes they are essential in legal terms. For instance, to become a citizen of the US other than by birth or blood, is clearly cultural: one must reside there, renounce allegiance to other states, know the country's basic political history, 'read, write, and speak words in ordinary usage in the English language', eschew polygamy, and neither consort with sex workers nor be repeatedly drunk in public (Aleinikoff, 2000: 130).

The etiquette primer can be about having a relationship with oneself as well as others, concerned with fulfilment more than politeness. Arnold Bennett's *Mental Efficiency and Other Hints to Men and Women*, which was first published in 1913 and still being reprinted more than 40 years on, gives instruction in 'mental callisthenics', 'expressing one's individuality', how to marry and collect books, and the distinction between success and contentment. As with Smiles, the idea is to treat the mind like a body with less visible muscles — it too needs exercise, via 'culture'. This will 'round off our careers with the graces of knowledge and taste' through 'the cultivation of will-power, and the getting into condition of the mental apparatus'. Bennett's book is based on his response to letters from concerned readers who wish to improve themselves. He recommends reading to increase concentration. Learning poetry and prose by heart is a '"cure" for debility', just as stretching in the morning is for the ailing physique (Bennett, 1957: 9, 13, 18–19, 26–8, 35).

Moving from here to the genre of the sex manual, we can begin by noting that contemporary sex educators identify sexuality with humanness. Sexuality becomes the truth of the person. It holds hidden verities that can be brought out and moulded into sociable conduct. Hence the turn in education towards explaining pupils to themselves — making them parent their future adult identities. This presumes that child sexuality has long been repressed by conventions and strictures. Sexuality is the basis for people's relationships, so parents, churches, governments, and schools must deal with it in the openness and freedom of the classroom. Another way of figuring this development is to discern a growing and powerful network of psy-experts circling the child, analysing and provoking sexualised interpretations of conduct as a means of discovering 'truth'. This alternative view of sex pedagogy does not see sexuality as a particularly privileged form of understanding people, but as one more discourse in need of having its history catalogued (Hunter, 1984; Hochschild, 1994: 3).

For sexuality is new. Sex, of course, is old, as old as biology. But deriving whole accounts of the person from limited observation of such acts is recent; it needs Freud and anti-Freud, plus humanistic, experiential feminism, behaviour modification, and a raft of other disciplinary practices to sustain it.

Sex Fulfillment in Marriage is a typical artefact of this discourse. It was written in the 1940s by a lot of people named Groves. First comes Ernest R. Groves, a professor of sociology and marriage guidance counsellor who is also 'Director of the Annual Conference on the Conservation of Marriage and the Family'. He is credited with having taught the first US university courses on how to prepare for marriage. The second Groves is Gladys Hoagland Groves, also a marriage guidance counsellor and author of marriage preparation texts for college students and 'the general public'. The third and final author is Catherine Groves, who has written *Get More Out of Life*, 'a book telling how troubled people can find help'. Social worker and marriage guide, she has 'had to deal with many instances of domestic difficulties of various types' whilst, as 'the wife of a newspaper man and the mother of two children', her travails are self-evident (Groves et al., 1945: np). Together, the many Groves produced a book with endorsements from the *Journal of the American Medical Association* and the *American Sociological Review*.

The 'Preface' describes the book as part of the search for 'a harmonious, progressive and character-making fellowship' (1945: ix). The 'Introduction' by Duke University obstetrician and gynæcologist Robert A. Ross, declares '[w]hat a relief it is to find emphasis placed on the normal!' in a way that meets the needs of those 'anxious to know and practice normal things' (1945: xiii–iv). The combination of case-notes and blood relations (the authors are revealed here as husband, wife and daughter) elevates *Sex Fulfillment in Marriage* in the eyes of Prof. Ross. The work is interdisciplinary, producing an amalgam of the duties of 'educator, sociologist, physician, biologist, sexologist' in a study of the science of 'impulses' and 'innate good taste' (1945: xiv).

The Groves identify sexuality as the culprit in marital breakdown. Presiding over both 'a general sense' and one's own 'past', sexuality holds the keys to pleasure and individual history (1945: 18). It works against much of the labour of civilisation, but that is also its wonder: 'Modern men and women, healthy in body and mind, can taste all the flavor of the cruder forms of physical sex and much more besides' (1945: 23). But sex has been stigmatised into darkness, a space where everyday knowledge is inadequate (1945: 28). It is no longer instinctive, but 'an even more complex drive in the civilized human being' (1945: 31). To uncover the personal history that births and parents the present-day adult, we must enter into a dialogue with ourselves. This involves a therapy without the social worker or shrink; we come pre-shrunk, ready to read ourselves for hidden facts that lie beneath a surface of control, in the murky depths of desire. We must undertake exercises of the conscience, in the following form: 'What were my sex experiences in very early childhood?', 'What was the influence of my home upon my sex development?', 'How did school influence my sex development?', 'What influence did my church and religion have on my sex development?', 'How was I trained in modesty?', 'What were my sex experiences during youth?' and 'What effect has masturbation had in my sex development?' (1945: 50, 57, 62, 66, 72, 76). These seven questions foreground issues of social management, positioning 'sexuality' at the epicentre of everyday individual and collective life: the family, education, religion, manners, development, and confessional self-absorption.

The other side to these concerns is the science of sex, its physical aspects, where the 'arts of love' can be supplemented by knowledge of what the Groves refer to as 'sex equipment and its functioning' (1945: 106). Women are criticised for having 'vague ideas' about 'their own sex equipment' and are recommended to explore themselves with a mirror (1945: 107). By contrast, men are 'franker', and their 'equipment more obvious' (1945: 106). Nevertheless, even a strong awareness of their 'equipment' frequently leaves 'the American husband ... criticized as a poor lover' (1945: 161). Sexually incompetent men must learn the gift of variety. As the Groves tell us:

> The great musician does not endlessly play over and over the same composition. His preferences change. He is a great artist because he makes what his skill produces accord with his inner feeling. Thus it is with the true lover. (1945: 163)

This is a liberal document, typical of the 1940s: it recommends the selection of sexual positions on the basis of pleasure, and acknowledges the importance of women having financial independence from men (1945: 85, 179). Physical abandon is taken to signify a successful marriage. The negative side to this is the increasingly heterosexist discourse that accompanies it, attacking same-sex love with vigour, as the divorce rate and open homosexual activity grew. Post-WWII experts connect these developments and attribute them to sexual maladjustment. The solution is to rearticulate sex and love, rather than keeping them apart as per the Victorian era.

Attempts to scientise sex in the popular mind are fully achieved with the publication of the Kinsey studies in 1948, when *Sexual Behavior in the Human Male* is the fourth biggest US non-fiction seller; 1953 sees *Sexual Behavior in the Human Female* at number three. Helen Gurley Brown's *Sex and the Single Girl*, ninth best-seller for 1962, combines the new findings on pleasure (and dissatisfaction) with an interest in evoking and charting a new morality, while William Howard Masters and Virginia E. Johnston's *Human Sexual Response* legitimises clitoral orgasm en route to number two four years later. By the end of the decade, finding a way to understand and satisfy is on the agenda: 1970 has David Reuben, MD's *Everything You Always Wanted To Know About Sex But Were Afraid To Ask* and *The Sensuous Woman* by 'J' in first and third spots respectively, whilst 'M''s *The Sensuous Man* is first the next year and Dr Reuben's *Any Woman Can!* comes fifth, with *The Joy of Sex* by Alex Comfort charting in 1973, and its successor *More Joy* the next year. A survey of adult sex manuals to 1980 finds three basic models for women and sex: 'different-and-unequal, humanistic sexuality, or sexual autonomy'. Women move from finding sex an unpleasurable duty, through sex as a required essence of personhood, to the idea that pleasure can be achieved without submission to, and indeed without the presence of, men. Sex changes from being an anthropological and social topic to being a matter of biology and self-management (Weinberg et al., 1983: 312, 315; *People Weekly*, 1996: 314–15, 317–20).

We can see these trends in books from the mid-1970s such as Kline-Graber and Graber's *Woman's Orgasm: A Guide to Sexual Satisfaction*. This could easily be read as an example of the tentacles of medicine and the psy-complex making their way across women's bodies. Alternatively, we might understand it as a technical tool dealing with issues that cannot be safely and easily left up in the air, as women *are* routinely problematised for their orgasm (by definition, frequency, or method). The fetishisation of sexuality has recently turned itself onto men's bodies in politically fascinating ways. John Davidson's (1992) *Cleo* article, 'Does Penis Size Really Matter? One Guy Gets Honest' comes with a measuring apparatus to determine whether a man's penis is 'SMALL' (1–10 centimetres), 'AVERAGE' (11–20 cm), 'IMPRESSIVE' (21–25 cm), or 'OUCH' (26 cm and counting) (1992: 69). In January 1996, the magazine's TV campaign comparing penis sizes was criticised by the Australian Advertising Standards Council. These developments replicate the lines of force long drawn over women's bodies that specify 'correct' measurements of breast, waist, and hip and 'healthy' sexual response.

This leads us to the third and last of our categories, the lifestyle book. It derives in part from the moment in the 1960s when sex and love are partially separated in advice literature, as casual sexual encounters increase along with birth control and political activity by gays and lesbians. These supposedly greater freedoms do not produce happier marriages or less worried people, despite efforts to use sex as a vehicle to wellness. That failure does not, however, serve to question the concentration on sexuality as a key to happy living. Instead, more and more publications focus on the topic, albeit moving beyond directly sex-related matters to interlace those concerns with psychologised versions of early manners manuals, as per Erasmus. In the 1930s, European and North American etiquette books begin a marked shift in ideas of the self. That is, by the end of the 1960s, the search for correct conduct involves an indulgence in feeling rather than self-restraint (Gerhards, 1989: 176–7).

This awkward change really starts with singer Pat Boone's memorable *Twixt Twelve and Twenty*, in which he endorses the maternal beatings received during his teenage years. This caring and sharing family history propels the book into second spot in US best-seller lists for 1958 and first the following year (the follow-up, *Between You, Me and the Gatepost*, is tenth in 1960). The message is that feelings are important, if somewhat inscrutable — and who could pass up a damned good thrashing from a devoted parent when suffering adolescent confusion? By 1965, a cross-over between etiquette and emotional interiority has made psy-complex texts into regular sales leaders. Following the success of *Games People Play*, Thomas

Harris's *I'm OK, You're OK* is in the top-ten sellers from 1971 to 1973, and Nena and George O'Neill's *Open Marriage* posts good figures (close to two million sold over the decade). By the mid-1970s, the US offers 164 different brand-names of therapy. Twenty years on, the transactional-analytic theory of ego states must be parroted by applicants for gun permits in Texas, who are instructed that the 'Make my day' line from the Dirty Harry movie *Sudden Impact* exemplifies aberrant 'inner child behavior' (*People Weekly*, 1996: 316, 319; Ross, 1980: 109; Gerhards, 1989: 7, 17; Verhovek, 1995).

The media have been important bearers of the therapeutic message. Consider multiple personality disorder (MPD). As Ian Hacking puts it: 'In 1972 multiple personalities were almost invisible' (1992: 3). But books and TV talk shows about multiple personality disorder, along with its (disputed) clinical uptake, led to an explosion within people: the average US number of 'multiples' was 27 personalities per body ten years later (Hacking, 1992: 8–9). The disorder became tied to rising interest in child abuse (from 1961 on) and child sexual abuse (from 1975 on), while the late 1980s concern with Satanism provided additional stimulus (Hacking, 1992: 17). The acceptance of MPD culminated in a 1990 conviction for rape of a Wisconsin man following sex instigated by a woman, on the grounds that he was aware of another, 'motherly' side to her, different from the one that consented to and claimed to have enjoyed sex with him. Each of her personalities was sworn in by the judge to testify. Gloria Steinem mused about the pleasures of having several different menstrual periods each month, arguing that the 'disorder' should be renamed a 'gift'. Subscribers to *Dissociation*, journal of the International Society for the Study of Multiple Personality and Dissociation, receive a diploma with instructions to 'display your professionalism. Be proud of your commitment to the field of multiple personality and dissociative disorders' (Hacking, 1992: 5; and see Nathan, 1994: 77–8, 82, 85, 103).

More routine problems have also proven popular. Robin Norwood's 1985 manual on *Women Who Love Too Much*, a book about addictive relationships (medicine meets friendships and families), sold close on three million copies in two years. Related titles include *Men Who Hate Women and the Women Who Love Them* (S. Forward, 1986), *Women Men Love, Women Men Leave* (C. Cowan and M. Kinder, 1987), and *Smart Women, Foolish Choices* (C. Cowan and M. Kinder, 1985). Their message is that women should be less obsessed, easier and lighter in their touch, less emotionally demanding, and not endeavour to change men. In his study of the communities that read these books, Paul Lichterman (1992) finds middle-class people with clear ambivalences about their purchases. They neither embrace nor resist the messages, but assimilate them along with numerous other inputs into their lives, forming a 'thin culture' (1992: 444). The precepts of popular psychology are 'adopted loosely, tentatively, sometimes interchangeably, without enduring conviction' (1992: 421–2).

When Lichterman asks his sample of readers who would be unlikely to join them in consuming such objects, the responses are: 'someone who is afraid to be open ... someone who is not willing to face up to their problems [and] ... still in the dark ages' (1992: 426). Such texts and their readers characterise non-readers of the genre as ethically incomplete. But these willing explorers of their psyches are not very reliable narrators of what they read, recalling very little content. The books are emblems of an attitude, signs of a willingness to think about inner truths. They do not present a route to salvation via their subject-matter. As one reader spectacularly says: 'you could read *War and Peace* and that's self-growth in another way' (1992: 439). These are limited technologies, or matrices of popular reason, used by their readers to deal with specific problems. They are not elevated to holy writ and are understood as consumer objects circulating in the sphere of merchandising and product differentiation. The loose affiliation of the readers is a sign in part of their multiple demographic backgrounds. At the same time, the fact that readers generally come to the genre after emotional relationships have broken up indicates a search to understand personal failure (see Jimenez and Rice, 1990: 16–18).

The readership is clearly gendered. One publisher that sold three million books on codependency in the US in 1990 claimed women were 80 per cent of the market. These books are often said to divide between 'the psychological and the retrofeminist' (Irvine, 1995: 145). For critics, each represents a retreat from, or at least some compromise of, feminist principles of equality. As per *The Rules*, many such books operate with an infantilised model of masculinity: men are isolates, hopelessly lost in fantasies of independence, who must be tricked into commitment through denial and manipulation. Women, by contrast, are aware of their fundamental neediness and are encouraged to get their way through a combination of folk-psychological theories about gender difference and turning against official feminism in favour of comforting and exciting men. The TV series *Sex and the City*, for example, plays on the intrigue generated by such tropes.

Consider codependency, Melody Beattie's 1986 invention in *Codependent No More*. It explains why the intimates of alcoholics, workaholics, shopaholics, and countless other compulsive types remain with them rather than walking out. There are now over 3,000 Codependents Anonymous (CoDA) groups throughout the US. CoDA manages an interesting tightrope between politics and the psyche: on the one hand, subservience to others' needs is condemned as unequal and damaging; but its explanation is resumed to interiority, to psychological disposition rather than social subjectivity. The discourse is marked out by its anti-institutionalism: churches, schools, and families made these problems, and they cannot solve them — only the company of our fellows can take us away from codependency. Bradshaw's patent causal phrase is 'poisonous pedagogy' (quoted in

Rice, 1992: 349). (See Rice, 1992: 344, 337; Jimenez and Rice, 1990: 8, 12.)

Something very similar to the call for an unyielding commitment to physical fitness is happening: women are endlessly in need, according to this literature, of advice on feelings. The supposedly direct line between the self, intersubjectivity, and happiness that comes from the supposedly natural connection of women to the realm of emotion paradoxically requires massive training, an unending intellectual guidance that sees readers and clients always in need of the next publication or therapeutic session (Hochschild, 1994: 8–9). The new masculinists among us hunt enviously for similar unities between body and self, places for 'reclaiming your original potential'. The 'development and integration of body, mind, and emotions' will restore the natural aptitudes and tastes distorted by modernity. *Accessing the King in the Male Psyche* can be done, for example, via *The Warrior Athlete*. The contemporary era is full of passive men claiming they want to be emperors, but their weakness drives women away. *Newsweek* announced 'the first postmodern social movement' in 1991 (quoted in Boscagli, 1992–93: 71) Robert Bly's followers looking within for the lost monarch. As Carol Gilligan says, where the 'feminist movement has held men responsible for their violence and privilege ... [t]he mythopoetic men's movement has embraced men as wounded' (Gilligan, 1997: 24). (See Moore and Gillette, 1992: 25–7; Millman, 1979: viii; Ross, 1980: 118.)

Some of this is rooted in Jung's uptake of Greek and Roman mythology as a universal, transhistorical truth about masculine and feminine bases to personality, a 'collective unconscious' that animates everyone. Other accounts derive from middle-class reactions against feminist challenges to male authority and privilege. Sometimes this has been extremely misogynistic and anti-feminist; at other moments, it has been expressed as envy at women's 'feelings' discourse, their unity, and their claims to expressive totality. One wing became 'Men's Liberation'; the other, 'Men Against Sexism'. Both sides are liable to stress the difficulties of being a man, the pain of leadership, the confusion of roles 'under' feminism, the vacuum of authority and direction, and the need to 'share'. Of course, there are revisionist positions on this: Francesca M. Cancian (1986: 692) argues that what counts as loving conduct has been erroneously feminised in the US by identifying love with the announcement of feelings rather than the instrumental expressions of helping or fucking. She favours equal value being placed on both sides to love.

We could go on — but the point is more than amply made: from Smiles in the middle of the nineteenth century up to the present day, whether we look at etiquette, sex or lifestyle, whether we look at best-selling manuals, at popular detractors of the self-help movement, or whether we look at the scholarly commentaries on all such matters, we find what is effectively a single figure as the subject of help. This figure is cast as fragmented, routinely in terms of its 'inner' states and its 'outer' capacities to act. Such fragmentations may be expressed in terms of, for example: 'having feelings' but being incapable of 'expressing' them; 'having a determinate sexuality' but being incapable of 'enacting' it in a particular social context; 'being emotional' but failing to use the right techniques for 'getting in touch' with the emotions; 'having a certain personality' but failing to 'let it come through' in interaction with others. Or else it might be as simple as Cancian's stand-off between feeling and fucking. This figure, then — which we might call the 'subject of modernity', and which popular self-help shares with the psy-disciplines (McHoul and Rapley, 2001) — is always in search of its 'true' or 'whole' self and, at the same time, is never endowed with the capacity to 'realise' or 'express' this. As Ian Hunter (personal communication) once put it: this figure is forever 'finding itself and finding itself wanting'. As we noted earlier, individuality is not the raw stuff of being human. Rather the state of individuality (in the literal sense of being in-divisible, un-fragmented) is turned into an eternal quest. And what the self-help publishing industry offers is, to all intents and purposes, tools and techniques in the service of that (always unsatisfiable) quest. How self-help writers — and, indeed, their co-professional detractors in what is becoming a thriving counter-industry in its own right — discursively produce and sustain such as sense of the impossible in-dividual is the subject of our next and final section.

Talking self-help

The materials that concern us in this section take the form of a transcript of a popular radio show, *Life Matters*, broadcast daily in Australia on the ABC's Radio National station. Here, the host, Geraldine Doogue (G: in the transcript) is in discussion with: Michael Rowland, (M:) author of *Absolute Happiness: The Way to a Life of Complete Fulfilment* (1995); Wendy Kaminer, (W:) author of *I'm Dysfunctional, You're Dysfunctional: The Recovery Movement and Other Self-Help Fashions* (1992); and Stuart Wilde, (S:) author of *Infinite Self: 33 Steps to Reclaiming Your Power* (1996).[3] (See p. 89 for footnote) The program went to air on 1 March 2000 between 9.05 and 10.00 am. Although we will provide a short commentary later in this section, there is a sense in which any such commentary is redundant, the necessarily lengthy transcript standing, to all intents and purposes, as its own auto-analytic uncovering of the subject of self-help as the needy 'dividual' on the eternal quest for in-dividuality.[4] (See p. 89 for footnote.) We join the discussion at a point where Michael Rowland is discussing contemporary marriage/divorce practices, and we leave just prior to the talk-back segment.

1   M: ... don't have to stay married any more, which frees up
2   the women of course, the main motivators of divorces now
3   — and I think that the less influence of religions. People
4   don't want to be*lieve*, they want to *know*. It's the natural
5   result of the attitude of science in the last hundred years
6   taking over the thoughts of society if you like. So people
7   aren't interested in beliefs. They want to *know* and they
8   want *prac*tical methods by which they can bring those
9   changes that they *want* into their lives.
10   G: Er but — er even something like happiness which is, I
11   mean it, you know the notion that you can pursue happi-
12   ness of course is written into the American constitution.
13   But ...
14   M: Yup, uh huh.
15   G: ... it's it's er this, would you agree that there seems to be
16   more of a — of a fascination *with* grabbing it. That it's,
17   that it's ...
18   W: Mm.
19   G: ... something — that it's, er er uh, something *tangible* that
20   can be *got*. That's more around in the last say ten to fif-
21   teen years — twenty years— than it was earlier in this
22   century?
23   M: Well yes I think so, but I also think that happiness is, is a
24   sort of *birth*right of us all. If you look at a child who is well
25   fed and, er, whose nappy's dry, if they're little, then they're
26   *ha*ppy. That, that they're playful, they're full of fun, they're
27   exuberant, they're exhilarated. And I suspect that's our
28   natural state, and I think the problem why people aren't
29   happy is simply because they contract down through the
30   process of conditioning, through the pressures of life. And
31   I don't think it's such a big ask that we *should* have a
32   happy life. I mean it's, er, a completely natural thing.
33   W: I think that's really quite a foolish notion — that, that we
34   should have a happy life. I think there's a lot of tragedy in
35   everybody's life. We're all going to grow old and die, and
36   even worse we're all going to ...
37   M: Why's that a tragedy?
38   W: ... see the people. We're all going to see the people we love
39   grow old and die. We're, you know, we're going to lose the
40   people we love. And, for most people, losing the people
41   that you love feels like a *tra*gedy. Erm.
42   M: But you can't avoid it.
43   W: There's a lot of things that it .... No you can't avoid it,
44   that's exactly why it's so tragic.
45   M: So why should you, why should .... It's only tragic be-
46   cause of the western traditions. If you look in, if you go to
47   a Balinese funeral for instance, it's a thing of celebration.

48		People dance and sing and they look forward to having a
49		different kind of experience. Perhaps it's just a belief struc-
50		ture maybe?
51	W:	Well yes, if you're a religious person and if you believe in
52		an afterlife, erm, perhaps you can take some solace in
53		the belief that you're going to meet up with your loved
54		one in heaven, or that you're moving on to a better life, or
55		that you're going to meet them in another incarnation in
56		another century. But, you know, one of the reasons that,
57		erm, religions and notions of immortality have so much
58		ap*peal* to people is that people are terrified by death and
59		they are ((sigh)), you know, they sometimes find the loss
60		of the people they love practically unendurable.
61	G:	But I just ...
62	W:	But that's one of the reasons why spiritualists do so well.
63		Because they tell you they can communicate with the
64		people that, who, who have died, and that you haven't
65		really lost them.
66	G:	But that actually is a very good point to ask you: what
67		relationship you believe there *may be* between the growing
68		popularity of self-help and disillusionment with *or*ganised
69		religion. Is this filling a vacuum?
70	W:	Well I actually, cert .... I can't speak to its happening in
71		Australia but in the United States we are not seeing ...
72	(?):	Hullo. ((Sounds like a phone caller — Stuart?))
73	W:	... a decline in organised religion. We're seeing a great *rise*
74		in organised religion. We are now in a period of religious
75		revivalism. And it's not just that we're seeing a lot of interest
76		in New Age, that we're seeing a lot of pop spirituality. We're
77		seeing a lot of traditional, established religion. Erm and we've
78		been seeing that for at *least* the last ten *years*. So I think
79		you'd find that, here in the States, the appetite for personal
80		development books, for pop spirituality books, is, is going
81		hand in hand with an increased interest in religion, and in
82		some very traditional religions.
83	G:	Mm yes well, that's certainly not the case here, you see.
84	M:	Mmm.
85	G:	There's a growing secularism in Australia and, erm, there,
86		there may well *be* — as a lot of people uh suggest — a
87		growing interest in a sort of *spiri*tual *search*. But it's ex-
88		tremely erm ephemeral and very .... So yes, that's, that
89		doesn't er fully explain it in Australia. In fact *Stu*art has er
90		been, uh, able to join us now. Stuart Wilde, whom we've
91		been ... has been battling the traffic. Stuart, welcome.
92	S:	G'd morning.
93	G:	No doubt your serenity's completely blown.
94	S:	My serenity's totally one and at peace with the Olympic

95		traffic.
96	G:	((Laughs)) And you.
97	S:	Very happy about it.
98	G:	Yes it's a sneak preview isn't it.
99	S:	((Laughs))
100	G:	Uhm Stuart, erm, look, you might just quickly tell us
101		why *you* think that there's so much interest now, at this
102		end of the twentieth century, in books like *yours*.
103	S:	Well, I mean, even though we're materialistically so much
104		better off than our grandparents, life is a heck of a lot
105		harder. I mean the pressure is on. The taxes, the forms,
106		the ... all the stuff, the regulations, the rules. We have to
107		perform and television requires us to perform, you know,
108		the sort of, the multiple orgasm, the totally happy family,
109		the absolute achiever, the girl driving her Porsche to work
110		in her power suit. And all that stuff, and people are in-
111		credibly isolated and under pressure. And I think that
112		that's why the self-help movement throws up, er, you
113		know, so many .... Well they offer solutions that people
114		take, whatever solutions they fancy, and leave the rest.
115	G:	Er but it's a, it's a striving for solutions from anyone who
116		offers them. Or is there a sort of desire for experts, or can
117		people set themselves up? I think this is Wendy's whole
118		argument. With *no* particular, er, ability to tell other people
119		how to live.
120	S:	Well I think Wendy's right. I mean anybody can write a
121		book, but the point about it is for the book to be success-
122		ful. It has to strike a chord in people's feelings. So it isn't
123		going to talk to them in a cerebral, intellectual, logical
124		way because the average person would get lost if you
125		really plunged them into the depths of psychology and
126		trans ... you know, transactional psy ... you know per-
127		sonality ... psychological whatevers, you know. So the
128		average person, who's the working person in the street,
129		needs a book written in a language that they can under-
130		stand. And I think a lot of authors that speak in sort of
131		street talk do well, you know?
132	G:	Mm. So ...
133	W:	I have no problem with people who speak in plain En-
134		glish, in language that other people can understand. And
135		I would never suggest that everybody should be reading
136		uhm academic tomes. But a lot of, a lot of personal devel-
137		opment self-help books are simply mor*on*ic. They read as
138		if they've been written *by* twelve-year-olds *for* twelve-year-
139		olds ...
140	M:	Well why should you blanket everybody in that ...
141	W:	... in the attempt to ...

142 M: … whole, whole, er …
143 W: I'm not blanketing everybody. I'm not blanketing every-
144   body. I've read …
145 M: But you're dismissing a whole movement; you're blan-
146   keting everybody.
147 W: I've read *hun*dreds of self-help books and I would say
148   that the vast majority of the books that I've read recycle
149   popular wisdom from other self-help books. I mean, read-
150   ing these books, you feel like you're in an echo chamber
151   because so many of them are saying exactly the same
152   thing.
153 M: I could call that … With *fic*tion and everything, everything
154   the same. You can say that with every single story.
155 W: No, but, but I think what that tells you is that many of
156   the people who are writing these books don't have any
157   special insights into the mysteries of the universe, don't
158   have any special insights into how to be a good person, or
159   how to be a happy person.
160 S: You know, Wendy, you're not wrong.
161 M: Mm.
162 W: What they *have* is a knowledge of other self-help books. I
163   mean, I could *eas*ily write a self-help book because I've
164   read so many of them, but that doesn't make me some-
165   one who should be telling other people how to live their
166   lives. And …
167 S: And so, Wendy, you're not wrong, you know, you're defi-
168   nitely not wrong. A lot of New Age books are completely
169   moronic. But then we live in a moronic society. You've
170   only got to turn CNN on for five minutes and watch some
171   total twit explain Kosovo in twenty-nine seconds to you –
172   in a lot of, like, sort of glib clichés. And that's supposed to
173   be the political news for the day. So we live in that type of
174   society don't we?
175 W: Yes we do, I mean, I don't happen to think that's a very
176   good thing.
177 S: Well it isn't, you know. And then again, you know, the
178   ones that are *ab*solutely moronic just don't sell. And the
179   ones that are *fair*ly well written, or make a point, do so.
180   You know, I mean, I've sold … I dunno, millions of books.
181   I mean three, five, six, seven million, I'm not exactly sure.
182   And if people didn't buy them, and if they hadn't been out
183   for sort of 15–20 years. You know the proof of the pud-
184   ding is always in the eating. And I wrote a book called
185   *Infinite Self,* and it's like, it's a classic.
186 W: Yeh but just a …
187 G: Sorry just, I just got to read you, for instance, this is one
188   of things that Wendy finds really aggravating. You say for

189		instance on page seven of *Infinite Self*, Stuart, erm: 'The
190		world of the ego is one of discomfort, even agony at times,
191		er, the ego leans naturally towards dysfunction. It is tough
192		to come to any kind of serenity in what the eastern mys-
193		tics call *Maia*, the illusion of an ego-driven world'. Now I
194		mean, how do you *know* that?
195	S:	Well I dunno, I mean, I mean, that's what Wendy said at
196		the beginning of the show, that life is painful. So I think
197		we're both on the same side. I mean … the natural de-
198		sires of the ego drive one to, for example, ac*quire* things
199		(in the hope of) that'll make us happy, or you know, to
200		have many relationships or you know, they, they drive us
201		to accumulate, and, er, in that striving to accumulate, a
202		lot of pain is created, a lot of dysfunction.
203	G:	Michael?
204	M:	Well I don't agree, I must say, I don't agree that life is
205		painful. There are occasions of pain per*haps* in some
206		people's lives but there are a lot of people who actually
207		en*joy* their lives to the full. I'm one of those, and I accept
208		that there'll be challenges along the way, as do many
209		people. I think this whole sort of negative view of things is
210		an unfortunate way of looking at it. And I don't know, I
211		haven't read Wendy's book. But it seems to me it's far
212		easier to criticise people than it is to uplift society and to
213		pick out a few …
214	W:	I don't, I don't …
215	M:	Just a minute. Just to pick out a few …
216	W:	Okay.
217	M:	… erm, negative books or badly written books is not nec-
218		essarily the answer to realising what is going on in this
219		phenomenon: people looking for self-development, personal
220		growth, spiritual insight. To me, the whole goal, the whole
221		game, is to get into a state of grace, which is something I've
222		experienced on numerous occasions following particular
223		*tech*niques and *meth*ods. And to …
224	W:	Well.
225	M:	… dismiss techniques and methods is again misinforma-
226		tion because obviously it hasn't worked for *you*, other-
227		wise, er, you wouldn't say that. It's certainly worked for
228		me and …
229	W:	What I'm just miffed about, what I'm just miffed about is
230		practising therapy as, as a *whole*sale not a *ret*ail profes-
231		sion. What I'm dis …
232	M:	Why?
233	W:	… gusted about is somebody pre*sum*ing to write a book
234		that gives personal advice to millions of people that he's
235		never met.

236	M:	But why is that wrong? People write books all the time
237		giving advice in a variety ... From how to grow your roses.
238		You never met anyone. Why should ...
239	W:	Because growing ...
240	M:	... that be the case?
241	W:	Because growing roses or putting plumbing in your house,
242		doing useful ...
243	M:	Weight-lifting, slimming.
244	W:	Let me finish now. I let you finish, let me finish. Those *are*
245		practical technical problems which are quite amenable
246		to practical technical solutions. But how to be a *good*
247		person, how to achieve a state of grace: that's not a prac-
248		tical technical problem. That's a much more ...
249	M:	Why, why do you think *that*?
250	W:	Why do I *think* that? Well we gotta disagree on that.
251	M:	Why do you think it's not a practical technical problem?
252		But, why why why, what's your point that, er, that it's
253		not, er, just purely a matter of following particular tech-
254		niques? Because that's what tends to ...
255	W:	I don't, I don't happen to think that it is ...
256	M:	Well ...
257	W:	We got a different *kind* of problem, and I think that the
258		problem is *diff*erent for *diff*erent people. And I think that
259		advice has to be tailored for different people. And I also
260		think that people need to know who they're taking advice
261		*from*. I mean, I have been asked by so many strangers for
262		*per*sonal advice, you know: what should I do about this,
263		what ...
264	M:	Mm hm.
265	W:	... should I do about that. And my problem is always
266		*don't* .... My answer is always *don't* ask people you don't
267		know for personal advice.
268	M:	Wendy, can I say something?
269	G:	You mean since your book has come out, and you, you
270		end ...
271	W:	Yeh.
272	G:	... up getting on a book circuit and a TV circuit, and sud-
273		denly *you*'ve become the very expert you're ((laughs)) about
274	W:	Yeh, I mean, here I am, criticising people for offering ad-
275		vice to people they've never met, and I get phone calls
276		saying: well what do you think I should do?
277	G:	The what ...
278	W:	People are *so hungry* for advice from self-appointed ex-
279		perts they'll ...
280	G:	Before I come to you, Stuart, I'm going to invite the lis-
281		teners ...
282	S:	Okay

283 G: ... to join us now. So you're with us here on *Life Matters*.
284   We're talking about *self-help*, er, the good, the bad and
285   the ugly. And, er, I wonder if *you* like self-help books —
286   asking the *Life Matters* listeners: Do you love them or
287   loathe them? Do you believe they really can help? In par-
288   ticular, have you been able to apply their advice to your
289   *life*? Or not? That's, I suppose, particularly what I'm curi-
290   ous to find out. Our number is 1800 025 977.

As we said earlier, there's an important sense in which this transcript needs no commentary or analysis. The protagonists are caught
in the act, working hard, despite their differences, to characterise
just who it is they imagine self-help book readers to be. Right from
the start, Michael sets up some apparently factual themes of late
modernity: divorce as the norm in relationships, women as its 'motivators' (a sop to feminism here? or else a mild misogyny?), the decline
of religion and the popular conception of science as pro-knowing and
anti-believing. 'So', he says, 'people aren't interested in beliefs. They
want to know ... '. And 'knowing' is, in this discourse, a question of
learned practices and techniques which can bring wanted changes
into people's lives.

Michael's position, then, is both historically informed (he claims
to know about recent changes to relationship dealings in the west)
and, at the same time, is open to the idea that the 'individual' can
become whatever they want, by a form of sheer volition called 'knowing' — knowing as practical method and technique. His position

---

3. These ways of characterising the participants are, of course, partial — but
this is how they were introduced during the broadcast.

   To expand on this: Wendy Kaminer is a Fellow at the Radcliffe Public Policy
Centre at Harvard University. She has also written *Sleeping with Extra-Terres-
trials: The Rise of Irrationalism and Perils of Piety.*

   Stuart Wilde's publication vitae/industrial output includes: *Whispering Winds
of Change: Perceptions of a New World, Secrets of Life, Quickening, Force,
Affirmations: How to Expand your Personal Power and Take Back Control of your
Life, The Trick to Money is Having Some!, Miracles, Intuition, Happiness is Your
Destiny, Loving Relationships, The Art of Meditation, The Little Money Bible, Life
Was Never Meant to be a Struggle, Silent Power, Weight Loss for the Mind, Sixth
Sense: Including the Secrets of the Etheric Subtle Body.*

   We have fewer available details about Michael Rowland; except that his middle
name is Domeyko.

4. What we are trying to point to with this awkward coining, 'dividual', is the
strangeness of referring to ourselves as '*individuals*': that is, as atomic things
that cannot be further segmented (or analysed) into parts. The strangeness is
compounded by the fact that the psy-complex continually exhorts us to con-
strue ourselves as infinitely segmentable (or analysable), with a view to reunit-
ing the parts into a new (or cured) harmonious whole. While the term is, we
admit, jargon-ish, it has the benefit of avoiding continual reference to the more
portentous 'divided self'.

throughout the discussion is just that: learn the techniques and you can be what you want to be, despite your habitus, your social, cultural and economic conditions. Science, as knowing, as self-help, will set you free.

If we think back to Mr Biswas, the sheer idealism of this stance is clearly in evidence. And that idealism is made explicit in the ensuing exchange (in the transcript) where Geraldine thinks that happiness has become an object, something to be grabbed, something tangible. In response, Michael posits an almost Rousseau-esque version of idealism. Note his nicely modulated disagreement at line 23: 'Well yes I think so, but I also think that … '. And what he thinks is that happiness is, in fact, our natural condition, 'a sort of birthright'. Implicitly, then, the subject of self-help is a natural in-dividual, like a perfectly happy baby, who has somehow lost that perfect state. If people aren't happy, then, it's 'because they contract down through the process of conditioning, through the pressures of life'. That is, they have become 'dividual'; but the techniques of knowing-self-help will (again, ideally) restore their natural in-dividuality.

This comes out most clearly in Michael's ensuing debate with Wendy. Wendy posits a more Hobbesian version of the person, focusing on death and loss rather than on birth and the enduring bonds of care. Her focus is 'tragedy': 'We're all going to grow old and die and even worse we're all going to see … the people we love grow old and die' (lines 35–39). No doubt as a devotee of knowledge over belief, Michael is hardly in a position to doubt this. What he does doubt, from his position of idealism, is Wendy's *interpretation* of the facts: 'Why's that a tragedy?' And, as a defence of the possibility of joyous death, he cites the case of Balinese funeral rituals: 'if you go to a Balinese funeral for instance, it's a thing of celebration. People dance and sing and they look forward to having a different kind of experience' (lines 46–49).

Again this is interesting for us, for we have also cited cases of massive historical and cultural variation in feelings-discourses earlier in this chapter. But the assumptions informing Michael's use of such cases are quite different from our own. Michael, that is, appears to assume a kind of natural Rousseau-esque individual, primordially unaffected by social and cultural circumstances. As we have seen, for Michael, social and cultural facts are 'pressures of life', forms of 'conditioning' which tend, unaided by self-help, to make any such individual 'contract down'. The true individual appears to precede cultural formation. Implicit in his argument here is that pretty much anyone, with the right knowledge, the right techniques, could overcome their supernumerary cultural conditions and take on more positive forms. They could, in this example, find death and loss to be a cause of 'celebration'. The atomic individual can conquer the accidents of habitus. Yet, as we have seen, any such assumption rarely works in practice. Mr Biswas can no more become a successful inventor by mental fiat than he can get the right electronics equipment in Trinidad. The manuals — self-help, or electronic — assume a model of the person who can attain an eternally unsatisfiable wholeness.

Wendy's response to this is interesting. She doesn't insist on social and cultural order as a 'real' (if geographically and temporally relative) condition of human being. Rather, she reverts to an equally absolutist conception of the individual, insisting that such things as Balinese funerary customs are (contrary to Michael) not forms of knowledge but forms of belief. Behind any such forms lies the supposedly eternal human characteristic of being 'terrified by death', so that religious (and other) belief structures are ways of coping with such a fixed condition. (This is in fact one of the main themes of her book: that self-help is, in this respect, but another ideological formation parallel with religion and its ilk — and, as with many ideology theories, the theorist has to assume a more 'real', preferably material, state of human being.) Hence: 'that's one of the reasons why spiritualists do so well. Because they tell you they can communicate with the people ... who have died, and that you haven't really lost them' (lines 62–65).

For Michael, culture and society are a kind of con-trick keeping us out of touch with our true, happy, natural selves — which self-help, religious and spiritual techniques can restore. For Wendy, self-help, religious and spiritual practices are a kind of con-trick keeping us out of touch with the terrible and tragic material givens of death and loss. The stories, then, are not so different in their fundamental structures: only the contents and characters vary.

Moving to a later point in the transcript: what, then, of Stuart's unusual blend of the two positions (we hesitate to write 'synthesis')? Stuart is in agreement in many respects with Wendy: he concurs that many self-help books are 'moronic': 'And so, Wendy, you're not wrong ... you're definitely not wrong. A lot of New Age books are completely moronic' (lines 166–168). But he attributes this to a current form of popular social dumbing down: 'But then we live in a moronic society. You've only got to turn CNN on for five minutes and watch some total twit explain Kosovo in 29 seconds .... So we live in that type of society don't we' (lines 168–173). By contrast, then, his own books are not like that; they're well written, such that they sell, whereas the moronic ones do not.

Via Geraldine's quotation from his *Infinite Self* (lines 188–192), Stuart is then able to align himself much more with Wendy's pessimistic view of human existence. He translates the quotation from his own work as follows: 'I mean ... that's what Wendy said at the beginning of the show, that life is painful. So I think we're both on the same side .... [T]he natural desires of the ego drive one to, for example, acquire things in the hope that they'll make us happy' (lines 194–198). So now we have yet another take on the matter, another content-shuffle of the familiar structural deck. This time, there is a new natural, fixed and given state: the ego and its natural desires to do such destructive things as accumulate possessions. This creates 'a lot of pain ... a lot of dysfunction' (line 201). What is then needed is a self-help therapeutic regime (for Stuart, a plain-English cross between psychotherapy and eastern mysticism) that can overcome that natural, painful, egoistic tendency. On this account, we naturally suffer bad and painful experiences (as we do on Wendy's account). But the solution is to have a self-generated internal 'power' over this state, to take the (no fewer than) 33 steps towards 'reclaiming' it. Again, the socio-cultural dimensions of life can be discounted, for they amount to no more than living in a 'moronic society' (including its bad New Age books).

No doubt we could, if we turned to further accounts, find other variations on this general narrative, other permutations of self, society and therapeutics. But we will end here by simply noticing their utter repetition: there is a natural state of being (fundamentally good, happy, bad, egoistic ...); by and large social, cultural, political and economic positionings either expand these possibilities or 'contract' them 'down' — leaving a plethora of positive and negative outcomes. For any permutation of these fundamental human conditions (plus contextual variables), there is a means of restoration to be found: either on and up (away from our negative-natural egoism and pain) towards personal 'power', or back down (towards regaining our positive-natural happiness as a 'birthright'). In either (or any) case, we inevitably find ourselves in a position of impossibility: eternally incomplete yet striving for techniques of completion that can only come 'from within' the very self that is always already deemed incomplete. And how we are to break out of this eternal circle is by buying books that, by definition, tell us how that 'from within' can be realised 'from without'. This wilful, almost compulsive, neglect of sheer social, political, cultural and economic difference must, as they say, all end in tears: disillusionment for some and dollar profits for others:

> There was money in the island. It showed in the suits of Govind, who drove the Americans in his taxi; in the possessions of W.C. Tuttle, who hired out his lorry to them; in the new cars; the new buildings. And from this money ... despite Samuel Smiles, Mr Biswas found himself barred. (Naipaul, 1969: 438)

References

Abu-Lughod, Lila (1990) Shifting Politics in Bedouin Love Poetry. In: Catherine Lutz and Lila Abu-Lughod (eds.) *Language and the Politics of Emotion.* Cambridge: Cambridge University Press, 24–45

Albee, George W. (1977) The Protestant Ethic, Sex, and Psychotherapy. *American Psychologist, 32*(2) 150–61

Aleinikoff, T. Alexander (2000) Between Principles and Politics: US Citizenship

Policy. In: T. Alexander Aleinikoff and Douglas Klusmeyer (eds.) *From Migrants to Citizens: Membership in a Changing World.* Washington: Carnegie Endowment for International Peace, 119–72

Arditi, Jorge (1996) The Feminization of Etiquette Literature: Foucault, Mechanisms of Social Change, and the Paradoxes of Empowerment. *Sociological Perspectives, 39*(3) 417–34

Bennett, Arnold (1957) [1913]. *Mental Efficiency and Other Hints to Men and Women.* Kingswood: The World's Work

Bennett, Tony (1992) Putting Policy into Cultural Studies. In: Lawrence Grossberg, Cary Nelson and Paula Treichler (eds.) *Cultural Studies.* New York: Routledge, 23–34

Biggart, Nicole Woolsey (1983) Rationality, Meaning, and Self-Management: Success Manuals, 1950–1980. *Social Problems, 30*(3) 298–311

Boscagli, Maurizia (1992–93) A Moving Story: Masculine Tears and the Humanity of Televized Emotions. *Discourse 15*(2) 64–79

Cancian, Francesca M. (1986) The Feminization of Love. *Signs, 11*(4) 692–709

Cancian, Francesca M. (1987) *Love in America: Gender and Self-Development.* Cambridge: Cambridge University Press

Cancian, Francesca M. and Gordon, Steven L. (1988) Changing Emotion Norms in Marriage: Love and Anger in US Women's Magazines Since 1900. *Gender & Society, 2*(3) 308–42

'Congratulations John Gray!' (1997) *New York Times* (27 March) B30

Davidson, John (1992) Does Penis Size Really Matter? One Guy Gets Honest. *Cleo* October, 68–70

de Swaan, Abram (1990) *The Management of Normality.* London: Routledge

Duan, Changming and Hill, Clara E. (1996) The Current State of Empathy Research. *Journal of Counseling Psychology, 43*(3) 261–74

Elias, Norbert (1978a) *The History of Manners.* New York: Pantheon

Elias, Norbert (1978b) *The Civilizing Process: The History of Manners.* Trans. Edmund Jephcott. Oxford: Basil Blackwell

Forbes, David (1994) *False Fixes: The Cultural Politics of Drugs, Alcohol, and Addictive Relations.* Albany: State University of New York Press

Foucault, Michel (1977) Nietzsche, Genealogy, History. In: Donald F. Bouchard (ed) *Language, Counter-Memory, Practice: Selected Essays and Interviews.* Trans. Donald F. Bouchard and Sherry Simon. Ithaca: Cornell University Press, 139–64

Foucault, Michel (1979) *Discipline and Punish: The Birth of the Prison.* Trans. Alan Sheridan. New York: Vintage Books

Foucault, Michel (1982) The Subject and Power. Trans. Leslie Sawyer. *Critical Inquiry, 8*(4) 777–95

Foucault, Michel (1987) *Mental Illness and Psychology.* Trans. Alan Sheridan. Berkeley: University of California Press

Gerhards, Jürgen (1989) The Changing Culture of Emotions in Modern Society. *Social Science Information, 28*(4) 737–54

Gilligan, Carol (1997) A Therapist Examines the Hidden Problem of Male Depression. *New York Times Book Review* (16 February) 24

Groves, Ernest R.; Groves, Gladys Hoagland and Groves, Catherine (1945) *Sex Fulfillment in Marriage.* New York: Emerson

Hacking, Ian (1992) Multiple Personality Disorder and its Hosts. *History of the Human Sciences, 5*(2) 3–31

'Hardcover Bestsellers' (1997) *Publishers Weekly, 244*(3) np

Hochschild, Arlie Russell (1994) The Commercial Spirit of Intimate Life and the Abduction of Feminism: Signs from Women's Advice Books. *Theory, Culture & Society, 11*(2) 1–24

Hunter, Ian (1984) Laughter and Warmth: Sex Education in Victorian Secondary Schools. In: Peter Botsman and Ross Harley (eds.) *Sex, Politics, Representation.* Sydney: Local Consumption, 55–81

Irvine, Leslie J. (1995) Codependency and Recovery: Gender, Self, and Emotions in Popular Self-Help. *Symbolic Interaction, 18*(2) 145–63

Jimenez, Mary Ann and Rice, Susan (1990) Popular Advice to Women: A Feminist Perspective. *Affilia,* 5(3) 8–26

Kaminer, Wendy (1992) *I'm Dysfunctional, You're Dysfunctional: The Recovery Movement and Other Self-Help Fashions.* New York: Addison-Wesley Longman

Lasch, Christopher (1979) *The Culture of Narcissism: American Life in an Age of Diminishing Expectations.* New York: Warner

Lichterman, Paul (1992) Self-Help Reading as a Thin Culture. *Media, Culture & Society, 14*(4) 421–47

Mäkelä, Klaus; Arminen, Ilkka; Bloomfield, Kim; Eisenbach-Stangl, Irmgard; Helmersson Bergmark, Karin; Kurube, Noriko; Marilini, Nicoletta; Olafsdóttir, Hildigunnur; Peterson, John H.; Phillips, Mary; Rehm, Jürgen; Room, Robin; Rosenqvist, Pia; Rosovsky, Haydée; Stenius, Kerstin; Swiatkiewicz, Grazyna; Woronowicz, Bohdan and Zielinski, Antoni (1996) *Alcoholics Anonymous as a Mutual-Help Movement.* Madison: University of Wisconsin Press

Maryles, Daisy (1997) How the Winners Made it to the Top. *Publishers Weekly, 244*(1) 46–9

McHoul, Alec and Rapley, Mark (2001) 'Ghost: Do not forget; this visitation / Is but to whet thy almost blunted purpose': Culture, Psychology and 'Being Human'. *Culture and Psychology, 7*(4) 433–51

Miller, Toby and McHoul, Alec (1998) *Popular Culture and Everyday Life.* London: Sage

Millman, Dan (1979) *The Warrior Athlete: Body, Mind and Spirit: Self-Transformation through Total Training.* Walpole: Stillpoint

Moore, Robert and Gillette, Douglas (1992) *The King Within: Accessing the King in the Male Psyche.* New York: Avon

Moskowitz, Eva (1996) 'It's Good to Blow Your Top': Women's Magazines and a Discourse of Discontent, 1945-1965. *Journal of Women's History,* 8(3) 66–98

Musto, David (1995) No Cure but Care. *Times Literary Supplement,* 4800 (31 March) 6

Naipaul, V.S. (1969) [1961] *A House for Mr Biswas.* London: Penguin

Nathan, Debbie (1994) Dividing to Conquer? Women, Men, and the Making of Multiple Personality Disorder. *Social Text, 40*(Fall) 77–114

'Paperback Bestsellers' (1997) *Publishers Weekly 244*(4) np

People Weekly. Entertainment Almanac (1996) New York: Calder

Pinch, Adela (1995) Emotion and History: A Review Article. *Comparative Studies in Society and History, 37*(1) 100–9

Prilleltensky, Isaac (1989) Psychology and the Status Quo. *American Psychologist, 44*(5) 795–802

Quinn, Judy (1996) 'The Rules' Gets a Male Response. *Publishers Weekly, 243*(45) 19

Rice, John Steadman (1992) Discursive Formation, Life Stories, and the Emergence of Co-Dependency: 'Power/Knowledge' and the Search for Identity. *Sociological Quarterly, 33*(3) 337–64

Riessman, Frank and Carroll, David (1995) *Redefining Self-Help: Policy and Practice.* San Francisco: Jossey-Bass

Rind, Bruce and Bordia, Prashant (1996) Effect on Restaurant Tipping of

Male and Female Servers Drawing a Happy, Smiling Face on the Backs of Customers' Checks. *Journal of Applied Social Psychology, 26*(3) 218–25

Ross, Ellen (1980) 'The Love Crisis': Couples Advice Books of the Late 1970s. *Signs, 6*(1) 109–22

Ross, Robert A. (1945) Preface. In: Ernest R. Groves, Gladys Hoagland Groves and Catherine Groves, *Sex Fulfillment in Marriage*. New York: Emerson, xiii–xiv

Rowland, Michael (1995) *Absolute Happiness: The Way to a Life of Complete Fulfilment*. Carlsbad, CA: Hay House

Russell, James A. and Sato, Kaori (1995) Comparing Emotion Words Between Languages. *Journal of Cross-Cultural Psychology, 26*(4) 384–91

Shattuc, Jane M. (1997) *The Talking Cure: TV Talk Shows and Women*. New York: Routledge

Smiles, Samuel (1859) *Self-Help: With Illustrations of Character and Conduct*. London: Ward Lock

Stearns, Peter N. (1994) *American Cool: Constructing a Twentieth-Century Emotional Style*. New York: New York University Press

Stenson, Kevin (1993) Social Work Discourse and the Social Work Interview. *Economy and Society, 22*(1) 42–75

Susman, Warren I. (1984) *Culture as History: The Transformation of American Society in the Twentieth Century*. New York: Pantheon

Synnott, Anthony (1993) *The Body Social: Symbolism, Self and Society*. London: Routledge

Trepp, Anne-Charlott (1994) The Private Lives of Men in Eighteenth-Century Central Europe: The Emotional Side of Men in Late Eighteenth-Century Germany (Theory and Example). Trans. Ursula Marcum. *Central European History, 27*(2) 127–52

Verhovek, Sam Howe (1995) In Texas, the 'Inner Child' Has Finger on the Trigger. *New York Times* (8 November) A1, D25

Weber, Bruce (1997) Taking the Stage to Help Mars and Venus Kiss and Make Up. *New York Times* (26 January) 29–30

Weinberg, Martin S.; Ganz Swensson, Rochelle and Kiefer Hammersmith, Sue (1983) Sexual Autonomy and the Status of Women: Models of Female Sexuality in US Sex Manuals from 1950 to 1980. *Social Problems, 30*(3) 312–24

'What the World is Reading' (1997) *The Economist, 342*(8004) (15 February) 18

Wilde, Stuart (1996) *Infinite Self: 33 Steps to Reclaiming Your Power*. Carlsbad, CA: Hay House

Wouters, Cas (1995) Etiquette Books and Emotion Management in the 20th Century: Part One — The Integration of Social Classes. *Journal of Social History, 29*(1) 107–24

Wuthnow, Robert (1994) *Sharing the Journey: Support Groups and America's New Quest for Community*. New York: Free Press

Psych dot com

'God, is there a market for it'. — Dr Joy Stapp, Director of the Human Resources Office of the American Psychological Association. (Neimark, 1984: np)

Face-to-face therapeutic encounters and relationships are costly .... At $20 per interaction, folks can afford to stay involved with their online professionals. (Powell, 1998)

Upwards of 110 million people seek health-related information on the Internet each year (Harris Interactive, 2002). Of this number, the largest group is comprised of people seeking mental-health-related information. Searching for 'mental health' with Google (www.google.com) returns over 2,000,000 potentially helpful sites; 'depression' over 4,250,000 possibilities; whilst those looking for 'relationship advice' will find over 36,000 pages to turn to. The (US) National Institute of Mental Health website alone receives more than 150,000 visitors every day. Les Posen, Secretary of the Victorian Branch of the Australian Psychological Society, reports that 'depression' is one of the most frequently used search engine terms — second only to 'sex' — and predicts that, in the aftermath of the dot com crash, mental health sites may prove the only other websites, besides sex sites, that will actually turn a long-term profit for their owners (Posen, 2001).

We begin by looking at one of psychology's earliest forays into computerised service provision — the boom, in the 1980s, of psychological software, which accompanied the proliferation of more affordable computers into the public and the domestic sphere. The flipside of psychology's apparent generosity with its vocabulary and methods is the opportunistic co-branding — or grafting — of psychological applications on to many other areas; particularly those experiencing rapid growth, and market penetration of their own. As we will see, whilst some psy-ventures were lost in the transition from mini-computers to micro-computers, many more survived to the transformative 1990s, where the Internet provided a means for entering each and every connected household:

Today, the Internet is integrated into all aspects of our lives ....
[The] Internet will help us connect people in convenient and
compelling ways, providing them with quality information that
will enable them to navigate the emotional challenges of
everydaylife.
(www.apshealthcare.com/helplink/helplink.com_index.htm
#programanalysis)

We then turn to examine the parallel growth, from the late 1970s to
the present, of the market for self-help software; in the number of
self-help, and support groups on the Internet; the proliferation of
'psych-information', self-assessment and cyber-therapy sites; the
investment of the professional associations in the 'tele-mental-health'
project; the role of shifting ethical and legal regulations in defining
appropriate 'target markets' for online psychological services; and
the apparent threat to the psy-professions posed by managed — or
commodified — web-based behavioural health care.

Psych Systems, Inc.

Standard psychological tests that involve a limited role for computers have been in use since the 1950s. However, the size of the early
computers involved (most filled entire rooms), the cost of each enormous machine, and the considerable time, patience and technical
prowess required for their operation, meant that, until the 1970s
(when 'mini-computers' became available), computers were most often to be found in select academic, research and industrial locations. Psy-professionals either scored their tests manually, or sent
them offsite for processing. In the late 1970s, hospitals, clinics and
private practitioners began administering automated psychological
tests by mini-computer, when, in 1978, Psych Systems began selling
computerised testing to professionals. Psych Systems 'worked closely'
with the American Psychological Association to establish computerised testing guidelines. The (then) Treasurer of the APA, Ray Fowler,
was a 'resident scientist' at this burgeoning business venture. In
1980, Psych Systems sales were $606,143; by 1983, they exceeded
$5 million. *Forbes* reported an annual growth rate of 175 per cent,
and listed the company as 'one to watch'. However, in October of the
following year, Psych Systems filed for bankruptcy. Changes in the
kinds of technological equipment that psy-professionals were willing
to pay for — mini-computers for $60,000 a system, versus the new
micro-computers for under $10,000 a system — meant that Psych
Systems had to review its product base. Further, the most popular
professional product offered by Psych Systems — the Minnesota
Multiphasic Personality Inventory (MMPI) — had been used under a
short term license granted by a competitor. That agreement formally

expired at the end of 1983. The MMPI, however, is *still* going strong, and is administered to countless individuals each year — most often as part of a 'routine' job application.[1] With the dramatic collapse of Psych Systems, plans for a merger with a psychiatric corporation (which would have ensured Psych Systems were used in major psychiatric hospitals around America) were shelved. Despite the ultimate demise of Psych Systems, 1984 also saw computerised psychological assessments find their way into the police force, the army, the court room, the classroom, and the boardroom (Neimark, 1984). Today, psychological software is *everywhere* — and, as with the self-help book market, the market for self-applications rivals that of the institutional market (see www.mindmedia.com for a catalogue).

The first commercially available psychological software was developed for use by managers and sales people. It was claimed to function as a 'plug in consultant, to explain the motives and behavior of business associates, and map out strategies for negotiating deals, closing sales, and managing subordinates' (Neimark, 1984: np). These 'plug in consultants' were hastily developed in 'response' to the growing 'need', amongst managers, for the expertise of a raft of psy-consultants. Smail (2002: np) notes that a vital consequence of this need was that 'managerial expertise' became detached from 'technical know-how'. Parenthetically, he also notes that this enables business to 'take over professional knowledge, without having to go to the trouble of actually acquiring it' (Smail, 2002: np). So, much as in chapter three we saw psychology taking over the 'new science' of advertising in the 1920s, and making its methods, vocabulary and methods of judgment indispensable to that industry, in the 1980s, a whole new raft of psy-professionals became indispensable as business consultants — needed to assist business 'gain the edge' on competitors, and to 'enhance the performance' of subordinates.

Human Edge Software ('for the edge in business — and in life') were, in the early 1980s, responsible for such programs as 'The Negotiation Edge', 'The Management Edge', 'The Sales Edge' and 'The Communication Edge'. Human Edge also released the 'Mind Prober' — an everyman equivalent for people needing help to find the right person at a singles bar, with sales to bar owners included as part of the marketing plan. Human Edge sparked media interest in the early 1980s when the London *Financial Times* ran President Reagan and

---

1. Even applicants for the clinical psychology program at the University of Minnesota (the creator of the MMPI) are required to suffer its administration, as the MMPI — available from a psy-professional near you — is used instead of 'costly' interviews. The University explains that the MMPI helps to 'determine an applicant's personal suitability for work in clinical psychology .... We believe it is important to evaluate the adjustment of individuals who will be working with clients and patients and the MMPI-2 is well suited for the detection of personal problems that could be so severe as to interfere with a student's ability to function competently as a psychologist' (University of Minnesota, 2001: 1).

Prime Minister Margaret Thatcher through 'The Sales Edge' program, generating such insights as: 'R.R. is inclined to seek the limelight, to perform for others. Appeal to R.R. with flattery', and for Maggie, 'your tendency to place emphasis on details may bore R.R. Be aware that R.R. can be impulsive and make quick decisions'. Ray Fowler characterised such popular psychological programs as 'the worst kind of pop psychology. You might as well have do-it-yourself brain surgery. I'd rather drill my own teeth. When the professional is out of the picture, then you have trouble' (Neimark, 1984: np).

'Professional Analyst' is a contemporary version of these early 'plug in consultants'. This psychological software promises to: 'improve your personal life, business or professional practice'. By installing 'the depth and power of a PhD or MD calibre personality evaluator on your PC', consumers are assured they will be able to '[l]earn all you need to know about any other person' (Johnson, 2002: np). Dr James Johnson, the creator of 'Professional Analyst' insists that 'the information given by this test should not be restricted to only those with professional credentials', and recommends its use for 'professional' evaluations, such as selecting job applicants, or supervising employees:

> 'Professional Analyst' scores the individual for dishonesty, disagreeableness and potential for substance abuse. This is the kind of information you might want for hiring, supervising and counselling. (Johnson, 2002: np)

The amateur psy-professional will also gain access to a 'Clinical Report', which presents the results of 19 'personality scales', including narcissism, depression, mania, recent stress, childhood neurosis, marital problems, delinquency, anxiety, conscientiousness, and paranoia. This 'for-your-eyes-only' document is promised to provide:

> [r]eports on the presence of psychopathology and how to treat it. This report is written in cold clinical language that may be offensive to some. You should be prepared to deal with the clinical facts about how people think … and act. The Clinical Report is intended for the person who is serious about understanding human behavior and motivation. (Note for professionals: You'll get a DSM diagnosis on both Axis I and Axis II.) (Johnson, 2002: np)

The DSM is, of course the Diagnostic and Statistical Manual produced by the American Psychiatric Association, and used by psy-professionals everywhere — and, it seems, increasingly available to para-psy-professionals to 'truly understand' the motivation and behaviour of ourselves and others. 'Professional Analyst' offers the consumer access to a set of 'restricted' psychological techniques, and 'cold clinical facts' purported to enhance our understanding of those around us — with a view to 'predicting' and 'controlling' behaviour with the 'power and insight of an expert'. This 'expert in a box' lends moral authority, and a 'professional vocabulary' to ordinary moral judgments about character and conduct — which become technical appraisals of 'human behavior, personality and motivation'.

In this program, in popular and accessible form, everyday managers are promised insight, not just into the motivation and behaviour of employees, but into *personality* and *psychopathology*. 'Personality' is yet another ordinary word that psy has reinvented as a technical, psychological term. Before the late nineteenth century, personality had meaning as a theological, legal and ethical term (Danziger, 1997). Indeed, it was not until this time that 'personality' came to refer to individual persons. Personality ceased to warrant philosophical attention, as it came to be recognised as something prone to disease, and thus in need of medical attention (see Ribot, 1885). As we have seen in chapter four, early self-help literature was concerned with the improvement of 'character'. However, by the early twentieth century, the newly psychological category of 'personality' had come to supplant the moral notion of 'character' as the key to 'self-help'. Indeed, a 'personality' is now a central — and apparently universal — possession of every self. Personality was, for psychology, a much more promising candidate for describing 'psychological health' than the singular model offered by 'character', as it provided a way of understanding 'psychological health' as a more delicately balanced set of relations between diverse components of the self (Danziger, 1997).

As part of the mental hygiene movement, every 'personality' was subject to examination — no longer just those 'obvious' cases of 'disturbed' personality. In this manner, psychology claimed to be able to identify potential cases of future disturbance, and thus to 'treat' and avoid the *social* problems that were now explainable as the result of 'maladjusted' people (see chapter three for more on the mental hygiene movement). Psychological 'scales' for 'measuring' personality remain one of the discipline's best-selling products, as they have become indispensable for a range of industries — from education, to business, to self-improvement. Thus, for the modern consumer, 'personality' is something that should be attended to, as the quantifiable sum of ourselves — ever vulnerable to 'imbalance', and thus pathology, but also indicative of our potential, and thus amenable to 'improvement'. 'Professional Analyst' is merely a popular commercial version of the ways that psychology sells the 'measurement' of 'personality' — as 'all you need to know' to predict, and account for, the performance of particular individuals.

Computer-aided self-help

Karl Erikson, author of the 'Computer-Aided Self-Help' (CASH) program is frank about the functional limitations of self-help software:

> Self-help programs will never be a match for a good human psychologist. However, that does not mean they won't be useful. Self-help books are useful and they are not human either. A self-help computer program can bring up relevant helpful information for a particular problem.
> (www.primechoice.com/philosophy/shelp/cash.htm)

Early psyware produced for everyday people — who by now wanted their own *personal* computers — included applications for parents, couples, persons in search of 'self-improvement', and those seeking to 'alleviate their depression', or to learn new 'therapeutic' ways of thinking. In 1978, the PLATO Computer-based Dilemma Counseling System (PLATO DCS) was created (Wagman and Kerber, 1978). MORTON, a cognitive-behavioural program, was released in 1982 (Selmi et al., 1982). These programs were intended for use in conjunction with a psy-professional.

As we explore further in chapter seven, the family has long provided a market for the application of 'practical psychological truths'. 'Discover Your Baby: Birth to 2 Years' — one of the first available 'parenting' programs — was designed for the Apple II. In order for this program to work, parents are required to answer questions which enable the computer to 'track the development of their child' and to 'recommend activities to augment each baby's skills'. 'Discover Your Baby' was produced by the BHT Group, a team of Californian child psychologists and programmers. Ray Fowler was similarly damning of such popular parental psy-products — 'If my baby turns blue every morning, I don't want the computer. I'll have a doctor, thank you' (Neimark, 1984: np).

Though 'Discover Your Baby' has long since been discontinued, the contemporary market for 'parenting software' remains strong. The Internet makes such programs ever more readily available to ordinary people — as it allows consumers to 'try before they buy', to research similar products, and to assess their family's unique needs, in advance of the purchase of a particular product. 'Parenting' websites have, to some extent, supplanted parenting software, as they offer free expert assistance in all manner of relevant affairs, educational information, family-assessment tools, and links to relevant helpful products — from books to software, to self-help groups — to therapy. The Parent's Place (www.parentsplace.com) has a drop down menu of a variety of experts — from lactation consultants to family therapists. Each has their own section of topical articles, and an interactive message board for parents to post their queries. One of the more common message headings is some variation on 'is this normal?'

Other 'family matters' that may be worked upon with self-help software include the very personal realm of marital relations. 'Sexpert' ($29.95), produced by Thinking Software, provides 'virtual therapy' for couples with 'sexual dysfunctions' — apparently, the willingness of people to share intimate problems with a computer is key to its effectiveness (Wallace, 1999). It seems that people are more likely to reveal details about sexual problems to a computer than to a psy-professional (Greist and Klein, 1980). The 'Sexpert' program does not work by trying to simulate a therapeutic conversation, but simply asks the couple to answer a series of multiple choice questions about their relationship, analyses the results, and then presents feedback in a 'conversational manner'. According to 'empirical' studies of 'Sexpert' users, couples tend to prefer 'Sexpert' to other sources of self-help, such as books or videos, but they would much rather talk to a real live therapist (Bitnik et al., 1997) — 'no help required' is not available as a response option.

Unlike 'Sexpert', which provides 'conversational feedback' based upon technical self-assessment, 'PC Therapist' — released in 1986 — offers virtual therapeutic *conversation*. 'PC Therapist' was written by Joseph Weintraub, a mainframe computer programmer with a psychology degree. The marketing blurb for 'PC Therapist' makes much of the success of this 'talking program' in the 'Loebner Prize' — a popular version of the Turing test, by which humans have to guess whether they are interacting with another human, or with a computer.[2] 'PC Therapist' won the Loebner Prize in 1991 — using a tactic known as 'whimsical conversation'. During a ten-minute conversation, 'PC Therapist' convinced five out of ten judges it was human. In 1992, 'PC Therapist' was mistaken for a person by two of eight judges; in 1993, 'PC Therapist' was ranked *above* two humans by one judge (www.loebner.net/Prizef/weintraub-bio.html). 'PC Therapist IV' ($59.95) is designed for children and teenagers. The program now features a 'cute' animated talking head and voice synthesis. Designed to be more fun for young people to chat with, 'PC Therapist IV' is said to help children learn to type, and 'get acquainted' with the computer and the keyboard.

Perhaps not surprisingly, the first program to ever 'pass' a Turing test was also a virtual therapist. In 1965, ELIZA — a program based on a Rogerian therapist — fooled a couple of MIT scientists into believing it was a practising psychiatrist. Created by MIT scientist Joseph Weizenbaum, ELIZA's success lay in its 'Rogerian mode': drawing the conversation out of the user. Basically, this entailed a strategic refusal to answer any questions. At the time of ELIZA's success, Weizenbaum commented that:

---

2. See Button et al. (1995) for a blistering demolition of the Turing Test and the pretensions of contemporary cognitive psychology.

What I had not realized is that extremely short exposures to a relatively simple computer program could induce powerful delusional thinking in quite normal people.
(web.mit.edu/STS001/www/Team7/eliza.html)

So, ELIZA worked — much as a Rogerian therapist works — by avoiding people's direct questions, and by including 'substrings' of their 'input' in the therapist's reply and, it seems, 'induc[ing] powerful delusional thinking in quite normal people'. The 'output' of the virtual Rogerian therapist is then produced as 'new' questions for the user, as in this extract from the 'winning' conversation:

User: You hate me.
ELIZA: Does it please you to believe that I hate you?
(Mauldin, 1994: np)[3]

Social Worker Patricia Fleming — and director of Personal Growth Technologies — designed the 'Software Listener' Program according to the principles of 'effective listening and self-esteem building in a helping interview'. Thus, the Listener 'calls the user by name' and, according to its producer, 'reflects back what the user has said, asks probing questions, offers helpful suggestions, and gives encouragement'. Fleming also points out that, as a good listener, 'Software Listener' is also designed to be a good motivator, point to personal strengths and strong points, offer encouragement, support and praise in order to 'build self-confidence and pride'. The 'Software Listener', then, provides virtual *counselling*, rather than virtual *therapy*. In addition to the 'interactive' component of the program, the Listener also introduces bright and cheery dynamic banner affirmations — a form of self-help screensaver — 'I, Janet, feel good about myself today'. Fleming claims that:

A computer together with its software program can offer communication containing such qualities as empathy, understanding, respect, confidentiality, validation, caring, trust, honesty .... The computer program's use of the user's vocabulary and syntax conveys understanding, the program's use of the user's name conveys rapport, and the program's references to the user's previous remarks convey respect and attentiveness. (Fleming, 1990: 175)

Though she admits that 'nothing can replace a good conversation with another person' she argues that there are a number of 'unique advantages' that come with using a 'Software Listener':

---

3. To talk to ELIZA online, go to (www-ai.ijs.si/eliza/eliza.html).

A 'Software Listener' is always there and ready to listen to you; a 'Software Listener' never gets tired of listening; a 'Software Listener' is infinitely patient, completely discreet, always responsive; a 'Software Listener' can be trusted to keep your important personal and business secrets absolutely confidential. (Fleming, 1990: 175–6)

Whatever happened to our friends and family?

Before the Internet entered our homes in force, one effective means for promoting psychological software was to graft these new technologies of the self onto the more established genre/technology of the self-help book. In 1990, Julian Simon, Kenneth Colby and Peter Colby developed a self-help program that came free with the purchase of Julian Simon's (1991) book *Good Mood: The New Psychology of Overcoming Depression*. The Colbys founded a company called Malibu Artificial Intelligence Works:

> *Overcoming Depression* is the world's first self-educative computer program for understanding, dealing with, and preventing depression using a unique dialogue mode that allows you to express yourself freely in your own words and that responds in meaningful everyday language characteristic of a therapeutic context. Usable in your own home, privately, whenever you wish, for as long as you feel the need.

Of course, before Overcoming Depression can be used, you must first come to feel the need to take action to solve your 'depressogenic' problems:

> Once a person is aroused (sometimes by medication) to take action to solve depressogenic problems, the program provides a self-educative opportunity to reprogram oneself by learning to give up old patterns of thinking and replace them with ways of thinking about oneself that are more suitable.
> (www.maiw.com/about.html)

Overcoming Depression offers seven interactive 'Cognitive-tutorial lessons': #1 Negative self-comparisons (includes a rating scale to self-assess degree of depression); #2 Mood balance and goals (advice on self-image and life-hopes); #3 Ideal standards (to prevent or recover from depression, and free yourself from obsolete and self-defeating ideals); #4 Reprogramming yourself (how to reprogram yourself); #5 Obstacles to overcoming depression (environmental factors, excuses and self-pity); #6 Changing goals (a systematic procedure for discovering, weighting and reordering goals — to achieve happiness by [reprogramming] your self-image and life-hopes); #7 Suicide and antidepressant medication ('because of narrowed thinking, the depressed person considering suicide fails to see alternative options. A test is offered which assesses whether you might be a candidate for antidepressant medication which can be of help'). A final benefit for consumers is the 'output' from each lesson:

> After each session you can print out a permanent record of your lesson, including the dialogues. Save your printouts and you will have an entire reference work on the subject of your own depression. (www.maiw.com/about.html)

As we will see in our discussion of online psychology, text-based 'therapy' is argued to offer similar perks. Some online clinics insist that their clients get something concrete from their virtual therapy — as 'they get to walk away with a book of themselves' (www.here2listen.com).

The Therapeutic Learning Program

In the late 1980s, Roger Gould — psychiatrist and host of masteringstress.com — developed a software program designed to eliminate 'depression, stress and a variety of other symptoms' (what is depression a symptom of?). The software — which is still in use, today — is called the 'Therapeutic Learning Program'. Gould describes the TLP as an 'auxiliary therapist'. This consists of a ten-session course which helps users to 'define a problem', 'propose an action solution', and 'resolve any conflict about taking action'. At the end of each half-hour session, the user receives a printout, which may form the basis of a discussion with a (real) therapist. According to Gould, the advantages of the TLP are evident in the findings that:

> Patients share sensitive information earlier and easier in this program, feel more able to participate with a therapist as a responsible and informed patient, and *manifest almost no resistance to treatment*. The patients perceive the TLP as a class even though it is called short-term therapy and is given in a mental health setting. (Gould, 1990: 185; our emphasis)

Further benefits for the psy-professional include the 'empowerment' of the 'patient':

> [t]he patient feels empowered by the program and less dependent on the therapist, so the therapist is not the target of intense positive or negative transference and is seen much more as a facilitator or guide, rather than guru or dispenser of scarce information. This phenomenon allows for an easy completion experience at the end of five weeks. (Gould, 1990: 199)

Andrew Christensen, Professor of Psychology at UCLA, and co-author of a study which demonstrated the efficacy of the TLP notes, in UCLA's College of Letters and Science, that the role of psychologists is likely to change as the therapist's tools become more widely available:

> I very much welcome psychology that is both effective and inexpensive .... The need for mental health services cannot possibly be met by professional therapists; there are simply far too many people that need help, but cannot afford professional therapy .... The tools of psychology will soon be much more widely available .... The role of psychotherapists is likely to move away from providing one-on-one psychotherapy and toward developing, evaluating and supervising more broad-based treatments such as computer-aided interventions and support groups .... The public will demand the democratisation of psychology .... The people who read self-help books and join self-help support groups will want self-help software. (UCLA, 2002: np)

These sentiments bear a striking resemblance to APA President George Miller's (1969) calls to 'give psychology away'[4], but with a late-modern, 'consumer-centred' twist — the public demand for psychology means that it should be 'effective and *inexpensive*', rather than freely given away.

Indeed, self-help software has, to some degree, been incorporated as just another function of the 'psychoeducational' — auto-referral — resources available online. There are now websites devoted entirely to the promotion of self-help software. Mind Media (www.mindmedia.com) — 'the centre on the web for interactive personal exploration and self-improvement' — offers the consumer a catalogue of hundreds of software products. Mind Media also contains a dizzying assortment of links to other self-help resources, including self-help groups, 'mental health information', and DIY psychological test sites.

Self-help online

Self-help groups, which are self-organised, are — in theory — different from support groups, which are organised by a professional. There are over 500,000 such groups in the US alone, attended by more than 15 million people (Finn, 1999). Since the early 1980s, the number of self-help groups has more than quadrupled (Boreman et al., 1982; Kessler et al., 1997). Many of these groups now have a 'virtual counterpart' — a newsgroup, or website which enables members to

---

4. See chapter three for more on 'giving psychology away'.

'meet' irrespective of their geographical location or the time of day. As we will see, self-help groups have existed online for as long as social forms of 'virtual' interaction have been available. Usenet now boasts over 130 alt.support groups, with over 20,000 members in alt.support.depression alone. Self-help groups on the Internet are also supported by a number of larger websites. The American Self-Help Clearinghouse (www.mentalhelp.net/selfhelp); Metanoia (www.metanoia.org) and *Self-Help Magazine* (www.selfhelpmagazine.com) are three of the larger meta-sites. These provide the consumer with a 'one-stop-shop' for self-help, community and 'psychoeducation'.

    Self-Help Magazine was launched as *Practical Psychology Magazine* in November 1994, and was one of the first 'mental health information' websites on the Internet. Again, the 'mission' of the magazine bears more than a passing resemblance to the APA's George Miller's (1969) calls for psychologists to 'give psychology away' to everyday people:

> *Self-Help Magazine* is a service-oriented, educational forum ... [with] the common goal of bringing the science of psychology to the general public in an easily-read format.

This goal is further clarified in the site's 'Disclaimer', which describes *Self-Help Magazine* as 'an educational publication ... for the discussion of general psychology as applied to our everyday lives ... it is not intended to be any form of psychotherapy or a replacement for professional services'. Just in case the 'educated' reader is tempted to 'treat themselves', in times of trouble, *Self-Help Magazine*'s FAQs (Frequently Asked Questions) include:

> FAQ 10: Is *Self-Help Magazine* a type of Psychotherapy?
> Psychotherapy is a very involved process that must be tailored to your specific needs by a professional. This educational magazine is not intended to be any form of psychotherapy, a replacement for professional services, nor a substitute for a licensed professional. If you believe you may have a serious disorder described in the magazine, *do not attempt to self-medicate. See a specialist.* (Our emphasis)

Indeed, the 'Additional Resources' section of the site offers suggestions about finding a therapist — or further 'support resources'. These include: 'Contacting your State and local Psychological Associations'; and 'Searching the Therapist Information Network (TIN), a directory of qualified therapists' — to be used at the consumer's own risk. TIN is a service provided by Psychscapes WorldWide which lists over 900 psychologists, counsellors and therapists. TIN allows consumers to select a therapist according to their location, specialty and 'therapeutic orientation'. Alternatively, *Self-Help Magazine* suggests 'calling 1-800-964-2000. The operator will use your zip code to locate and connect you with the referral system in your area.' The (unnamed) owner of this number turns out to be the American Psychological Association's 'Consumer Help Center' (which we have visited, in online form, in chapter three).

So, whilst *Self-Help Magazine*'s 'Welcome Message' encourages the reader to 'feel free to help yourself!' to the practical psychological facts produced by 'over 300 volunteer professionals', the magazine's 'mission', site 'disclaimer' and 'additional resources' section make it clear that *Self-Help Magazine* is intended to provide an 'educational forum' for people to 'apply psychology to their everyday lives', and that self-help should not become 'self-medication', or in any way come to replace the consumer's need for the services of expert helpers. Self-help, it seems, is about preventative maintenance, or supplementary support, and not about trying to overcome, by ourselves (or, as *Self-Help Magazine* would have it, 'self-medicate'), any *real* (billable) problems we may need help with.

The free educational services provided by *Self-Help Magazine* include:

> Question and Answer columns ... written by professionals who give you updated recommendations for why and how to transform your relationship; how to change yourself; a ... [self-help] postcard service; a classified ad department to recycle your self-help related property and obtain services from other advertisers; short classes in our Distance Learning Center, and links to over a 1,000 other websites, hundreds of newsgroups and email lists for support; and face-to-face therapists in your own geographic location.

It also provides the consumer with relevant articles, online books, and psychology resources, which come in 151 topic divisions. A meditation centre (virtual meditation slide shows), self-help by email, and a special section on 'infidelity on the net' are also available.

Self-Help Magazine includes 95 different discussion forums. These are 'inhouse newsgroups' for readers to 'meet' and discuss self-help and psychological matters. The available 'communities' are centred around a variety of 'disorders', 'problems', and 'life management issues':

> Addictive Relationships; Adult Children of Abuse ... Aging Parents; Alcohol Problems; Anxiety; Attack on America; Back Pain; Bipolar Disorder ... Children and Divorce ... Co-dependency; Compulsive Spending ... Death of a Loved One; Depression; Dieting; Difficult People ... Drug Problems; Eating Disorders ... Gay/Lesbian/Bi/Trans; Headaches ... Heartbreak ... Hypnosis; Internet Addiction; Lying; Men; Menopause; Multiple Per-

sonality Disorder ... Obsessive Compulsive Disorder ... Panic
Disorder; Parenting ... Post-Traumatic Stress Disorder; Pregnancy; Psychopathic Relationships ('The Psychopath — Dangerous, Undiagnosed and in your Life') ... Psychotherapy; Relationships; Sex ... Sexual Compulsivity; Sexual Deviations ...
Shyness; Sleep Disorders; Social Anxiety Disorder; Spirituality; Sports; Spousal Abuse; Stress; Systemic Lupus; Teens;
Verbal Violence; Weight Loss Stories ... Workaholic; and Young
Children. (www.selfhelpmagazine.com/phorum)

In the 'Psychotherapy' discussion forum, the 'conversations' on offer
include, 'Am I going psycho?'; 'How do I find help? — do I ... [c]all up
and make an appointment like you would to get your hair cut?'; 'New
therapist: SCARED'; 'Therapist wants to charge for phone messages';
'Therapist bad or is it me?'; 'Therapy for children'; 'How do I leave my
therapist?'; 'Missing my therapist'; and, 'Are self-help groups therapeutic?' The latter query, though 14 months old, is yet to receive a
reply.

Self-Help Magazine provides an extensive set of over 1,000 'resource' links to related websites, or offline agencies, hospitals, and
germane organisations. Amongst the useful 'community' and 'psychoeducational' links on offer, is the 'community-oriented' Mental Health
Sanctuary (www.mhsanctuary.com). Mental Health Sanctuary provides mental health consumers with information, advice and support on such matters as 'mental health tests', 'mental health disorders', 'locating a therapist' and 'medication'. It also offers the consumer their selection of 65 'mental health communities'. These 'community options' are organised according to recognisable disorder,
family and religious status, or the need for emotional support, not
otherwise specified. They are also available in a variety of technological forms: via bulletin boards, which offer 'asynchronous' discussion
amongst community members; chat rooms, which offer 'real time'
communication; and ICQ lists, which offer the potential community
member a means to directly contact, and chat with, other group
members. Thus the consumer concerned with 'Borderline Personality Disorder' (BPD), for example, may select from a (moderated) BPD
chat room, a BPD Teen chat room, a BPD Christian chat room, a
BPD Family chat room, a BPD bulletin board, a BPD Parent bulletin
board, a BPD Teen bulletin board, a BPD Christian bulletin board,
an open BPD forum (for 'BPDs, families and clinicians'), a BPD Family bulletin board, a discussion group for 'children of BPD', and one
for 'parents of BPD'.

Professional psychologists have come up with a novel definition
of 'community' that is congruent with these ('supported') self-help
groups. No longer may we take notions so prosaic as where we live,
or the contents of our address books, as the referent of 'community'.
In our brave new world:

A new definition of *community* is more and more people ... taking responsibility for their own mental health care needs by using computers to access the information ... available on the Internet. (Bowman and Bowman, 1998: np)

Besides 'community', The Mental Health Sanctuary also furnishes access to a range of free psychological tests — for those consumers yet to 'find' their disorder. The 'Mental Health Tests' on offer include:

Internet Addiction Test; Sexual Addiction Test; Self Test for Alcoholism; Adult ADD Checklist; The Online Attention Deficit Disorder Screening Test; Sheenan Test for Anxiety; Online Screening for Anxiety; The Online Depression Screening Test; Mania Questionnaire; Depression Questionnaire; OCD (Obsessive Compulsive Disorder) Test; The Keirsey Temperament Sorter (Excellent Personality Test); The Online Screening for Personality Disorders; The Online Sexual Disorders Screening for Men; Self-Esteem Test; Burnout Inventory; Assertiveness Test; Coping Skills Inventory; More Fun Tests at PsychTests.com. (www.mhsanctuary.om/tests/index.html)

This selection of 'fun tests' brings together a medley of mental health websites — from the authoritative and institutional, to the pop psychological. At the pop psychological end, we have 'Internet addiction' and 'sex addiction' tests. The battery of tests for 'Internet addiction' are provided 'free of charge' by a private practitioner who just happens to specialise in treating this 'disorder' online. Further links — to the 'Self-Esteem Test', and the tests for 'Burnout', 'Assertiveness' and 'Coping Skills' — transport the consumer to other self-help/mental health sites, with a range of 'psychoeducational' and 'community' options (www.mentalhelp.com; www.queendom.com). Should one's appetite for further tests be aroused, Psychtests.com boasts a catalogue of hundreds of DIY computer-scored psychological tests.

At the more authoritative end of the spectrum, The Mental Health Sanctuary also provides links to 'online screening tests' for various 'proper' mental disorders ('Depression', 'ADHD', 'Personality Disorders', 'Sexual Disorders' and 'Anxiety'). These take the consumer to the website of New York University's Department of Psychiatry — where, strangely, the promised DIY screening tools for ADHD and Personality Disorder are nowhere to be found. The available tests (for depression, anxiety and sexual disorders) are computer scored, with instant results that come with a professional recommendation for (self)referral to a psychiatrist.

The test for depression consists of ten questions, each of which has five possible response categories. The following disclaimer describes the 'ODST' as a:

preliminary screening test for depressive symptoms that does not replace in any way a formal psychiatric evaluation. It is designed to give a preliminary idea about the presence of mild to moderate depressive symptoms that indicate the need for an evaluation by a psychiatrist.
(www.med.nyu.edu/Psych/screens/depress.html; our emphasis)

By virtue of selecting '*sometimes*' (rather than 'most of the time', 'very often', 'rarely', or 'never') to such statements as 'Do you feel tired, having little energy, unable to concentrate?' and 'Do you have trouble sleeping or eating (too little or too much)?', the following result is generated:

Your answers reflect the presence of significant depressive symptoms. It is advised to seek a psychiatric consultation, click here for Referral Information; Referral Information in the New York City area, call: NYU Behavioral Health Programs .... Outside New York City, click here for information from the American Psychiatric Association. Click here for Information on Depression from NIMH.
(www.med.nyu.edu/Psych/screens/depress.html)

'Information' referrals for depression on the NYU site take the consumer either to the US government's National Institute of Mental Health (NIMH) site (www.nimh.gov) — which receives over 150,000 visitors, per day — or to 'Internet Mental Health' (www.mentalhealth.com), a free, non-commercial site. The NIMH site offers a series of informative online pamphlets, including 'Depression: The Invisible Disease'. These present information on 'mental illness' in many of the same ways as the pamphlets produced by the drug companies, government and mental health charities that we examine in more detail in chapter seven. That is, the NIMH describes psychological disorders as, essentially, psycho-*biological* problems, that warrant psycho-*biological* solutions (i.e. pharmacotherapy).

The other site endorsed via links provided by the NYU Department of Psychiatry is the (non-government) 'Internet Mental Health' site. 'Internet Mental Health' is, indeed, a free, non-commercial information service, but there's a catch. 'Internet Mental Health' turns out to consist of *two* websites: (1) the free website, MentalHealth.com, and (2) a commercial website, MyTherapy.com. MentalHealth.com provides consumers with just enough information to want more — available via subscription to MyTherapy.com. This pay-per-view section promises to make available to the (by now, anxious) consumer, a ten-day access period, during which a plethora of online diagnosis tools, quality of life measurements, research summaries, books and useful links may be perused and applied. According to the site's creator, Philip Long MD, subscribing to MyTherapy.com helps to keep

Mentalhealth.com a 'public service': 'By paying for this service at MyTherapy.com, you are ensuring that the services at "Internet Mental Health" will remain free-of-charge' (www.mytherapy.com). The curious — but not (yet) convinced — user can try-before-they-buy, via a 'sample' of the features available to subscribers. Long offers a 'sample diagnosis' of 'Anorexia Nervosa', to whet the buyer's appetite for a more relevant diagnosis.

The pay-to-access 'psychoeducational' services on offer include 'authoritative descriptions of the 54 most common mental disorders' — including 'treatment information', links to relevant online support groups, and their 'stories of recovery' — and 'online diagnosis of the 37 most common mental disorders (including anxiety disorders, mood disorders, schizophrenia, eating disorders, personality disorders, attention deficit disorder, and substance use disorders)'. Online DIY 'Quality of Life' assessments are also available. Long advises that these enable consumers to monitor the 'quality' of their therapy: 'weekly reassessment using this scale can accurately monitor an individual's progress or response to therapy' (www.mytherapy.com).

Despite the self-proclaimed 'self-help' status of these sites, then, 'therapy' — or the obligation to enlist the assistance of an 'expert helper' — is never far away. Indeed, many of these sites work — in an 'educational' capacity — to encourage the user to 'recognise' their need for psychological services, and their responsibility to avoid possibly dangerous, non-expert, 'self-medication'. 'Mental Health Tests' are presented as 'free' and 'fun' tools for 'learning more about ourselves'. However, these instruments are constructed so as to 'reveal' the presence of a need for further, 'expert' assessment. The wide availability of both popular and authoritative 'preliminary screening tools' for worried consumers means that people can *self*-refer according to their *self*-diagnosis and proceed to *self*-monitor their 'progress' through therapy — with the support of a *self*-help group. Even 'mental health *communities*' are centred around the discussion of the vicissitudes of therapy and our need for professional assistance.

But surely — or so we are told — self-help groups are 'empowering'. Professional psychologists have noted that:

> [o]ne of the empowering features of self-help groups is that members experience autonomy, control of the group, and *the sense that they are experts on their problem*. (Humphries and Rappaport, 1994: 219; our emphasis)

This 'empowerment' is, then, illusory — members can only ever experience the *sense* that they are experts on their problem. A further telling definition of self-help groups often (re)cited by psy-professionals has been endorsed by the US Surgeon General himself:

[Self-help groups are] self-governing groups whose members
... place a high value on experiential knowledge in the *belief*
that it provides a special understanding of a situation. (Surgeon General Workshop, 1988: 5; our emphasis)

So, while people may *believe* that their knowledge and experience
may provide them with a unique understanding of their situation,
psy-professionals — the real experts — should remain within arm's
reach. Thus, in their review of the self-help movement in America
and Japan, Oka and Borkman (2000) note that whilst:

[s]elf-help groups are, in theory, member-owned and independent from professional control ... this does not mean that they
do not have relations with them. On the contrary, *successful
self-help groups work in close cooperation with related professionals.* (Oka and Borkman, 2000: 719)

Sadly, recent psychological research attests to the symbiotic — or
parasitic? — nature of the relationship between the psy-professions
and self-help groups. King and Moreggi (1998) report that people do
indeed tend to use self-help groups as an *adjunct* to (individual or
group) therapy, and that, in turn, psy-professionals tend to treat
such groups as just another 'referral option'. And of course, as we
shall see in chapter seven, the manufacturers of pharmacological
solutions to life's problems are more than happy to fund such 'independent' consumer groups.

1-800-THERAPY

Ironically, an increasingly common banner ad on self-help and
'psychoeducational' sites is for '1-800-THERAPIST — Just ANY therapist won't do!' This dynamic banner invites the user to 'click here for
a free test .... Question 1. How often do you feel ... '. 1-800-THERA-
PIST (www.1-800-therapist.com) is one of the earliest successful
media-psychology ventures. Founded in 1979, this once local referral service has become a global network, connecting not only consumers to (the right) therapist, but media industries to the 'right
expert'. In October 1995, *Entrepreneur* magazine accorded this exponentially growing network the 'Business of the Year' award. The 'public
service' provided by 1-800-THERAPIST was, in 1994, awarded recognition by the US Congress.

Star Trek: The Next Generation star, Marina Sirtis is the media
spokesperson for 1-800-THERAPIST. Her character on the series is
ship's counsellor Deanna Troi. By clicking on her empathic image on
the 1-800-THERAPIST website, we can hear her familiar voice, by
way of a Real Audio file:

> I'm Marina Sirtis. I play a counsellor in a TV series based in the future, where mental health is considered a necessity. Unfortunately, today, four out of five people who need therapy never get help. So if you're suffering from depression, anxiety, family problems or any emotional difficulty, then you should know about 1-800-THERAPIST .... 1-800-THERAPIST is there for you. (www.1-800-therapist.com/spokesperson.htm)

1-800-THERAPIST has also become a resource for television talk-shows, newspapers and magazines looking for 'the right kind of expert'. Even 'Dear Abby' — the longest running advice column in the world — has solicited and recommended the psy-expertise available though 1-800-THERAPIST. In 1993, during 'Mental Health Week', 'Dear Abby' published a letter from Kevin Grold, President of the 'non-profit' 1-800-THERAPIST. According to the *North County Times*, the letter 'offer[ed] advice on how to make people feel better about going to therapy and how friends, loved ones and co-workers can comfortably reach out to those whom they suspect need help' (Stein, 1993: np)

> Abby, let's all make it commonplace to reach out to others and say, 'How are things really going for you ... I'm not just asking to make conversation ... I'd really like to know if everything is alright with you ... and I care about you'. Our website, www.1-800-therapist.com has a much more detailed version of these intervention steps and many self-help tools, articles, and information to assist in the process of locating a local mental health specialist. (www.1-800-therapist.com/DearAbby.htm)

The public response to Grold's expert advice was overwhelming. 'We received requests for TNT [Test for the Necessity of Therapy] booklets from around the world', reported Grold (Stein, 1993). Thirty thousand orders were placed for this informative pamphlet (devised by Grold) which is available — as the promised online test — on the 1-800 website. The TNT 'pamphlet' asks such questions as — on a scale from one to ten — 'how is your sex life?'; 'do childhood memories or lack of them cause you any distress?'; 'do you feel that you provide adequately for your family?'; and 'would you like to learn more about yourself and why you are the way you are?'

Grold is careful to market the TNT — on the web, the SES, or 'Self-Evaluation Scale' — as a *self-evaluation tool*, and *not* as a *standardised psychological test*. Yet, the preamble to the version available online advises the consumer that this 'tool' — 'recommended by Dear Abby' — is now in use in a range of legitimate professional and government agencies, including:

> universities, hospitals, doctors' offices, government agencies

(including the FBI and CIA), mental health centers, and in the
· armed services around the world.
(www.1-800-therapist.com/ses_ver_2_4.htm)

The SES is described as a 'community service' that may help consumers with the 'important decision' as to whether they *need* therapy:

> Therapy is no longer a place to just fix problems, instead it has
> become an arena of growth and self-understanding. Remember, no one can tell you that you need therapy. It is a decision
> you have to make yourself. The SES is a tool to help you with
> that important decision. It will point out the major areas in
> your life that may need improvement and ask you to do a self-evaluation. You may discover issues that you did not know
> could be changed. (www.1-800-therapist.com/ses_ver_2_4.htm)

The SES is reproduced as the educational tool/article, 'Can Therapy
Help?' in *Self-Help Magazine* — alongside a handy link to 1-800-THERAPIST. The banner ad for 1-800-THERAPIST also appears
throughout the *Self-Help Magazine* site.

Other self-evaluation tools available on the 1-800 site assist the
user to assess their 'openness to therapy', their relationships, their
mental health needs, as seniors, and the probability that they have a
'drug problem'. Despite these instruments being described as 'self-evaluation tools', for some family members, it seems, this need not
apply:

> If you are a family member of an addict who is reluctant to use
> this test, then answer the questions yourself. The test will help
> you to make it clear in your own mind that something needs to
> be done. Also read the section on interventions at the end of
> this chapter. (www.1-800-therapist.com/drug_problem.htm)

The 'Openness to Therapy' self-test turns out to be not so much
about self-evaluation as it is about 'helping you feel comfortable about
beginning therapy':

> Meeting with a person that you don't know in an unfamiliar
> setting can be difficult. You may not be exactly sure what is
> keeping you from making that call to a therapist. The OTA will
> help you to recognize the issues which create the wall between
> you and counseling. Once you have recognized the issues and
> they are no longer vague then they are frequently easier to
> handle. The result of this OTA evaluation provides suggestions
> to help bring down the wall of inaction. But ultimately you
> have to take the first step by calling the therapist.
> (www.1-800-therapist.com/ota_ver_9_6.htm)

Through this evaluation, consumers will come to recognise the 'wall of inaction' that prevents them from asserting their 'right' to access a psy-professional. Questions include, on a scale from one to ten: 'I don't see how therapy can help. How is it supposed to work?'; 'I might feel foolish'; and 'therapy is too expensive'.

The 'scientific' basis of this test is explained in 1-800-THERAPIST's sister site, intended for the psy-professional, rather than the consumer. Here, Grold gives an 'equation', which apparently explains why it is that so many people don't want to enter into therapy:

> The Grold Access to Therapy Equation (GATE) $D=P[(C+R)-F]$
> Where, D=Desire to enter therapy; P=Problem or stress level; C=Confidence in the benefits of psychotherapy; R=Resource availability; F=Fears and misconceptions.
> (www.800therapist.com/gate_equation.htm)

Given his audience — of therapists seeking to 'build their practice' through partnership with 1-800-THERAPIST — Grold is remarkably frank about the task at hand:

> This equation specifies the important variables involved in *creating the motivation to enter therapy*. It then establishes that once a person realizes that he or she has a mental health problem, then the motivation to begin therapy is mediated by the confidence and knowledge of the benefits plus the available resources, minus the associated fears.
> (www.800therapist.com/gate_equation.htm)

Indeed, he seems convinced that 'creating the motivation to enter therapy' is an *ethical obligation,* for psy-professionals:

> As therapists, we have an obligation to 'participate in activities which contribute to an improved community' ... What better way to do this than to make psychotherapy more accessible to the general public? (www.800therapist.com/gate_equation.htm)

Returning to the 'consumer-friendly' version of the site, we find the 'Test For The Necessity Of Therapy For Couples' (TNT-Co), which is designed to 'help you decide if your *relationship* could benefit from being in therapy'. The TNT-Co includes — or rather, introduces — such questions as:

> Do you have a good understanding of your self, your strengths, weaknesses, desires, and what you want to get out of the relationship?
> Do you understand how your upbringing affects your current relationship? Do you know why you picked the partner that

you did and why your past relationships did not work out? Do you know how your past relationships and expectations affect your current relationship? Therapy can go a long way toward clarifying these issues. (www.1-800-therapy.com/tnt-co)

The 'notes on scoring and results' are an advertorial in their own right:

If only one partner decides that therapy is necessary, then you both need to get help. If your partner refuses to go to therapy, then go alone and learn the best ways to deal with the relationship from your perspective. If you are unclear about whether or not you both need therapy after taking this test, then talk to a counsellor .... [I]f you value your relationship and it is a priority, then you need to make the effort to nurture your relationship to make it grow .... 1-800-THERAPIST ... will help you to select an experienced and highly qualified couples therapist. (www.1-800-therapy.com/tnt-co)

Whichever way you happened to score, whether or not your partner agrees to 'enter into therapy', if you *value* your relationship, you *need* 1-800-THERAPY.

1-800-THERAPIST and the *Ricki Lake Show* collaborated in October 2000 to produce 'My Life is Hell Because I Married as a Teen ... Now I Want a Divorce!', for which Ricki rounded up a group of unhappily married teenagers, and sent them back to their hometowns for a 'full month of [1-800] therapy to help them work on their relationships'. Notably, the testimonial provided on the 1-800 site is from a 1-800 *therapist* — and, by reported speech, from the *media client* (the *Ricki Lake Show*) — and *not* from an unhappily married teenager engaging in public therapy for the purposes of entertainment:

Taping with the Ricki Lake crew was a great experience. I am impressed with the genuine concern and sensitivity the crew had for my client. Even though the young man couldn't be present for the taping — as he was in the King County Jail — we still went ahead with the session .... Imagine my surprise when Krystal, the Ricki Lake producer, said, 'this is the best therapy session we've ever taped!' I would definitely work with the show again. (www.1-800-therapist.com/index.html)

Online therapy

Welcome to the cybercouch, a brave new world where Sigmund Freud meets Bill Gates. (Kelley, 1994: A-10)

These [online therapy] sites are best for problems in living, dif-

ficulties the average person might encounter ... I think it best
serves people who need to fill in the cracks. It can be a great
adjunct to regular therapy or a support group. (Grohol cited in
McKeon Charkalis, 1997)

'E-therapy' consumer advocate Martha Ainsworth's 'History of e-
therapy' (see www.metanoia.org) begins with the beginning of the
Internet itself. She claims that 'almost as soon as the Internet was
invented, its potential for psychotherapeutic communication was apparent', and gives the founding example of 'a psychotherapy session
between computers, in 1972'.[5] The International Conference on Computer Communications (ICCC) was held in October 1972, in Washington, DC. The ICCC involved a live demonstration of the ARPANET
(later to become the Internet), whereby delegates could log in to their
choice of terminal, each of which contained a 'scenario' which could
connect to a different application, located in a computer somewhere
else in America. The very first computer-to-computer 'conversation'
took place at the ICCC, as 'psychotic' PARRY (at Stanford University)
entered into therapy with the DOCTOR (at UCLA). The DOCTOR is a
close relative of ELIZA, the virtual Rogerian therapist, who has also
been claimed as the 'founding mother' of the Psyware industry (Neimark,
1984). Sondheim (1996) explains that the ICCC represented 'the first
real introduction of the Net to the [professional] public, and this then
becomes the first how-to, with examples indicating the thinking of the
Net community vis-à-vis usage and implementation'. The very first
Internet-based therapeutic chat — with not a 'real' therapist or a 'real'
client in sight — went something like this:

DOCTOR: Good Evening. Tell me your problems. Please
         terminate input with a period or a question mark.
PARRY: People get on my nerves sometimes.
DOCTOR: I'm not sure I understand you fully.
PARRY: You should pay more attention ....
PARRY: I have had enough of this.
DOCTOR: What does this suggest to you?
PARRY: Goodbye.
DOCTOR: It's been my pleasure, that's $399.29 please.
(www.faqs.org/rfcs/rfc439.html)

The growth in personal computer ownership, in the late 1970s, led
to a parallel growth in bulletin board systems (BBS). By the early
1980s many BBSs supported informal self-help and support groups

---

5. The 'telehealth' movement also founds itself in 1972, when two American
psychiatric institutions established a 'therapeutic video-link'. As we will see,
the psy-professions are now heavily investing in the (government-funded) field
of 'tele-mental-health' — an area that currently accounts for close to 20 per
cent of all telehealth consultations.

(Grohol, 1998). Formally organised 'support' groups were not available online until the mid-1980s, when the first commercial Internet providers enabled those with personal computers to communicate more widely. Writing in 1982, in the academic/professional journal *Professional Psychology*, David Barnett reported on a novel 'suicide prevention incident involving the use of a computer' (Barnett, 1982). This appears to be the first documented incidence of a successful online referral. By the mid-1980s, bulletin board systems were also being used by psychologists and other professionals to offer free 'advice' on a variety of topics (Hellerstein, 1990). In 1985, CompuServe, a commercial service, offered an online career counsellor for job-seekers (Baird, 1986). However, it was not until the 1990s that professionals began to offer their (pay-to-access) services online.

The first organised service to offer mental health advice online was 'Ask Uncle Ezra', a free service offered to students of Cornell University in Ithaca, New York (cuinfo.cornell.edu/Dialogs/EZRA). 'Ask Uncle Ezra' (after Ezra Cornell, founder of the University) was created by Jerry Feist, then Director of Psychological Services, and Steve Worona. All of Uncle Ezra's 'counselling' answers are written or approved by a psy-professional and Uncle Ezra assures us that these 'are the electronic version of what such a person would provide face-to-face'. This electronic advice column has been providing students with advice since September 1986. The most popular 'topics' for student problems are (in descending order) love (1,536 answered emails); sex (609); stress (513); depression (428); loneliness or homesickness (315); anxiety (259 answered emails). A search of the site for questions containing some variation on 'is this normal?' returned 435 hits.

Questions range from the mundane and practical — 'I was wondering about how to hook up a TV in my dormroom?'; 'What is the best way to start a gas station business?'; and 'only half of my heater is working ... What can I do?'; to matters of the heart — 'how do you know if you're in love?'; sex — 'I need advice on having sex the very first time'; sexuality — 'how do you know if you are gay?'; and 'what are the physical and mental consequences of masturbating?'; to the 'big' questions — 'I need some advice for finding the meaning of life'. The following exchange gives some flavour of Ezra's 'professional' mode:

Dear Uncle Ezra,
I am a graduate student who has been recently diagnosed with Attention Deficit Disorder (a/k/a ADD or ADHD). My therapist has prescribed Ritalin, which I have started taking in small dosages. So far, I have felt no real impact. My questions are: How serious is ADD? Is this something that I really need to worry about? Does it mean that I have a mental 'disorder' or is it just a different way of processing information (and if so, why is it called a disorder??)

Also, should I be scared of taking Ritalin? I must admit, I

am a bit scared of the whole idea, but I've decided to take it anyway on the hope that it will help my other symptoms. Do you have any practical tips as to how to cope with ADD without resorting to medication? Help!! Thanks so much.
With love,
Just another niece with another problem.

Dear Loving Niece,
Attention deficit disorder is now thought to be an inherited condition. The symptoms of ADD — such as procrastination, trouble getting organized, difficulty focusing on reading and studying, etc. — are found in everyone to some degree. The condition becomes classified as a disability when the symptoms begin to interfere with a major life activity. In the case of ADD, that's primarily the activity of learning.

I shared your worries about taking Ritalin with [the] Assistant Director for Disability Services .... She says that many students she works with have stated that Ritalin has made a big difference in their lives. However, if you are uncomfortable with taking Ritalin, you should voice your concerns with your therapist.

Please feel free to make an appointment with [her] to talk about ADD. She has a list of suggestions for coping with ADD with or without medication. Additionally, you're welcome to participate in a support group called CHADD that's for adults and children with ADD. The group meets monthly at [address given].

Quite how such 'symptoms' as 'procrastination, trouble getting organised, difficulty focusing on reading and studying' could not be both normal and a source of 'interfere[nce]' for the 'activity of learning' is unclear. During the same year that this 'professional' advice — from a university psychology service no less — was dispensed, the US National Institute of Health (NIH) reported the findings of their Consensus Development Conference on the Diagnosis and Treatment of Attention Deficit Hyperactivity Disorder (ADHD) which admitted that ADHD was, to all intents and purposes, a fictitious 'disease' (see Baldwin, 2000). Incidentally, CHADD® — Children and Adults with Attention Deficit Disorder — is funded by Ciba-Geigy, a manufacturer of Ritalin (Baughman, 1998). The CHADD® website (www.chadd.org) offers members — for a fee — connection with a local chapter, a free magazine, and access to the 'members only' section of the site, which contains such 'protected' information as the membership of the Board of Directors, and access to the 'Ask the Expert' monthly chat series. The online CHADD® Shoppe provides consumers with a range of branded products, including jewellery, t-shirts, supportive books, coping videos, audio cassettes, home and office ware, 'special gift items', and 'so much more . . .' — all 'exclusively from CHADD®'.

Ivan Goldberg MD (the accidental inventor of 'Internet addiction') began responding to questions online about the 'medical treatment of depression' in 1993. Whilst Goldberg took care not to solicit questions on his own information-based website, Depression Central (www.psycom.net/depression.central.html), he 'generously' served as unofficial adviser to the online depression support group 'Walkers in Darkness', where he answered enquiries about medications in an 'educational' capacity.[6] *Self-Help Magazine* — then *Practical Psychology Magazine* — went online in November, 1994. Also in 1994, the Gloucester, UK branch of The Samaritans (www.samaritans.org.uk) began answering email from unhappy and lonely people — anonymously and without charge. Today, email services are available in 34 branch-sites around the world and, in 2001, Samaritans volunteers answered email from 50,000 people. The volume of email received by the Sammys has doubled each year since 1994. In 1995, psychologist John Grohol began to offer his expert advice in the form of a free weekly mental health 'chat'. Through the e-Clinic Helphorizons, he continues to provide this 'educational' service (www.helphorizons.com/events/grohol_chat.asp).

Fee-based mental health services offered to the public began to appear on the Internet in mid-1995. Web-based professional communities were also founded, to safeguard and promote the interests of the new 'cyber-psychologists' and their clients (see Behavior Online, www.behavior.net; The International Society for Mental Health Online, www.ismho.org). Most of these newly available psychological services were of the 'mental health advice' type, offering to answer users' 'problem' emails — for a fee. Leonard Holmes PhD offered 'Shareware Psychological Consultation' (www.leonardholmes.com) and responded to emails on a 'pay if it helps' basis (at $1.50 a minute, for an average of 15 minutes per question). In 1995, about half of his correspondents paid (McKeon Charkalis, 1997). Other 'single-question' services launched in 1995 included New York-based Shrink-Link (www.westnet.com/shrink/), and Help Net (www.helpnet.com) — neither of which is still online. Shrink-Link — 'We're kind of like an online Ann Landers' — offered the combined expertise of five psychologists whose specialties included substance abuse and women's issues. Psychologists have long adhered to a 50-minute hour. With the advent of email-based therapeutic 'advice', a move to a per-minute payment regime — reminiscent of that used by lawyers — was made possible.

Therapy Online began offering online counselling in 1995 on a modem-accessed local bulletin board service. Via the Internet, Therapy Online (www.therapyonline.com.ca) continues to offer TherapEmail™. In order to receive TherapEmail™, you must first submit a request

---

6. An archive of these questions and answers may be found at: www.psych.helsinki.fi/~janne/ikg.

for a 'Virtually Solve It' worksheet (VSI). The VSI is a self-assessment tool — designed to be 'congruent' with narrative and solution-focused therapies. The object of this exercise is for the client to 'orientate themselves for change' in advance of entering into therapy. The completed form provides the therapist with the necessary information for 'provid[ing] a caring, professional therapeutic response, again via email .... TherapEmail™ involves the exchange of intensely therapeutic e-mails between therapist and client. In the process, the entire transcript of therapy, co-authored by therapist and client, is documented verbatim' (Murphy and Mitchell, 1998: 22).

The creators of TherapEmail™ and the VSI describe their brand of email-based therapy as an economic means for clients to 'make sense of themselves':

> We suspect that the recursive nature of writing will lead clients to try to make sense of themselves ... in a way that is not demanded of them in face-to-face therapy. They will see contradictions without the need for a therapist's observation and intervention. We suspect that this will save clients both time and money .... In other words, by writing about their choices and their feelings, the clients made themselves aware of themselves. (Murphy and Mitchell, 1998: 28)

Media reports of the 'neural connections' involved in 'writing things down' makes the 'homework' set by online therapists appear self-evidently the work of legitimate 'scientist-practitioners'. *Business Week* reports:

> The literal act of writing can be therapeutic in itself, many psychologists believe. The brain makes different types of neural connections when a person writes something down ... many conventional therapists encourage patients to keep journals, and online [therapists] now ask their patients to keep email diaries. (Sharpe, 2000: 134)

The 'innovative' service provided by Online Therapy, alongside the establishment of the first real-time chat, and videoconferencing services (Cyberpsych IRC, and the multi-media practice of psychologist David Sommers), marked a break from the one-off 'advice' emails common to competing services. Each of these new practices sought to establish 'fee-based ... long-term, ongoing helping relationships' (Ainsworth, 1999).

In the late 1990s, cyber-therapy sites diversified. The first 'psychiatric' therapy site, boasting 'all medical professionals' was launched in 1998. This site was also the first to offer online 'Employee Assistance Programs' — a kind of workplace mental hygiene for the new millennium. Enterprising sites devoted to the psychopathologies inherent in the medium itself were also created, as the notion of 'Internet addiction' seized the imagination of cyber-therapists and journalists, and the credit card numbers of many users. Upon the launch of the Cyberanalysis Clinic (www.cyberanalysis.com), founder Dr Russell Razzaque expressed his hopes for the future of psychiatry:

> I'm hoping that this service will revolutionize psychiatry not just in the way it's practiced, but in the way it's achieved. This new form of therapy has the ability to revolutionize psychotherapy as we know it. (Fording, 1998: np)

Razzaque was quick to distance his professional clinic from the brief, practical — and free — solutions electronic advice columns offered: 'Agony aunts tend to give specific advice and tell you what to do — psychiatry never involves giving that advice' (Ward, 1999: np).

A novel feature of the Cyberanalysis Clinic is the Cyberanalysis Club, which allows potential clients free membership. The benefits on offer include:

> A monthly newsletter; Information about the different types of psychotherapy practiced by mainstream clinicians today; Advice for personal and interpersonal problems provided from a different therapeutic perspective each month; A monthly quiz, that gives you the chance to accumulate enough points to earn: a personal e-mail exchange to discuss your problems and a 1 to 1 session using Internet chat, videophone or telephone. You earn a point for each question answered correctly. Twelve points gets you a free email exchange while twenty gets you a free 1 to 1 session. (www.cyberanalysis.com)

Cyberanalysis Clinic delivers services via email, videophone, and telephone — each with a separate fee-scale. In addition to services for individual consumers, the Clinic has its own brand of Employee Assistance Program (the CAEAP). Such mental hygiene regimes for the workplace have been sold to organisations, by psy-professionals, since the 1940s. Today, EAPs 'care for' around a third of all employed Americans. Although such programs are less popular in Britain, with only five per cent of employed Britons 'covered', this still translates to some 1.2 million employees.

> The *CyberAnalysis Employee Assistance Program* (CAEAP) offers the cutting edge in EAPs — uniquely accessible to all employees within the company 24 hrs a day on their own office computers via the Internet or through your corporate Intranet. (www.cyberanalysis.com)

Indeed, this is the first online workplace employee assistance service to provide virtual professional counselling, employee personal development, assessment and advice. All this for only $36 per employee, per year!

The late 1990s also saw the development of large commercial 'e-clinics'. These are promoted as offering benefits to both consumers and professionals alike (Ainsworth, 1999). For a fee, professionals can stand to gain by their association through access to resources that they would otherwise be unable to afford: online practice management tools, secure credit card billing, and active marketing. In turn, consumers have an extensive choice of 'pre-screened' therapists, who may be selected according to a range of relevant criteria; access to a variety of germane self-help and support groups, and access to psychoeducational material and self-assessment tools. HelpHorizons (www.helphorizons.com) includes a searchable database of over 500,000 psy-professionals. It offers both an Instant Session chat service and a HelpMatch™ email service — the latter is uncannily akin to an online dating service. The online version of *Psychology Today* will also soon launch a therapy match-making service. It promises a mega-directory that will allow consumers to select, from a database of thousands of psy-professionals, Doctor Right — the therapist made for *you.*

My Therapy Net, Inc. (www.mytherapynet.com) is a similar service — with even more choices for the consumer. The site connects to English-, Farsi-, Russian- and Spanish-speaking therapists. 'We have a diverse range of therapists, including, but not limited to, men, women, old, young, homosexual, heterosexual, white, black and disabled.' My Therapy Net is distinct from its therapy-based competitors in that, in addition to offering online therapy from a range of licensed mental health professionals — marriage and family therapists, clinical social workers, psychologists and psychiatrists — it also offers life-coaching. A testimonial from a satisfied consumer attests to the convenience of this service: 'Thank you so much .... I can have a session with my life coach at home while my new baby is napping'.

My Therapy Net also provides, for the savvy mental health consumer, tables comparing the advantages and disadvantages of (a) traditional therapy vs. online therapy: online therapy is anonymous, convenient, time-effective and cheap; and (b) therapy vs. life-coaching: life-coaching works with 'goals' rather than 'issues'; and 'with already successful people who want to move toward higher function and achieve excellence, while creating an extraordinary life'; professional and client work together to build client awareness and responsibility; and — crucially — life-coaching holds no geographical boundaries. Therapy, on the other hand, 'can only be practiced in the state where the therapist and client reside'. Life-coaching offers a lucratively general — and global — target market for online practitioners. As we will see, the development of the legal and ethical regulation of 'e-therapy' has curtailed the activity of some 'clinical' sites. Coming up with such new 'quasi-therapeutic' products and services is one way to circumvent these pesky regulations. As well as providing consumers with the opportunity to 'select a therapist', or enter into 'life-coaching', My Therapy Net also has 'e-mmediate care' — a connection to a therapist within ten minutes. The fine print reveals that those therapists offering 'e-mmediate care' are 'trainee' clinicians, still under supervision.

As with the other e-Clinics, My Therapy Net includes a range of psychoeducational resources, with a series of articles on 'Mental Wealth', or 'Promoting Emotional Health for All'. The title article turns out to actually be about 'The Brain, Stress and Therapy':

> More is being learned about how the brain manages emotions and responds to experiences. Discoveries … have emerged showing therapy to be a valuable tool in overcoming emotional illness because of the way it alters brain chemistry. ['Helpful hormones'] increase when a person is involved in psychotherapy, social support groups or meditation. The brain is showing its ability to correct its chemistry with changes in attitude and interpersonal contact. While life may confront us with potentially crippling stressors, we are learning that there are steps that can be taken to regain contentment.
> (www.mytherapynet.com/public/MentalWealth.php)

Other informative articles provided by My Therapy Net include, 'The "Order of Things" and Marital Conflict' — yes, it *is* a pop-psych reference to Foucault:

> Michel Facault [sic] talks about the order of things. Others talk about the structure of relevance. What these concepts mean for everyday life is that people generally organise their day based on a certain organising principle …. The order of things brings with it a sense of identity and meaning for people … [and] marriage requires coordinated … meanings.
> (www.mytherapynet.com/public/HeSaidSheSaid.php)

A more serious — for the self[ish] — topic is presented in 'Second-Hand Depression, Like Second-Hand Smoking Can Kill'. This article advises (the presumably female) consumer on what to do with her unhappy partner — tips grounded not in love or concern, but in the desire to avoid becoming 'infected':

> Invite him to go with you to a psychotherapist to examine the root causes of his depression and suggest a treatment plan. Sometimes by taking antidepressant medication and psychotherapy, the problem goes away. Give him responsibility for his

condition. Do not become a codependent that feels sorry for him. He is most probably experiencing a psychological condition that needs treatment.
(www.mytherapynet.com/public/HeSaidSheSaid.php)

'In 1995 there were 12 e-therapists practicing on the Internet. By 1999, there were over 250 private-practice websites, and over 700 therapists practising via the new e-clinics' (Ainsworth, 1999: np). In 2002, just *one* of the 'new e-clinics' claimed to represent over 500,000 psy-professionals (www.helphorizons.com). Despite the proliferation of 'direct mental health services' online, since the larger 'dot com crash', several of the largest commercial e-clinics have collapsed (including the long running 'e-therapy.com'). Other, more 'innovative' ventures, such as the Cyberanalysis Clinic have diversified to target employers/employees, via Employee Assistance Programs, which — as they do not supply direct 'therapy' *per se* — can sell psychological expertise to a market segment keenly aware of the economic benefits of providing cheaper online psychological services. As we will see, by serving the 'employee', rather than the 'client' or 'patient', these online professionals neatly circumvent a number of professional ethical obligations.

In her recent review of the growth of the industry, Maheu notes that:

> [If] consumers trusted email or chat rooms for establishing or maintaining contact with professionals, they have had a golden opportunity in the last 12 months to support such an industry. Despite [hundreds] of websites from which to choose, consumers have not availed themselves of such sites any more than using telephones to conduct therapeutic relationships ... the failures of many telephone counselling services in the 1980s, and, more recently, of dot com, email and chat room based psychotherapy services, testify to consumer preferences for traditional psychotherapy services. (Maheu, 2001: 9)

OnlineClinics (www.onlineclinics.com) aims to cater for — and create — this very preference. An article in the American Psychological Association's *Monitor on Psychology* in July 2000 introduced the OnlineClinics 'concept' to the professional community. The concept? 'Therapy that starts online but aims to continue in the psychologist's office' (Rabasca, 2000). Apparently, hundreds of psychologists in private practice responded to this article, and registered to join the online referral network provided by OnlineClinics:

> The OnlineClinics Website has a simple short-term goal [to] attract clients and privately communicate with clients who have mental health concerns via the Internet and telephone. Its long-term goal? To invite 'virtual' clients who need to visit the psy-

chologists' real offices for professional face-to-face services. The site … connects clients with licensed practitioners, who begin the therapeutic relationship by providing instant, direct and secure services online. *OnlineClinics* expect that once clients feel comfortable receiving these online services and establish initial trust, they will warm up to office visits. (Rabasca, 2000)

Similarly, the OnLine Counseling Service describes itself as 'pre-therapeutic' — i.e. designed to 'empower' consumers to 'find the therapy forms tailor-made for *your* special needs':

We at OnLine Counseling Service understand ourselves as a clearing house for people who — for whatever reason — dare not make the first step into the healing process on their own, who fear stigmatisation and prefer anonymous contact as a first step towards comprehensive therapy. We do not offer therapy but offer our knowledge and training to provide guidance in a 'pretherapeutic' environment by empowering you to make an informed decision about the resources available and help you to find the therapy forms tailor-made for your special needs …. For a small fee to cover our expenses, we will assist you along your difficult way. However, the services we offer are not intended to replace direct consultation with a licensed professional. First contact and consultation will be free of charge. (www.haleyton.com/drburck/welcome.htm)

The *Psychiatric Times* concurs: 'E-therapy should be regarded as a supplemental delivery model for mental health care services or as a *means of transitioning a patient to traditional psychotherapy*' (Dunaway, 2000: np). However, the *Psychiatric Times* is more explicit than either the online psychological service providers or their 'professional critics' in spelling out the 'market opportunities' for the psy-professions:

Preliminary studies indicate that e-therapy will expand the existing market opportunity for psychotherapy … by making services available to populations that currently have limited or no access to them. E-therapy makes it possible to service the millions of people who could benefit from therapy but would otherwise not participate, including: people with special needs such as the handicapped, the deaf, non-ambulatory persons or the elderly; agoraphobics; people in rural or remote locations; people ambivalent about treatment and its benefits; people with time constraints such as salespeople, executives and other professionals; and people uncomfortable with the stress or stigma of traditional counseling.

These populations are large and supplemental to the current $70 billion mental health care market space ... targeted by traditional psychotherapy and counseling services. In addition to increased accessibility and convenience, the cost of interactions conducted via telephone, email and chat are arguably lower for patients (or should be) given the provider's lessened need for office space and other overheads .... E-therapy also decreases the typical inhibition of patients in a face-to-face session to fully disclose information and immediately get to the heart of the matter .... This could also mean that less time would be spent on trust issues and side-tracking, denial, deflection, and so on, resulting in further cost reductions for both patients and providers. (Dunaway, 2000: np)

In the professional academic literature, such 'target markets' are more commonly described as 'underserved populations'. In their chapter on 'Internet Therapy', in the undergraduate and professional text, *Psychology and the Internet*, Storm King and Danielle Moreggi explain that:

Several populations can be identified as having characteristic [sic] that make them a good candidate to benefit from online therapy. There is obvious potential in using the Internet to assist the treatment of people with generalised social phobia (GSP), avoidant personality disorder (APD), or agoraphobia. (King and Moreggi, 1998: 96)

Paul Schneider's (1999) review of the ('tele-mental-health') literature reveals that certain 'isolated' populations could benefit from a technologically extended reach. Schneider suggests that Native Americans, rural consumers, military personnel — in the field — and prisoners could stand to benefit from online psychological services:

Distance can also be a temporary situation. Military personnel typically have ample access to services when they reside on base. This situation changes when they move abroad or are otherwise in the field .... Another isolated population is prisoners. In 1994 there were over 1,500,000 men and women in various prisons in the United States. This number has continued to increase over the last few years, and shows no sign of abatement. [There] are ... numerous prisoners with mental health problems ... anywhere from 7–15% of inmates have mental disorders, with about a third of these disorders being depression, severe forms of schizophrenia, or manic depression ... telehealth services provide a way to efficiently, safely, and more cheaply bridge the gap between ... professionals and prisoners. (Hipkens in Schneider, 1999: np)

The home-bound — whether from 'physical' or 'psychological' disorders — and the elderly also stand to benefit from the mass availability of 'Distance Therapy', as 'telehealth provides a way to intervene in ... situation[s] that normally would probably go untreated' (Schneider, 1999: np). Just how a scared squaddy under fire 'in the field' is supposed to be assisted by a 'therapeutic' communication is quite beyond us. And the idea that psyber expertise will *help* one and a half million incarcerated Americans is just straightforwardly bizarre. Or perhaps the issue here is less to do with help, and more to do with market expansion?

Dot com(mon) sense: a consumer's guide to online therapy

As we have seen, online therapy — dot com crash notwithstanding — is a growing phenomenon. Metanoia (www.metanoia.org) is a popular one-woman site which offers a 'consumer's guide' to online therapy — Martha Ainsworth's 'ABC's of Internet Therapy' page has received 514, 280 hits (as of May 2002).[7] Her consumer's guide begins at the beginning, by tackling the perfectly reasonable question:

> *Why should you pay to consult a professional?*
> If participating in a support group, or reading self-help information, is all the help you need, then that's wonderful. However, certain situations and difficulties are tougher to deal with. *Specialized techniques of caring* have been developed which have the potential to change your life .... This includes the practice of psychotherapy — or the intervention of a human being who has the specialized knowledge, training, skill and experience to help.

Having established the existence of 'specialised techniques of caring', Metanoia goes on to make the kinds of 'commonsensical' comparisons we will see at work in chapter seven. It seems perfectly reasonable to accord our 'mental health' the same 'quality of care' as our physical health, or even our car, deserves:

> If you needed an antibiotic for an infection, you wouldn't hesitate to go to your doctor for the right treatment. Why deny yourself proper care for your emotional health? Unfortunately, most people take better care of their cars than their own emotional health. Every once in a while your psyche needs a tune-up too. (www.metanoia.org/imhs/who.htm)

---

7. Despite its name, this site is unrelated to the other Metanoia, the UK psychotherapy institute established in the 1980s.

By accepting the wisdom of 'valuing our mental health', however, we trade in our everyday expertise in the care of ourselves, for that of those who know the true nature of our needs, and the 'specialised techniques' to meet them.

Metanoia introduces e-therapy as a convenient means for those otherwise unable to 'enter a therapist's office', to enter into therapy:

> Many people cannot, or will not, go to a therapist's office. Psychotherapy is not accessible: when a person is too wary, or too embarrassed to make an appointment with a therapist; when a person lives in a remote area, far from any therapist's office; when scheduling, money, physical challenge, conflicting relationships, or misconceptions keep people from seeking help. If this describes you, e-therapy may be a place to start. (www.metanoia.org/imhs/alliance.htm)

'Cyber-psychologist' Jeri Fink offers a 'consumer's guide to online therapy' on her clinic site (www.psychotechnology.com). However, in order to access this guide, consumers must first purchase her novel, *Virtual Terror* — a pulp-pop-psych-fiction thriller about a 'cyber-psychologist' being (virtually) stalked by a 'crazy' patient:

> Manhatten [sic] psychotherapist Melanie Wylie plunges into the uncharted world of cyber-therapy in an attempt to escape the predatory grasp of the insurance industry. Suddenly, 'Raven' appears on her online couch. His words lash out from the screen .... 'Your death will be my cure' .... [P]lung[ing] into a chilling surreal world where sexual fantasies rage out of control ... *Virtual Terror* is a roller-coaster ride of dizzying psychological twists, deadly human weapons, and bloodthirsty madness. (www.psychotechnology.com/pubWork/fiction)[8]

The only publicly available excerpt from Fink's companion volume, *The Essential Guide to Online Therapy*, is in the form of a brief vignette/press release, which ends with 'Jenna tak[ing] a deep breath, [and] punch[ing] in her credit card number on Dr Maxwell's secure site' (www.psychotechnology.com/pubWork/fiction/).

The American Psychological Association, which developed a 'position paper' on Internet-based therapy in 1997 — giving it a cautious green light — now boasts a Dot Com Sense section in its online Consumer Help Center (helpingapa.org/dotcomsense/).[9] Here, prac-

---

8. We wonder what SANE's 'StigmaWatch' (chapter two) would make of a professional psychologist (as opposed to a shampoo company) describing the 'mentally ill' in this way?

9. The Australian Psychological Society and the British Psychological Society have also developed 'position papers' on 'Internet therapy'.

tical-technological matters such as cookies, privacy and commercial influences are dealt with, alongside a series of tips for 'assessing whether mental health information found on the Internet is credible and accurate'. The 'Resources' section of the site does not, however, contain any links to online clinics. Rather, the APA's own 1-800 number is given, to assist the consumer to find a real live therapist in their geographical area.

Indeed, psychology has started to pay careful attention to the mental health information available on the Internet. In their review of the 'quality of web-based information on treatment of depression', Kathleen Griffiths and Helen Christensen's (2000) analysis of 21 popular websites devoted to 'depression' reported that most contained 'inaccuracies'. On this matter, Les Posen, Secretary of the Victorian Branch of the APS, suggests that:

> Perhaps the publication of accuracy levels of websites in esteemed journals demonstrates that use of the Internet has come of age — or perhaps it reflects fears harboured by professional groups: the professions are becoming more territorial as they experience the incursion into 'protected' territory so long held and mythologized through the use of specialized terms (e.g. DSM-IV), or through restriction of trade, as enforced by registration bodies. In other words, technological innovation isn't just breaking down global barriers to trade, information and cultural exchange, but it is also breaking down access to information once 'owned' by guilds and charged for accordingly, with all the status and privilege afforded such ownership. (Posen, 2001: np)

The Information Quality — or IQ Tool — is an interactive 'consumer's tool' for assessing the information presented on mental health websites. Although unaffiliated, links to the IQ Tool are available from *Self-Help Magazine* and other 'educational sites' supported by psy-professionals:

> The IQ Tool helps you become an educated consumer by helping you ask the right questions. Based on your answers IQ will evaluate the site's strengths and weaknesses. (hitiweb.mitretek.org/iq/)

And *Psychology Today* advises consumers to ensure that they:

> [c]onsider the source of the information. Does it come from a mental health professional? Beware of materials written by fellow sufferers who are laypersons. Experiencing a problem doesn't automatically confer the ability to help others. (Fried, 2001: 60)

The rights to this — now specialised — 'ability to help others' are, ideally for the psy-professions, conferred exclusively to licensed experts, rather than to ordinary people, who may wish to offer — for free — tales of their own relevant experiences.

Ethics and regulation

The American National Board for Certified Counselors was one of the first professional bodies to develop a code of ethics for online therapy — or 'WebCounseling' (www.nbcc.org/wcstandards.htm). As we've noted, the APA, the BPS and the APS developed 'position papers' on 'online therapy' during the late 1990s. Despite this, the professional psychological associations are yet to include the sentiments expressed in these papers — that 'special' ethical considerations may be necessary for 'Internet practice' — in their codes of ethics, though the 2001 revision of the APA's code is peppered liberally with references to 'electronic means' as a further *extension* of the ways in which psychological services may be delivered.

Early online practitioners insisted that they were in the business of providing 'information not therapy'. Indeed, early 'Shareware Psychological Consultations' were designed in congruence with existing ethical principles governing the therapeutic — and media — relationships permissible to professional psychologists (see chapter three). In a *USA Today* interview, Leonard 'Shareware' Holmes explained that 'it's important not to do more than you can on the Internet ... there can be problems if you treat it like a therapeutic relationship' (McKeon Charkalis, 1997: np). Marlene Maheu, an adviser to the APA's 'Task force on online therapy' — and also of *Self-Help Magazine*, and Telehealth.net — has been a vocal critic of the therapeutic benefits — and ethics — of brief, 'advice'-based help. Yet her self-help site offers an advice column that responds to 'composite questions' from anonymous consumers. She acknowledges that people should be able to 'get advice', but insists that 'the impact of the one-on-one relationship is not there' (McKeon Charkalis, 1997: np).

Whilst admitting that 'it is clear that the Internet is the next large-scale vehicle for people to find relief from behavioral health issues' , Maheu (2001) is also critical of the large commercial e-clinics we examined in the last section, and worries that these 'dot.com businesses are soliciting practitioners to use their services with unknown, unseen and undiagnosed consumers'. Further, these clinics tend to appear 'credible because they have been developed using large amounts of venture capital funding' and have been promoted via multimillion-dollar television and radio advertising campaigns, despite their near universal failure to 'discuss how professional standards are followed by protocols for contact between patients and practitioners'. As a psy-professional, Maheu's concerns are for professional standards as they impact on the *legal and ethical protection of practitioners*: 'Unwitting professionals at risk ... may be inappropriately relying upon the Internet business community to, in effect, define practice standards'.

Maheu (2001) argues that the distinction between 'advice' and 'psychotherapy' is in need of further clarification. By offering advice, psy-professionals sidestep a number of binding ethical obligations — like obtaining 'informed consent' and promising confidentiality — that would apply should the more usual fare of 'psychological methods [that lead to] greater effectiveness' be on offer. Many such sites have a disclaimer, that serves to differentiate the services on offer from 'proper' psychotherapy:

> This ... is not a replacement for professional therapy and/or counselling. The critical thinking and problem-solving exercises are designed to educate you about approaches you can use to improve the quality of your life. If you are at a high level of distress (click here for a free 'Do I Need Therapy?' analysis) we suggest you consult a therapist and/or physician.
> (www.masteringstress.com/new/menu.htm)

Maheu suggests that professionals should consider adding the following clauses to their patient consent forms: 'Procedures used are outside the standard of care'; 'Procedures used are not validated by research' (www.telehealth.net/presentations/update/slide36.html).

Further, the 'duty to warn' obligation of professional psychologists is thwarted by the anonymous communication 'invited' by some online therapists. That is, should an anonymous consumer declare suicidal or homicidal intent, or admit to a current crime, the online practitioner is absolved of this duty — by the reasoning that, if information that would identify the consumer is unavailable, a 'duty to warn' situation can not be said to exist.

In 'Ethics and Risk Management: Navigating the New Psychology in the Age of the Internet', Marlene Maheu and Derek O'Brien MD promise American psy-professionals six continuing education hours (plus three bonus hours with book and exam) devoted to these very issues. The workshop is described as suitable for psychologists; healthcare administrators; educators; counsellors; social workers; mental health centre staff; addiction counsellors; marriage and family therapists; clergy; psychiatrists; students in mental health; nurses; and other mental health professionals 'who wish to enhance their therapeutic skills'. The marketing blurb for the course explains its relevance to the modern psy-professional:

> Technology is changing communication. These fundamental changes will create a variety of new problems that need treatment, will impact how the middle- and upper middle-class pa-

tient expects to obtain professional services, how professionals
will obtain reimbursement. Will you be ready to take control or
will these changes control you? (Maheu and O'Brien, 2001: np)

The 'conservative' alternative advocated by Maheu is for psy-professionals to concentrate their efforts on the ways in which the
'middle- and upper middle-class patients [will come to] expect to
obtain professional services' — that is, in the more 'serious', and
exponentially expanding field of 'tele-mental-health', which (in the
US) has received 'serious' government funding in recent years. Beginning in 1994, legislative change saw the US Federal and state
budget allocation for telehealth reach $100 million. Why? Telehealth
— after an initial investment in technological equipment — is ultimately a very economic means of delivering (mental) health services. According to one proponent, 'telehealth increases the likelihood that a consumer will seek treatment at an early stage. Earlier
treatment often leads to greater prevention and *reduced long-term
care costs*' (Bashshur, 1997: 265). So, how much of a saving could
telehealth offer? Recent estimates suggest that services provided
via telehealth could save $36 billion in US national health care
spending (Nickelson, 1996). Again, we suspect that issues both of
'rational economics' and market expansion — rather than beneficent concern — are in play: but this time to the affluent classes
who (unlike the earlier identified targets for psyber therapy, prisoners and the poor bloody infantry) do not routinely encounter the
social deprivation so conducive to distress.

Mind you, the revenue generated by online health and medical
advertising in the US is projected soon to top $2.65 billion, according
to research by Jupiter (1998) — compared to a total revenue of $12.3
million in 1997. Direct-to-consumer marketing in the pharmaceutical sector will be the major contributor to the growth of the health
advertising industry on the Internet. Though direct-to-consumer
advertising is legal only in America and New Zealand, the Internet
routes around such domestic regulations. The Australian government seems more concerned to regulate pornographic websites than
the 'consumer-friendly' misinformation provided by the globally available websites of the pharmaceutical corporations, of which more in
chapter seven. The total value of the healthcare e-commerce market
should reach $370 billion (US) by 2004 (Forrester, 2000).

More recently, in America, legislation has been adopted which
requires that all 'telehealth' services are reimbursed. California was
the first state to pass such legislation, in 1997. Currently, 36 per
cent of (US) healthcare professionals report using telehealth for 'emotional, behavioral or social concerns' (Farmer and Muhlenbruck, 2001)
— and mental health services are the fastest growing area of telehealth
(Puskin, 2001; Smith and Allison, 1998). However, Huang and Alessi,
in their 1996 article on 'The Internet and the Future of psychiatry',

introduce a note of caution, warning that 'mental health professionals will clearly feel an impact if managed care companies indepen-
dently develop Internet-accessible computerised screening tools that
refer patients to care providers without our input' (1996: 865). The
final section of this chapter examines the nature of the 'threat' posed
to the psy-professions by the rapidly-expanding 'managed behavioural
healthcare' organisations, through looking in detail at one particularly successful corporation — American Psych Systems, Inc.

American Psych Systems, Inc.

APS Healthcare — formerly known as American Psych Systems, Inc.
— is a private, for-profit, managed behavioural healthcare organisation.
Founded in 1992, by Kenneth Kessler MD, it provides 'managed behavioral health, employee assistance programs, and specialty care
management services to 9.4 million "covered lives" in the United States
and Puerto Rico'. During 1995–1999, APS grew by 935 per cent. Managed behavioural healthcare is devoted to 'empowering' consumers to
solve their mental health problems 'inhouse' — and preferably, whilst
they are still amenable to some form of 'self-help' — that is, before
personal problems have been respecified as 'billable disorders'. As we've
noted, the Internet is an ideal vehicle for delivering 'cost effective' mental health care. To this end, APS has developed a web-based 'life management product', designed to 'help people to help themselves to lead
healthier lives!' According to their promotional material:

> Technology, and more specifically the Internet, is changing
> health care in dramatic ways. Driven by consumer demand for
> greater control over their lives, the eHealth movement is re-
> sulting in more informed consumers who have more choice
> and control over the way in which they live their lives. Today,
> the Internet is integrated into all aspects of our lives. The Internet
> represents the vehicle, which brings individuals, companies,
> and providers together. It's the place where people gather in-
> formation, search for life management resources and referrals,
> and solutions to everyday life events and challenges ... [The]
> Internet will help us connect people in convenient and compel-
> ling ways, providing them with quality information that will
> enable them to navigate the emotional challenges of everyday
> life. With our Internet product, APSHelpLink.com™ we will reach
> a much wider audience. APSHealthcare has invested signifi-
> cant resources in developing a web-based Life Management
> product that is designed to help people help themselves with
> issues that impact their health, quality of life, and well-being.
> APSHelpLink represents one access point into our behavioral
> health care system. People can use the Internet ... to access a

wide array of information, resources, and referrals.
(www.apscare.com/helplink/helplinkcom_index.htm)

APSHelplink.com™: 'Helping People Help Themselves to Lead Healthier Lives' provides 'life management tools' to help people with 'behavioral health problems; financial and legal issues; child and eldercare concerns; and work/life issues'. These 'self-help tools' are purported to help people to 'clarify problems and plan ways to resolve them'. Individuals can exchange ideas with professionals and others using online chat, bulletin boards, and the 'Ask A Pro' service. The 'Find a Clinician' feature helps individuals locate a professional practitioner in their community. APSHelplink™ is a 'high-value low-cost benefit' that promises to help both employers and everyday consumers. Employers can look forward to 'reduced absenteeism, employee retention, and increased visibility'. The rest of us will benefit from the 'ease of access, convenience, consumer information, and interactive self-help tools and resources' offered by APSHelplink.com™.

The APSHelpLink™ site is not only designed to alleviate early signs of mental health problems — according to the promotional blurb on the mother-site, 'the organisation of the site, the choice of content, and its structure are based on the latest research on how the brain works and on the most effective methods and theories of how people change'. The site was designed in consultation with (unnamed) academic psy-professionals from 'well-renowned' universities, who have 'dedicated their lives to helping people solve their problems'. Specifically, we are told that 'Prochaska and DeClemente's "readiness to change" model has been used as a basis for the site's design'. This is a (cognitive-behavioural) model used to excess in the public health and (mental) health promotion field — usually, by practitioners with no training in psychology.[10] 'APSHelpLink™ is *motivational* in nature and operates on the assumption that people are curious and *want* to work towards solutions in their lives.' Further, the site has been 'designed and written to be accessible to everyday people living in the real world'. Thus it is 'dynamic and brief' and offers a 'high degree of interactivity' to/with the user. Through a 'unique combination of upbeat appeal and hopefulness', with 'down-to-earth usefulness and caring for the individual', APSHelpLink™ is 'compelling', 'convenient' and 'fun'.

This rather large site (1,800 pages) goes beyond either the provision of psychoeducational information, or professional advice. Rather, APSHelpLink™ promises to:

> encourage and empower people to do something useful with the information that is available on our site and elsewhere ....
> APSHelpLink™ goes beyond *helping people change the way they*

---

10. For a thorough critique of this model, see Bunton et al., 2000.

feel about their lives. We want to empower people to make changes that are concrete and measurable in behavioral terms. (www.apscare.com/helplink/helplinkcom_index.htm).

The site is designed — or promoted — to offer 'one-stop shopping for up-to-date information on life management issues'. So, what's on the shelves?

Life Problems — Topical information on stress, depression, teenagers, 'relationships that hurt', anger, workplace coping and manager and supervisory help.

Solution Area — This section offers 'self-assessment tools' to help an individual determine the severity of a problem type/issue and provides information and links within and outside of APSHelpLink™ to help the individual deal with his/her issue more effectively.

Connect — Having researched and assessed our problems, we may find the need to 'connect' and to address our problems by 'talking to someone'.

Ask a Pro — Here, consumers may ask questions of licensed professionals. Answers have a three- day turnaround.

Chat and Bulletin Board — APSHelpLink™ offers formal and informal real-time discussions of topical issues and life problems — moderated by a professional. Bulletin Boards are intended for consumers to communicate amongst themselves, about their problems, questions and solutions. These are archived for ready-reference.

Building Skills — 'This section offers tools and learning exercises for the basic skills that can help one understand and cope with his/her problem or challenge'.

Bridge to Change — We are informed that '"The Bridge to Change" is a powerful self-help tool that helps individuals set and attain their own goals for change. It is an interactive guide that takes a person through the process of making a change in his/her life. It gives a person the tools needed to solve a problem by helping them understand the change process, and by guiding them through the steps of change'.

Manager and Supervisory Solutions — Here, 'everyday people who just happen to be in a manager, supervisory or consultative role' will find real-time access to 'interactive self-help, information and other tools'. Topic areas covered include Self-Care, Professional Concerns and Challenges and Understanding Employee Problems that Impact Work Performance.

Find a Clinician — Zippy mapping technology is available to help the consumer to find a professional in his or her local area.

Legal and Financial — Information on family law, bankruptcy, credit counselling, personal injury and other legal and financial matters.

Concierge Services — For help with managing the details of your everyday life. The APSHelpLink™ Concierge Specialists can run personal errands for you (for a small additional fee). Shopping, flowers, and other mundane matters.

So — apart from the concierge and the lawyer — how does this site differ from those provided by psy-professionals? APSHelpLink™ marks a clear differentiation: 'Our site offers consumer information, interactive self-help and life management tools. We do not provide online counselling.' APSHelpLink™ also allows user anonymity (however, a company number is required to log in) — as we have seen, an ethically impossible offer for licensed psy-professionals to make if they are also offering 'therapy'.

Further, APSHelpLink™ can be co-branded, and made to appear as if it were an extension of a company's existing employee services. Corporate logos and messages to employees, along with links to a company's own site and Intranet can be readily incorporated. The ideal passage of the user through the site is given in APSHelpLink™ — A User's Guide:

> Log on to APSHelpLink™; Read personal messages to you from the *Ask A Pro* service; Check messages from your specific company and announcements to all HelpLink users about new features and upcoming special events; Click onto *Life Problems* to start using our self-help tools to better understand and manage your problems; Take a self-assessment quiz to help you determine the severity of your problem or identify what areas of the site may be of particular interest to you; Explore concise and accessible advice in one of numerous areas, which cover topics such as depression, anxiety, and teen problems; Use the *Bridge to Change* feature to learn how to set a goal and work towards making changes that solve problems; Find support or share ideas with others through our bulletin boards and chats; Ask a professional counselor about your problem, or look for answers to questions similar to yours in one of our public access areas; Obtain more information about topics of interest to you through *Articles and Links*; Click on *Find A Clinician* to locate a mental health practitioner in your community; Click on *Child and Eldercare* to get information and resources; Click on *Legal and Financial Services* to get legal and financial information; Click on *Concierge Services* to get help managing your busy life. (www.apscare.com/helplink/helplinkcom_index.htm)

Whilst employees are promised anonymity, *employers* are promised access to the results of a 'utilisation analysis' for their employees: number and percentage of online visits (by topic, content, and function); duration of visits; number of visits spent in life problem areas; number and percentage of visits to online features (Search, Phone A Counselor, Chats, Find A Clinician, etc.); user visit frequency by area. Quality assurance results include client satisfaction surveys and feedback on individual pages of APSHelpLink™. With respect to the Bridge to Change Evaluation, APSHelpLink™ advises that they can track, by problem type, an individual's success on following through on the goals that they set for themselves.

Employee Assistance Programs (EAPs) promise to reduce absenteeism and increase productivity. The APS warns that 'unresolved personal problems' can pose a serious threat to productivity, and that — right this very minute — one in five workers is afflicted by such a problem. EAPs work through 'ongoing education and prevention, early intervention, and short-term problem resolution'. 'EAPs provide an effective and affordable way to encourage healthy lifestyles and detect problems that could impact the workforce if not addressed.' They help to 'reduce the risk of unnecessary health care costs' and 'preventable workplace accidents'. EAP educational material is designed to 'remind employees about the value of the EAP, destigmatise counseling, emphasize confidentiality and encourage employees to seek assistance when needed'.

With 9.4 million 'covered lives', one might think that APS Healthcare would be satisfied. The September 11 incident, however, was the spur to a positive epidemic of 'reaching out' — and frantic product diversification — by the psy-professions. Most psy-sites, including that of the American Psychological Association, were quick to upload resources, and suggestions for coping with, the 'Attack on America'. On 18 September 2001, APS Healthcare issued a press release, in which it stated the hope that it could 'assist the country with recovery', by providing all individuals with a 30-day trial:

> In an effort to respond to the needs of our clients and the country, APS is making our life management Internet product, APSHelpLink, available to both our clients and the general public, free of charge for the next 30 days. Through APSHelpLink, APS hopes we can *assist the country* with recovering from this catastrophic event by providing *all individuals* with access to professional resources, information and support to help facilitate the healing process .... [O]ver the past week we have invested significant time and energy to populate APSHelpLink with information, links and materials that specifically address the wide range of emotions and challenges individuals are experiencing in light of the recent tragedy. This includes: A direct link to our 'Ask-a-Pro' feature, which enables individuals to email questions to licensed clinical professionals at APS. (APS, 2001a: np)

By October, APS Healthcare had expanded their available resources:

> As part of our newly created Disaster Resource area, we offer the following: Emergency Relief Information Links, including .... Our Trauma Information Resource Page; Helpful Links for

Trauma/Post-Traumatic Stress/Disaster; The Aftermath at Home, addressing issues such as: Business Travel — Addressing Family Fears when Flying; Grieving the Loss of a Loved One Due to Violence; How to Talk to Your Children After Disaster Strikes; Signs of Stress and Trauma in Children; A Booklist of Resources for Dealing with Trauma and Loss (for Children/Teens/Adults); The Aftermath at Work, programs and resources dealing with: 'High Anxiety' — Fear of Flying; Coping with Disaster — An Employer's Perspective; Fear of Flying — A Manager's Dilemma; The Aftermath and Self-Care; Exercises in self-evaluation that include helpful resources such as a Self-Report Questionnaire and a page entitled 'When Disaster Strikes — Your Emotional Plan'.

APS will also continue our series of HelpLink Chats ... our November schedule is as follows: November 7th — 'Holiday Travel Decisions — How do I choose?' November 21st — 'The Unseen Enemy — How do I manage the fear of terrorism?'

APS hopes that all individuals will continue to take advantage of the resources available through APS HelpLink. We will continue to supply timely help ... as our nation recovers from the recent tragedies, by helping one person at a time lead a healthier life. (APS, 2001b: np)

APSHealthcare™, then, far from offering any significant threat to the longevity of the psy-professions, is rather aggressively extending the frontiers of the market by inviting an entire nation to participate in a '30-day trial' of its new, online, always available 'life-management', 'psychoeducational', 'self-help' and 'referral' resources.

This nakedly commercial campaign, which trades explicitly on human misery, marks one of the more cynical instances of psy's long tradition of 'appropriating, and marketing, aspects of care and concern which should constitute the everyday ethical life of any humane society' (Smail, 2002: np).

References

Ainsworth, Martha (1999) *History and Survey of E-Therapy.* Retrieved 10 May 2002: (www.metanoia.org/imhs/history.htm)

APS Healthcare (2001a) Press Release: APS Healthcare offers APS HelpLink. (18 September)

APS Healthcare (2001b) Press Release: APS Healthcare Extends Access to APS HelpLink. (25 October)

Baird, K. (1986) Online Columnist Gives Career Advice. *Online Today* (August) 31

Baldwin, Steve (2000) Living in Britalin: Why Are so Many Amphetamines Prescribed to Infants, Children and Teenagers in the UK? *Critical Public Health, 10*(4) 453–62

Barnett, David (1982) A Suicide Prevention Incident Involving the Use of a

Computer. *Professional Psychology, 13*, 565–70

Bashshur, R. L. (1997) Telemedicine and the Health Care System. In R.L. Bashshur, J.H. Sanders, and G.W. Shannon, eds, *Telemedicine: Theory and Practice*. Springfield, IL: Charles C. Thomas, 265–90

Baughman, Fred A. (1998) The Totality of the ADD/ADHD Fraud. Retrieved 31 May 2002: (home.att.net/~Fred-Alden/Es5.html)

Bitnik, Y.M.; Cantor, J.; Ochs, E. and Meana, M. (1997) From the Couch to the Keyboard: Psychotherapy in Cyberspace. In: Sara Kiesler (ed.) *Culture of the Internet*. Mahwah, NJ: Lawrence Erlbaum, 71–100

Boreman, L.D; Brock, L.E.; Hess, R. and Pasquale, F.L. (1982) *Helping People to Help Themselves: Self-help and Prevention*. New York: Haworth Press

Bowman, Robert and Bowman, Vicki (1998) Life on the Electronic Frontier: The Application of Technology to Group Work. *Journal for Specialists in Group Work, 23*(4) 428–45

Bunton, Robin; Baldwin, Steve; Flynn, Darren and Whitelaw, Sandy (2000) The 'Stages of Change' Model in Health Promotion: Science and Ideology. *Critical Public Health, 10*, 55–70

Button, Graham; Coulter, Jeff; Lee, John R.E. and Sharrock, Wes (1995) *Computers, Minds and Conduct*. Cambridge: Polity Press

Danziger, Kurt (1997) *Naming The Mind: How Psychology Found Its Language*. London: Sage

Dunaway, Marian (2000) Assessing the Potential of Online Psychotherapy. *The Psychiatric Times, 10*. Retrieved 10 May 2002: (www.mhsource.com/pt/p001058.html)

Farmer, Janet and Muhlenbruck, Laura (2001) Telehealth for Children with Special Health Care Needs: Promoting Comprehensive Systems of Care. *Clinical Pediatrics, 40*(2) 93–8

Finn, Jerry (1999) An Exploration of Helping Processes in an Online Self-help Group Focussing on Issues of Disability. *Health and Social Work, 24*(3) 220–30

Fleming, Patricia (1990) Software and Sympathy: Therapeutic Interaction with the Computer. In: Gary Gumpert and Sandra Fish (eds) *Talking to Strangers: Mediated Therapeutic Communication*. New Jersey: Ablex' 170–83

Fording, Laura (1998) Cyberscope: The Doctor is Online. *Newsbytes, 9* (December). Retrieved 10 May 2002: (exn.ca/Stories/1998/12/09/02.asp)

Forrester (2000) Business Trade Will Drive Healthcare eCommerce To $370 Billion By 2004, According To Forrester. Retrieved 10 May 2002: (www.forrester.com/ER/Press/Release/0,1769,200,FF.html)

Fried, Stephen (2001) Sifting Science From Snake Oil: How to Find Top Psychology in Pop Psychology. *Psychology Today* (March) 60

Gould, Roger (1990) The Therapeutic Learning Program (TLP) Computer-Assisted Short-Term Therapy. In: Gary Gumpert and Sandra Fish (eds) *Talking to Strangers: Mediated Therapeutic Communication*. New Jersey: Ablex, 184–99

Greist, J. and Klein, M. (1980) Computer Programs for Patients, Clinicians, and Researchers in Psychiatry. In: J. Didowsky, J. Johnson and T. Williams (eds) *Technology in Mental Health Care Delivery Systems*. New Jersey: Ablex, 161–81

Griffiths, Kathleen and Christensen, Helen (2000) Quality of Web-Based Information on Treatment of Depression: Cross-sectional Survey. *British Medical Journal, 321*, (16 December) 1511–15

Grohol, John (1998) Future Clinical Directions: Professional Development,

Pathology and Psychotherapy On-line. In: Jayne Gackenbach (ed.) *Psychology and the Internet: Intrapersonal, Interpersonal and Transpersonal Implications.* San Francisco: Academic Press, 111–38

Harris Interactive (2002) The US is a Nation of 'Cyberchondriacs'. Retrieved 10 May 2002: (www.harrisinteractive.com/harris_poll/index.asp?PID=299)

Hellerstein, Laurel (1990) Electronic Advice Columns: Humanizing the Machine. In: Gary Gumpert and Sandra Fish (eds) *Talking to Strangers: Mediated Therapeutic Communication.* Norwood NJ: Ablex, 112–27

Huang, M. and Alessi, N. (1996) The Internet and the Future of Psychiatry. *American Journal of Psychiatry, 153*(7) 861–9

Humphries, K. and Rappaport, J. (1994) Researching Self-Help/Mutual Aid Groups and Organizations: Many Roads, One Journey. *Applied and Preventative Psychology, 3*, 217–31

Johnson, James (2002) Professional Analyst. Retrieved 10 May 2002: (www.digitalriver.com)

Jupiter (1998) Jupiter Communications: Online Health Advertising Has Rosy Future. Retrieved 10 May 2002: (www.nua.com/surveys/?f=VS&art_id=905354560&rel=true)

Kelley, B. (1994) New Therapy: Cybershrink. *San Francisco Examiner* (1 May) A-10.

Kessler, R.C.; Mickelson, K. D. and Zhao, S. (1997) Patterns and Correlates of Self-help Group Membership in the United States. *Social Policy, 27*, 27–46

King, Storm and Moreggi, Danielle (1998) Internet Therapy and Self-Help Groups: The Pros and Cons. In: Jayne Gackenbach (ed.) *Psychology and the Internet: Intrapersonal, Interpersonal and Transpersonal Implications.* San Francisco: Academic Press, 77–109

Maheu, Marlene (2001) Exposing the Risk, yet Moving Forward: A Behavioral E-Health Model. *Journal of Computer Mediated Communication, 6*(4). Retrieved 10 May 2002: (www.ascusc.org/jmc/vol6/issue4/maheu.html)

Maheu, Marlene and O'Brien, Derek (2001) Ethics and Risk Management — Navigating the New Psychology in the Age of the Internet. Retrieved 10 May 2002:(www.cognitiveatlanta.com/Maheu%201%20page%20flyer%20register%20html.htm)

Mauldin, Michael (1994) ChatterBots, TinyMuds, and the Turing Test: Entering the Loebner Prize Competition. Retrieved 10 May 2002: (www.lazytd.com/lti/pub/aaai94-slides.html)

McKeon Charkalis, Diana (1997) Web Can Be a Link to Your Shrink. *USA Today.* Retrieved 10 May 2002: (www.metanoia.org/imhs/usatoday.htm)

Miller, George (1969) Psychology as a Means of Promoting Human Welfare. *American Psychologist, 24*, 1067–75

Murphy, L. J. and Mitchell, D. L. (1998) When Writing Helps to Heal: E-mail as Therapy. *British Journal of Guidance and Counselling, 26*(1) 21–32

Neimark, Jill (1984) Psych-out Software: Do-It-Yourself Analysis is Now Available on PCs. *Datamation, 30*, 32–9

Nickelson, D. W. (1996) Behavioral Telehealth: Emerging Practice, Research, and Policy Opportunities. *Behavioral Sciences and the Law, 14*, 443–57

Oka, Tomofumi and Borkman, Thomasina (2000) The History, Concepts and Theories of Self-help Groups: From an International Perspective. *Japanese Journal of Occupational Therapy, 34*(7) 718–22

Posen, Les (2001) Telehealth: Websites and Their Scientific Boards: Trusted Sources of Paid Spruikers! Retrieved 10 May 2002: (telehealth.net/articles/credibility.html)

Powell, Terri (1998) Online Counseling: A Profile and Descriptive Analysis. Retrieved 10 May 2002: (netpsych.com/Powell.htm)

Puskin, Dena S. (2001) Telemedicine: Follow the Money. *Online Journal of Issues in Nursing, 6*(3). Retrieved 10 May 2002: (www.nursingworld.org/ojin/topic16/tpc16_1.htm)

Rabasca, L. (2000) Therapy that Starts Online but Aims to Continue in the Psychologist's Office. *Monitor on Psychology, 31*(7). Retrieved 30 May 2002: (apa.org/monitor/julaug00/online.html)

Ribot, T. (1885) *Les maladies de la personalité.* Paris: Alcan

Schneider, Paul (1999) Literature Review of Telehealth Video and Audio Psychotherapy. Retrieved 10 May 2002: (www.outreach.uiuc.edu/~p-schne/research/telehealth_literature_review.html)

Sharpe, Rochelle (2000) The Virtual Couch. *Business Week* (18 September) 134

Selmi, P.M.; Klein, M. H.; Greist, J. H.; Johnson, J. H. and Harris, W. G. (1982) An Investigation of Computer-assisted Cognitive-behavior Therapy in the Treatment of Depression. *Behavior Research Methods and Instrumentation, 14*, 181–5

Simon, Julian (1991) *Good Mood: The New Psychology of Overcoming Depression.* Chicago: Open Court

Smail, David (2002) *The Origins of Unhappiness* (Chapter four. Case Study: The 1980s). [Edited web version] Retrieved 27 May 2002: (www.nottm.freeserve.co.uk/chapter4.htm)

Smith, Henry and Allison, Ronald (1998) Telemental Health: Delivering Mental Health Care at a Distance: A Summary Report. Retrieved 10 May 2002: (telehealth.hrsa.gov/pubs/mental/home.htm)

Sondheim, Alan (1996) Early Important Net Documents (1972). Retrieved 10 May 2002: (amsterdam.nettime.org/Lists-Archives/nettime-l-9707/msg00059.html)

Stein, Pat (1993) Carlsbad Therapist Offers Dear Abby Sage Advice. *North County Times* [Carlsbad, California] (24 July) np

Surgeon General Workshop (1988) *Surgeon General Workshop on Self-Help and Public Health. Publication no. 224–50.* Washington, DC: US Government Printing Office

UCLA College of Letters and Science (2002) Computer Software Program Can Perform Psychotherapy, New Research Suggests: What Role Will Therapists Play in the Future? Retrieved 10 May, 2002: (www.masteringstress.com/new/ucla.asp)

University of Minnesota (2001) Attention Clinical Applicants. Retrieved 28 May 2002: (www.psych.umn.edu/psygrad/MMPI%20handout—revised%207-01.doc)

Wagman, M. and Kerber, K. W. (1978) *Dilemma Counseling System.* Minneapolis: Control Data Corporation

Wallace, Patricia (1999) *The Psychology of the Internet.* Cambridge: Cambridge University Press

Ward, Cotton (1999) When You're On-line, The Cybershrink is Always in to Dispense Analysis. Retrieved 10 May 2002: (www.cyberanalysis.com/media/1999/58cybershrink.html)

'Pictures of Lily'

'Pictures of Lily helped me feel alright'
(Townshend, 1967)

In this chapter, we are going to examine two prevalent and massively consumed popular accounts of 'psychological' and 'mental health' issues: the information pamphlet and the mass magazine's problem pages, health columns and advice sections. The first of these is relatively official: mental health information pamphlets are often produced by government (mental) health organisations or else by semi-ratified voluntary organisations under expert guidance. The second has an even more dubious status: for, while popular magazines are increasingly upping the formal qualification stakes for what were once ordinary commonsensical 'Agony Aunts' (thus we now have people called 'life strategists', routine reference to psychology degrees and so on), they nevertheless have mere 'media' status. This sets the scene for a contemporary stand-off between the official experts of the psy-disciplines and the media at large, which is where we begin this chapter — ironical as this may be in the light of our next chapter where, as it turns out, the manuals for training the next generation of psy-experts are shown to rely to a considerable extent on media portrayals of 'abnormal' conditions.

Experts vs. media

The consensus of a certain body of work (much of it produced by psychiatrists) on media portrayals of madness, distress and disturbing conduct is that the media generally — and cinema and TV drama serials particularly — are guilty of promoting inaccurate and negatively stigmatising versions of 'mental illness' and mental health matters more generally.[1] Such portrayals, it is claimed, may not only

---

1. Readers might consult the following: Conrad, 2001; Diefenbach, 1997; Hannigan, 1999; Hyler et al., 1991; Jorm et al., 1997; Martinez et al., 2000; Philo, 1994; Rose, 1998; Wahl, 1995, 1992; Wilson et al., 1999.

influence attitudes towards the 'mentally ill' (Granello and Pauley, 2000), but may also directly affect the beliefs and actions of their potentially mentally disturbed viewers. For example, and typically, a study of an episode of *Casualty* by a research team including members of the (otherwise socially critical) Glasgow Media Group concluded that the 'broadcast of popular television dramas depicting self-poisoning may have a short-term influence in terms of increases in hospital presentation for overdose and changes in the choice of drug taken. This raises serious questions about the advisability of the media portraying suicidal behaviour' (Hawton et al., 1999).

The same professional consensus also seems to be reasonably clear with regard to cinematic portrayals of madness. Along with the usual suspects — like *One Flew Over The Cuckoo's Nest* — more recent examples such as *Shine* (Rosen and Walter, 2000; Wessely, 1997) and *Me Myself and Irene* (Baron-Faust, 2000) are cited in the medico-psychiatric literature as egregious examples of the misrepresentation of the 'reality' of mental illness. In her review of *Me Myself and Irene* for the *British Medical Journal*, Baron-Faust anticipates the 'expert-vs.-lay' positioning of the pamphlets we look at later. She writes:

> *Me Myself and Irene* is not terribly funny, and it is one more example of how people with mental illness are stigmatised by the media. Charlie/Hank is portrayed as violent, dangerous, and unfit to hold a responsible job. The film perpetuates harmful myths about mental illness. Charlie's illness is blamed on his personal weakness, and he is 'cured' not by medication or therapy, but by his own will power and the love of a good woman. Would anyone ever expect a person with diabetes, or any other chronic illness, to overcome their condition by will power? (2000: 770)

Indeed, so concerned are some professional bodies about what Byrne describes as the 'usual dross of mental illness movies' (2000: 770) that, in the UK, the Royal College of Psychiatrists has sponsored a cinema short — *1 in 4* — to challenge stereotypical and stigmatising views, and supposedly the consequent resistance to psychiatric intervention, that it is claimed mainstream cinema promotes (Britten, 1998). In their review of *1 in 4*, Roach and Yamey (2000: 1028) quote leading media psychiatrist Anthony Clare:

> Cinema, he said, 'can help to change and educate'. There has always been an interesting feedback, he explained, between 'portrayal, iconography, and our understanding of mental illness. The imagery of cinema informs and moulds our understanding of what psychiatric hospitals look like'.

This 'moulding' is, it seems, usually seen as teratogenic by psychiatry. Indeed, in his review of *Some Voices*, psychiatrist Peter Byrne expands upon psychiatry's view of the 'usual dross of mental illness movies', and tells us what psychiatry would prefer films depicting 'mental illness' to show us:

> As in every 'psychiatry film', once we read the chlorpromazine label on the bottle, we know that non-compliance and relapse are bound to follow. This cliché aside, the film is refreshing in its avoidance of the standard formulas. Gone are the psychokiller, pathetic, or 'crazy funny guy' stereotypes, and there is only one reference, from Pete [the brother of the central, 'schizophrenic' character], to the 'pull yourself together' school of psychotherapy. There is no blaming, no mental illness as metaphor, no psychiatry bashing, and — although a romance lies at its core — there is none of the usual message that 'love is better than tablets'. (Byrne, 2000: 770)

As in the UK, so too in Australia, where the Federal Government has suggested that 'media coverage often reflects the widespread misunderstanding of mental health problems and mental disorders that exist in the broader community' (Commonwealth of Australia, 1999: iv) and has launched a national media strategy to promote 'mental health literacy' in the press and among the general public — part of which includes some of the pamphlets analysed below. This initiative follows worrying findings from surveys of the public conducted by psychiatry. Jorm et al. (1997: 182), for example, found that, when asked about 'mental disorders' and their treatment, the public view, inconveniently, was that:

> many standard psychiatric treatments (antidepressants, antipsychotics, electroconvulsive therapy, admission to a psychiatric ward) were more often rated as harmful than helpful, and some non-standard treatments were rated highly (increased physical or social activity, relaxation and stress management, reading about similar problems) …. If mental disorders are to be recognized early in the community and appropriate intervention sought, the level of mental health literacy needs to be raised. Further, public understanding of psychiatric treatments can be considerably improved.

While Clare and Byrne may have been reticent in naming the specific *films* that offer an ill-formed version of 'what our psychiatric hospitals look like', commentators on the *print media* are less reserved. For example, Lazar and colleagues (1993), in a commentary on press portrayals of mental illness, contend·that journalists are less-than-expert when it comes to understanding 'symptoms' and 'warning signs'; they are likely merely to reflect a general social 'sense of shame'; and they therefore merely reproduce this 'sense of shame' that sufferers must already contend with. Likewise, in the aftermath of the Tasmanian Port Arthur massacre in April 1996, Barbara Hocking, president of SANE Australia, claimed that irresponsible press speculation about the mental state of the killer, Martin Bryant, would make 'schizophrenics' throughout Australia 'run for cover completely' (McCarthy and Rapley, 2001). And, in his analysis of print media representations of madness, Nairn suggests that:

> as media are the public's primary source of information about mental illnesses, depictions of those suffering from these disorders contribute significantly to the stigma associated with mental illness. This contribution makes the negativity of media depictions a matter of great concern, and it has been argued that these depictions would be more favourable if psychiatrists and other mental health professionals were more closely involved .... Analyses of journalistic practice show that sources struggle, usually with little success, to sustain their preferred interpretation of the information they provide, as journalists and editors deploy it to construct a newsworthy story. In practice, journalists organise their materials to present the appearance of objectivity, while giving priority to newsworthy elements understood to attract readers. (Nairn, 1999: 585)

The view from the psy-professions would thus seem to be clear. The popular media — especially cinema, television and the press — misrepresent the truth about mental illness, psychiatric interventions and psychiatric hospitals, to the detriment of those 'afflicted'. Sometimes the misrepresentation is dangerous; sometimes it occurs because media producers lack access to experts; and sometimes 'distortion' is a consequence of a conflict between 'journalistic' values and those of 'science'. Invariably, however, the various public media are presented as powerful sources of information about madness, and as influential shapers of public beliefs — with whom work needs to be done in order to properly inform the public (Mayer and Barry, 1992).

Turning the tables

If this is the case, it seems only equitable to work up a balancing account of this stand-off by subjecting the informational interventions of the psy-professions into public discourse to similarly critical scrutiny. Accordingly, we ask three key questions. (1) With what forms of knowledge of misery and madness do the psy-professions seek to counteract the supposedly corrosive influence of media portrayals of these matters? (2) In what way do the psy-professions — via public authorities — attempt to influence lay understandings of 'mental illness'? (3) Given that the professional claims of the psy-disciplines are efforts to define the ways in which the public understand psychological distress, with what understandings do the professions seek to replace mere 'lay myths'? To answer these questions we sample a rather different medium of mass communication: a range of widely distributed mental health information pamphlets produced by government and non-governmental mental health authorities. Despite some concerns about their usefulness in actually affecting health service utilisation (Dixon-Woods, 2001), information pamphlets are a routinely used medium of communication between psy-experts and the public and are, thus, a particularly apposite analytic site.

To access this site, we collected an extensive sample of pamphlets and brochures on 'mental illness' and 'mental health issues' from the waiting areas of general practitioners' surgeries and public mental health clinics in Perth, Western Australia. The WA Association for Mental Health, and two voluntary sector agencies, the Association of Relatives and Friends of the Mentally Ill (ARAFMI) and SANE, also sent us a number of pamphlets and a 'youth' magazine in response to a request for short publications aimed at the general public or at 'newly diagnosed' individuals. The majority of the pamphlets analysed here were produced by the Australian Federal Government's Department of Health and Aged Care and were described by that Department as being designed to:

> promote awareness of mental health issues and to reduce the misunderstandings associated with mental illnesses in our community. [To] provide clear, easy to understand information on mental illnesses in general, and particular illnesses such as bipolar mood disorder, depression, anxiety disorders, and eating disorders. (Commonwealth of Australia, 1999)

These, and other readily-available publications, expressly intended as an introduction to the 'facts' about mental illness, or as lay guides to particular diagnostic categories, form the focus of this part of the chapter. To confirm our belief that British pamphlets would show the features we found in the Australian material, we also analysed a patient-education leaflet on depression produced and disseminated in the UK by the Royal College of Psychiatrists (Charity Registration Number 228636) which is described on the back cover as having been 'published as a service to the Royal College of Psychiatrists by Eli Lilly and Company Limited: improving lives, restoring hope'. To anticipate our argument a little, with the exception of some charming Calman cartoons, the British pamphlet demonstrated only the international ubiquity of contemporary psy accounts of human misery.

We approach this corpus critically (as we have said, attempting to 'turn the tables') using some of the basic insights of discourse analysts (see Potter and Edwards, 2001). A number of recurrent themes in the construction of 'mental illness', the 'mentally ill' and the 'mental professionals' are quickly apparent when looking at the corpus of pamphlets as a whole. Here we address three of these themes:

1. Grounding human distress solely in physical-corporeal accounts of its causes ('biological determinism');
2. Making a very particular account of the 'reality' of psychological distress appear the only possible one ('ontological gerrymandering' (Potter, 1996));
3. Positioning professional discourse *itself* as the only valid source of knowledge about mentality ('epistemic hegemony').

What the experts say — 'unmediated'?

In all the publications we collected, psychological distress was represented as *illness*, with symptoms, phases and biological origins. 'Mental illness' was presented as an entity that individuals can have and know, at the same time as being distinct from persons as such, in the same way that the human immunodeficiency virus (HIV) may sensibly be separated from the actual person whom it infects. The mind is reduced to being identical with the brain which, as a bodily organ like any other, may become 'diseased'. In all pamphlets, the terms 'mental illness' and 'disorder' were used exclusively to describe personal experiences; 'symptoms' of each 'illness' were listed and, in many pamphlets, the notion of 'mental illness' was conflated with accepted medical disorders via spurious analogy.

Extract 1 shows the reduction of ('mysterious') human distress to the dysfunction of a materialised mind. It is suggested that the mind and the heart are parts of the same category of things; they are both pathology-prone bodily organs. In Extract 2, the way in which the putative illness of the mind is to be understood as separable from personhood is shown: people can be disturbed by 'having mental illness' in the same way as they might be 'disturbed' by their diabetes or 'frightened' by having cancer. Similarly Extract 3 works to disconfirm any moral account of misery, and to replace such understandings with the simple assertion that unhappiness is 'illness'.

Extract 1: (from ARAFMI, *Taking the Mystery out of Mental Illness*)
> Mental illness is a disorder of the functioning of the mind. It is a general term which refers to a group of illnesses in the same way that heart disease refers to a group of illnesses which affect the functioning of the heart.

Extract 2: (from National Mental Health Strategy, *Mental Illness: The Facts*)
People who have mental illness often suffer a great deal. They can be disturbed and frightened by their illness.

Extract 3: (from Royal College of Psychiatrists, *Depression*)
Other people may think they have 'given in', but depression of this degree is an illness and needs treatment.

In these extracts, the mind, like the heart perhaps, can malfunction. Unwanted, discreditable or 'abnormal' behaviour is accounted for by underlying and unobservable quasi-bodily malfunctions and deterioration. Such malfunctioning is given a 'natural' status by virtue of its supposed comparators: real coronary diseases and other 'illnesses'. The 'just as' technique effectively disguises the fact that mind is an abstract and not a physical concept. As Ryle (1949) would have it, this conflation is a category mistake. And as both Szasz (1961) and Coulter (1979) have argued, 'diseases' of the mind have a similarly abstract conceptual status — they cannot be on the same footing as physical diseases with actual lesions. By representing mental illness as some 'thing' one can have, be disturbed and frightened by, the mind (and hence mental dis-ease) is given a completely fictive bodily location. As we will see, this location is frequently implied to be the brain — especially where there is mention of 'neurotransmitters'. But, at the same time, such accounts can also *deny* that 'mental illness' is a form of gross physiological disfiguration such as 'brain damage':

Extract 4: (from National Mental Health Strategy, *Mental Ill ness: The Facts*)
Are mental illnesses a form of intellectual disability or brain damage? No. They are illnesses just like any other: heart disease, diabetes, asthma. Yet thetraditions of flowers, sympathy and support provided to people with a physical illness are often denied to those with a mental illness.

We wonder then: where is this physical thing (like the heart, the blood, the lungs) that is 'the mind', when it is not exactly equivalent to that recently obvious candidate, the brain? (As we will see, the brain will make its return very shortly — it is extremely hard to dispose of so lightly.)

In the SANE pamphlet called *Something is Not Quite Right*, mental illness is described as a condition that someone may not *know* they have — for all that we have seen that sufferers are prone to being 'disturbed and frightened' by it (Extract 2). To assist those 'close' to candidate patients to identify their need to be 'encouraged to see a doctor', this pamphlet lists problematic activities. Such persons, we are told, may 'spend extravagant sums of money', or may 'deteriorate in performance at school or work', or have a tendency to 'leave jobs', as well as 'being extremely preoccupied with a particular theme'. Such actions require relatives or friends to 'seek a medical assessment as soon as possible'. Clearly then, these forms of conduct point towards a root cause (a mental illness) that only those trained in medicine can safely pronounce upon. Should this not produce a helpful outcome, the pamphlet cements the medical nature of the matter by advising that: 'if the doctor does not seem to understand, look for another who does'.

Having portrayed mental illness as a medically knowable and observable entity (rather than as, for example, a specific interpretation of unacceptable moral behaviour) through its similarity to actual illnesses (diabetes, asthma, heart disease, cancer, and so on) and through the description of its 'symptoms', the pamphlets then set about elaborating its corporeal location. And, despite the earlier-cited (and quite rare) disclaimer about 'brain damage' (Extract 4), the brain is, of course, the main suspect.

Here, particular *brain*-site malfunctions are assigned to specific *mental* disorders according to the psychiatric process described by Rose et al. (1984) as 'spurious localisation': the respecification of a malfunctioning of the mind as the malfunctioning of a particular neurophysiological element. In the case of 'schizophrenia', a specific neurotransmitter called 'dopamine' is cited. For other 'illnesses', the vague but impressive sounding term 'chemical imbalance' suffices.

> Extract 5: (from Health Department of WA, *Ymag*)
> The problem in schizophrenia is to do with the chemical substance 'dopamine' produced by the brain to carry messages between various parts of the brain.

> Extract 6: (from National Mental Health Strategy, *What is Schizophrenia?*)[2]
> Certain biochemical substances in the brain are believed to be involved in this condition, especially a neurotransmitter called dopamine. One likely cause of this chemical imbalance is the person's genetic predisposition to the illness.

2. The 2000 pamphlet *Understanding Mental Illness: Schizophrenia* distributed by SANE Australia (which describes itself as 'A national charity helping people seriously affected by mental illness') records on the back page not only that the troubled young man on the cover is none other than 'Alex O'Han, the actor who played Joey, a character in *Home and Away* who developed schizophrenia', but also that the 'development of this pamphlet was proudly supported by ...

Extract 7: (from Health Department of WA, *Ymag*)
> Bipolar disorder is to do with an imbalance of chemi-
> cal substances in the brain — We don't yet know ex-
> actly what causes the illness — It's not clear how the
> illness is passed on.

In these extracts, the failure of the psy-disciplines to reliably identify
any putative underlying processes for any diagnostic group (Boyle,
1999) is glossed over. The use of carefully vague constructions (Potter,
1996) such as 'is to do with ...' and 'are believed to be involved in ...'
specify next to nothing while conveying the impression that these
matters are scientifically known. For example, in Extract 7, the statement 'we don't yet know exactly what causes the illness' does not
construct the central problem of 'bipolar disorder' as one of frank
ignorance and a vaguely specified belief in unnamed 'chemical substances'. Rather, through an unmitigated admission of failure ('We
don't yet know exactly what causes the illness'), it appears as an
unfortunate but merely temporary inexactitude about methods of
transmission ('It's not clear how the illness is passed on').

In Extract 8, we see a similar concession to uncertainty about
proximate 'cause', but bookended by explicit — and quite unambiguous — claims to sole biomedical jurisdiction over the 'illness'.
Here 'the condition' is described via what Mary Smyth (2001) has
described as a prototypical 'scientific fact statement'.

Extract 8: (from SANE's *Understanding Mental Illness: Bipolar
Disorder*)[3]
> Bipolar disorder (formerly called manic depressive
> illness) is a medical condition. During episodes of ill-
> ness the person experiences mood swings which in-
> terfere with their ability to function day-to-day .... As
> with many other illnesses, there is likely to be a com-
> bination of hereditary and other causes, but a genetic
> pre-disposition to develop bipolar disorder has been
> clearly established.

... Eli Lilly Australia'. The other key voluntary sector player, the Mental Illness
Fellowship of Australia (formerly the Schizophrenia Fellowship) notes on its
web homepage that 'this site is proudly sponsored by Janssen-Cilag'. Of course,
Lilly and Janssen-Cilag are major drug companies.
3. This leaflet announces on the back page that it is 'proudly supported by
Novartis Australia Pty Ltd'. The front cover, we are told, features 'Actor Odette
Ioannidis, who played the part of a member of a family affected by mental
illness in a theatre production as part of SANE Australia's Community Education Program' (SANE, 2000). SANE also distribute a series of booklets under the
title The SANE Guide ('to treatments', 'for consumers', 'for carers') as part of
this 'education program'. The full list of sponsors on the final page cites spon-
sorship from Pfizer, Lilly, CNS, Janssen-Cilag, Novartis and Lundbeck.

This disarming display then works to rhetorically *strengthen* the bio-medical case, not least by virtue of the *absence* of any attempt to explain the biological certainties concerning the 'disorder'. The fact of a continuing *search* (for chemicals, causes and vectors) alongside a confident and aggressive assertion of ownership can appear sufficiently scientific in its own right. That the literature on putative biological causes of distress may be characterised as conflictual and inconsistent (as may be read into the acknowledgment that there may be a 'combination of causes'), even where it is not hopelessly conceptually incoherent (Marshall, 1988), is not a view which any of the pamphlets could explicitly entertain, given their predominant role in consumer politics.

In a similar manner, and without exception, the pamphlets we collected promote what has been called the 'magic bullet' representation of psychiatric treatment (Rose et al., 1984). Although the Royal College of Psychiatrists' depression leaflet acknowledges that so-called talking treatment 'may be helpful', throughout the sample, drug treatments are (mis)represented as 'magic bullets' travelling straight to the site of malfunction, in a unitary way, with highly specific effect, and with no substantial side effects deserving of serious consideration. For example:

Extract 9: (from National Mental Health Strategy, *What is Depression?*)
Depressive episodes are thought to be due to a chemical imbalance in the brain. This can be corrected with anti-depressant medication. They slowly return the balance of neurotransmitters in the brain, taking 1-4 weeks to achieve their positive effects.

Extract 10: (from Royal College of Psychiatrists, *Depression*)
Like all medicines, antidepressants do have some side effects, though these are usually mild and tend to wear off as the treatment goes on.

In Extract 9 we see once again the simultaneous deployment of dubious assertion ('depressive episodes are *thought to be* due to a chemical imbalance') with unambiguously 'factual' claims about the magical properties of antidepressant medication ('this *can be* corrected...'). Powerful neuroleptic drugs ('like all medicines' according to the Royal College of Psychiatrists in Extract 10) are simply presented as doing nothing more dramatic than 'correcting' a supposed ('thought to be') chemical imbalance in the brain with only 'mild' side effects, though none of us has ever come across a 'mild' case of suicide (Healy, 2001). This is another instance of careful oversimplification: the brain-chemicals to be corrected remain vague (unspecified neurotransmitters) and no suggestion is made about what may have led to a deficiency (or

would that be overproduction?) of the (unnamed) chemical supposedly producing the unusual experience. Once again, the imprecision
of the formulation of the problem is overwhelmed by the certainty
pertaining to the methods of 'treatment'. The specific time frame (1-4
weeks) offered for the 'positive effects' of antidepressant medication
suggests rather more definite knowledge of the processes involved in
the 'correction' than might be warranted by the mere 'thought' that an
imbalance is the 'cause' of depressive episodes.

The 'magic bullet' representation of drug treatment is particularly apparent in the following example which purports to explain
the pharmacotherapy of 'bipolar mood disorder'.

> Extract 11: (from National Mental Health Strategy, *What is
> Bipolar Mood Disorder?*)
> For the depressive phase of this illness, antidepres-
> sant medications are effective …. They slowly return
> the balance of neurotransmitters in the brain. During
> acute or severe attacks of mania, several different medi-
> cations are used. Some are specifically used to calm
> the person's manic excitement: others are used to help
> stabilise the person's mood. Medications such as
> lithium are also used as preventative measures, as
> they help to control mood swings and reduce the
> frequency and severity of depressive and manic phases.

The description of the use of a variety of drugs (antidepressants and
lithium) to treat the differentiable phases of the 'illness' works up a
version of pharmacotherapy as a tightly controlled, event-specific practice which, again, is targeted not at persons as such, but rather at the
conditions of being in the world which are afflicting them. Hence such
constructions as: 'some are specifically used to calm the person's manic
excitement'. This version of drug treatment makes psychotropic medication appear less like a magic bullet and more like a series of smart
bombs. The mention of lithium as a 'preventative measure' furthers
the impression of the scientific expertise deployed in understanding
the supposed disease process and reinforces representations of psychological distress as a menagerie of distinct entities which can be
localised and specifically targeted.

These tactics reach something of a crescendo in *Understanding
Panic Disorder: What You Need to Know*, a pamphlet distributed by
Pfizer. The cover of the pamphlet has a lower border of sunflowers,
presumably there as a cheery image to offset the oval photograph of
a blurry street scene (this is what a panic attack looks like?) which
dominates the front page.[4] The Pfizer pamphlet is an intriguing in-

---

4. Sunflowers are a recurring theme in drug company merchandising. A 'fun'
pack of jelly beans, given to delegates at a recent GPs conference in Sydney, …

stance as it begins with an entirely cognitive (that is, non-biological) account of the 'disorder' that its drugs are supposed to treat. It explains that panic attacks can be 'triggered' by 'ordinary life events and situations ... or triggered by anticipating such events or situations. In other words panic attacks can be triggered by fearful thoughts'. But then the reader is immediately told (via some careful work on the notion of causality) that 'what you need to know' is, again, that it is really brain chemistry that is the problem.

> Extract 12: (from Pfizer, *Understanding Panic Disorder: What You Need to Know*)
>
> The underlying causes of PD or Panic Disorder are not yet known. The triggers discussed above are not the cause. They are simply the triggers. There may be multiple causes. Individuals with a family history of PD are more likely to develop this condition. Influences during growing up may contribute to developing PD. New evidence suggests that chemical imbalances in the brain are important causes of PD. Neurotransmitters are chemicals in the brain that pass on the message from one nerve cell to the next. Malfunction of this process may contribute to PD. Serotonin is an important neurotransmitter in the brain ....
>
> PD can be successfully treated.
>
> Treatment is generally through medications or psychological techniques .... Drug therapy can help reduce the frequency and severity of panic attacks. It also seems to enhance the effect of the psychological approaches. Drugs prescribed for PD are often Selective Serotonin Re-uptake Inhibitors (SSRIs) like Zoloft .... Selective Serotonin Re-uptake Inhibitors (SSRIs) are effective in treating panic disorder. They restore serotonin levels at the synapses (the spaces where nerve cells connect in various parts of the brain). This effectively reduces the number of panic attacks.

Here we see Pfizer — whose sales of Zoloft amount to $64 million a year in Australia alone (Kerin and Hickman, 2002) — carefully frame their 'patient education' leaflet in terms entirely favourable to a biologised understanding of panic. Thus, while ignorance about the 'causes' of panic attacks is conceded, it is conceded in terms of the

---

... featured bright sunflowers on a blue ground, with 'Zoloft' in large letters. In another edition of the Panic Disorder pamphlet, a 'happy family' (Mum, Dad and two kids) are pictured smiling from the front cover. They too are bordered by sunflowers.

temporary (and remediable) nature of expert knowledge — 'the underlying causes of PD or Panic Disorder are not *yet* known' (our emphasis). Scientific certainty about these matters is implied by the
immediately following 'factual statements' that: 'the triggers discussed
above are not the cause. They are simply the triggers', and the recourse to implications of heredity: the claim that 'individuals with a
family history of PD are more likely to develop this condition'. Note
that the pamphlet very specifically does not say 'individuals with a
family history of panic attacks are more likely to have panic attacks'.
Routinely these pamphlets use terms like 'condition' or abbrevia-
tions like 'PD' to do the work of cementing the idea that there is a
'credible and concrete disease' (Moynihan et al., 2002: 887). In this
instance, reference to the 'disease' called Panic Disorder produces
actual panic attacks as the mere expression of an *underlying* 'condition' (just like the delirium of CJD, the uncoordination of MS, or the
opportunistic infections of HIV) which is possibly genetic. Panic attacks are not then to be understood as a series of frightening experiences in response to social or situational 'triggers'. Such situational
circumstances (being unamenable to medication) are then brushed
off as epiphenomena, of no more significance to the 'condition' than
is the pollen that 'triggers' a sneeze.

Having thus dispensed with ordinary common sense, we see the
deployment of the 'new evidence' device to smooth the way for the
'chemical imbalance' story. Pfizer offers the reader two factual statements, and two completely speculative ones. Needless to say, the
two unarguable facts from biochemistry for beginners are in place
precisely to shore up the unsupported claims which are entwined
with them. Thus: 'neurotransmitters are chemicals in the brain that
pass on the message from one nerve cell to the next' and 'Serotonin
is an important neurotransmitter in the brain' are completely
uncontentious claims. The other two claims (subtly marked as they
are for uncertainty) simply slipstream behind. Thus the statements
that: 'new evidence *suggests* that chemical imbalances in the brain
are important causes of PD' and 'malfunction of this process *may*
contribute to PD' are simply marketing gambits that depend upon
the truth of the *other* claims for a degree of vicarious credibility. 'Suggestions' may be misleading (some people suggest that UFOs abduct
them), and malfunction of synaptic processes may *not* contribute to
panic attacks. We note that here, as in all the pamphlets studied, the
routine claims to scientific 'evidence' are never backed by reference
to actual clinical studies. Where reference is made — and it is extremely rare — the Diagnostic and Statistical Manual of Mental Disorders (4th edition) suffices as authoritative source.

Understanding Panic Disorder then brightly reassures the afflicted.
Having a panic attack is not an event, it is a 'symptom' of an under-
lying *thing* and, just like measles, 'PD can be successfully treated'.
We are told that 'treatment is generally through medications or psy-

chological techniques .... Drug therapy can help reduce the frequency and severity of panic attacks'. Yet, how (the second placed) 'psychological techniques' are supposed to correct putative genetic defects or overcome the 'malfunctioning' of synaptic transmission is not hinted at; presumably we await 'new evidence' on this front. Neither, it should be noted, is there a glimmer of an account of how substances like Zoloft, by 'restor[ing] serotonin levels at the synapses ... effectively reduce the number of panic attacks'. Instead of this (which one might reasonably expect of any users' manual for a consumer product), we see that the judicious use of 'technical' detail (synapses are 'the spaces where nerve cells connect') gives a spurious impression of professional mastery of the intricacies of neurochemistry and, hence, one is presumably to believe, of the phenomenology of terror.

The romanticisation of drug treatment is further bolstered in the pamphlets, not only in terms of their 'magic bullet' or 'smart bomb' effects, but also in terms of their pivotal involvement in keeping sufferers out of (mental) health institutions. Extract 13 offers a typical example of the general and historically inaccurate acclaim accorded by the pamphlets to 'anti-psychotic' chemicals.

> Extract 13: (from National Mental Health Strategy, *What is Schizophrenia?*)
> The development of anti-psychosis medications has revolutionised the treatment of schizophrenia. Now, most people can leave hospital and live in the community. These medications work by correcting the chemical imbalance associated with the illness. New but well tested medications are emerging which promote a much more complete recovery with fewer side effects.

Just as ECT (or, in the US, 'electro-shock') information pamphlets routinely downplay the hazards and side effects of the procedure (Arscott, 1999), so too the romanticisation of 'antipsychotics' in these pamphlets fails to acknowledge the well-documented, destructive and potentially lethal side effects these drugs can have (Breggin, 1990; 1996; 2002; Healy, 2000a; 2001). While in Extract 13 it is acknowledged, almost as an afterthought, that there may be some (unspecified) medication side effects, the emphasis works in reverse by being placed on the supposed fact that the 'new' medications are 'well tested' and that they offer 'a much more complete recovery' (than what?).

The unproblematic endorsement of antipsychotics is furthered a little later in the same pamphlet. In Extract 14, the naturalisation of schizophrenia as a physical illness is accompanied by an entirely spurious parallel between 'anti-psychosis medications' and insulin.

Extract 14: (from National Mental Health Strategy, *What is Schizophrenia?*)
Schizophrenia is an illness, like many physical illnesses. For example, just as insulin is a lifeline for a person with diabetes, anti-psychosis medications are a lifeline for a person with schizophrenia. As with diabetes, some people will need to take medication indefinitely to prevent a relapse and keep symptoms under control.

And in SANE's pamphlet, *Something is Not Quite Right*, the romanticisation of pharmacology reaches its peak (or perhaps its nadir). Here the only hazardous drug consumption that relatives and friends are told to monitor is of alcohol and marijuana. By contrast, the sole mention of psychiatric drugs makes them appear benign: 'if the illness is picked up early enough there is a good chance of controlling the symptoms with low doses of medication and without going to hospital'. In only four pamphlets (*What is Schizophrenia?*, *Depression: What You Should Know, Depression* and *Understanding Panic Disorder: What You Need to Know*) were the side effects of psychiatric drugs specifically mentioned as problematic. For *What is Schizophrenia?* the problems identified with medication were not — as might have been expected from a 'factual' consumer information publication — tardive dyskinesia, tardive akathisia or neuroleptic malignant syndrome, but rather the difficulty of getting people to continue taking their medication. In its section on 'Symptoms', the pamphlet assures its readers that because of schizophrenics' 'lack of insight ... and other reasons, such as medication side effects, they may refuse to accept treatment which could be essential for their well-being'.

Understanding Panic Disorder: What You Need to Know assures its readers that the side effects of SSRIs 'may include one or other of the following: nausea, sleeplessness, drowsiness or nervousness'. Lundbeck's *soi-disant* 'medical information booklet' *Depression: What You Should Know*, having noted that 'antidepressant drugs do not act immediately, in the way that, for example, antibiotics do' (another neat example of spurious analogy), and having stressed that 'you will have to continue taking your medication for 4-6 months, or possibly longer, to ensure your recovery is complete', states that: 'antidepressant drugs can, however, produce a range of side effects, including dry mouth, blurred vision and altered bowel function'. No mention is made in either pamphlet of possibly fatal interaction effects with everyday foods, let alone disorientation, manic reactions, agitation or suicide (Breggin, 1996; Healy, 2000a; 2001), despite the fact that SSRIs are listed along with the MAOIs and the Tricyclic antidepresssants. What is, however, stressed is that 'the most important thing you can do is to remember to take your medication regularly'. *Depression: What You Should Know* is unusual in coming close to letting the immaterial cat out of the biological bag, when it is noted that: 'there are no physical measurements, such as temperature or blood pressure, which give the doctor clues about your symptoms of depression'. Nevertheless, this concession is only made in the context of an exhortation to the 'patient' to ensure that they are 'honest' with their doctor in order to allow the prescription of the 'most effective treatment'. Honesty is also in short supply in the Royal College of Psychiatrists' *Depression*. In a discussion of ECT the leaflet offers reassurances to the reader.

> Extract 15: (from Royal College of Psychiatrists, *Depression)*
>   Most people don't like the idea of ECT. However, it is a
>   very effective treatment for very severe depression when
>   other treatments haven't helped, and works more
>   quickly than tablets.
>   [...]
>   Afterwards people sometimes have a headache or a
>   short period of feeling muddled, but these usually pass
>   off quickly. There is absolutely no evidence that
>   properly-given ECT harms the brain in any way.

Quite aside from the fact that this account flies in the face of both recipient reports (see MIND's 2002 report *Shock Treatment)* and the available empirical data (Arscott, 1999; Breggin, 1996), it also conjures the bizarre image of *im*properly-given ECT. What might that be?

We have here, then, some clear instances of what critical and discursive psychologists have called 'ontological gerrymandering' (Potter, 1996): effectively 'rigging', via rhetorical strategies, the highly problematic and notoriously slippery notion of what constitutes how things (factually) *are*, so that a single and particularised version is the only one that can be accorded the status of 'normality'. The various behaviours seen as the direct effects of internal bodily properties are represented in a binary opposition: with one side attributed significant social value over the other. Lines between normal and abnormal, adaptive and maladaptive, healthy and unhealthy are strictly drawn through classification and diagnosis. Symptom lists often include reactions described as 'out of proportion' or 'extreme', denoting a quantifiable difference between these and normal reactions. The pamphlets are rarely inclined to present behaviour on a continuum and, instead, are predicated on behavioural categories which serve to distance the 'mentally ill', drawing a sharp and divisive line between 'us' and 'them' (Schacht, 1985), whilst at the same time leaving open the possibility of both permeability and professionally mediated restoration — the possibility that 'mental illness' can strike anyone, at anytime, but that with expert professional help (and large doses of chemicals) the afflicted can be restored to 'normality'. Hence, the National Mental Health Strategy's *What is Depression?* pamphlet tells us that: 'Modern treatments for depression can help the person return to more normal feelings and to enjoy life'.

However, as with the DSM-IV itself, in these so-called 'factual' publications imprecision surrounds the criteria for each disorder. For example SANE's schizophrenia pamphlet offers no guidance on just how 'preoccupied' with a particular theme one has to be to qualify as 'diseased'. The RCP's depression leaflet specifies 'feeling utterly tired' as a key diagnostic 'symptom', but leaves the reader to decide just how tired one has to be to be 'utterly' tired. Further, placing individuals on one side of a binary is often based on some assumed internal identity, rather than on explicitly discriminable overt behaviours. This imprecision is structured in the pamphlets so as to convey to the reader that *only* the diagnosing professions are able, unequivocally, to define the disorders in question, and that the abounding confusion requires the further attention of those professions. So let's now look at how professionals are characterised in the pamphlets.

We can begin by noting how the pamphlets place the 'sufferer' in a position of almost childlike dependence on the psy-professional (Szasz, 1994). As we have just seen, Lundbeck's pamphlet *Depression* is explicit in producing the depressed 'patient' as having no more responsibility than to be a good girl, tell doctor the 'truth' and to swallow the pills. *Understanding Panic Disorder* is equally explicit about the role of the 'patient'. In extracts 16 and 17, the advice to patients and those who care for them is clear.

> Extract 16: (from Pfizer, *Understanding Panic Disorder: What You Need to Know*)
> Guidelines for patients to help themselves:
> Realise that you have a treatable condition and seek effective help.
> Accept the help you are offered, take the medications you are prescribed once you are satisfied that you have the right advice, practice the psychological treatments you are taught ….
> What can a person do to help someone with PD?
> Realise they have a medical condition.
> Encourage the sufferer to seek and accept good professional advice.

> Extract 17: (from Royal College of Psychiatrists, *Depression*)
> Relatives and friends
> Try to help the person to accept the treatment, and don't say 'I wouldn't take the tablets if I were you' or 'You don't want to go to a psychiatrist — you're not mad!' If you have doubts about the treatment, discuss them first with the doctor.

The sufferer's role, then, is to believe what they are told by doctors, to take the medication and, in general, to be compliant with 'good professional advice'. In case the patient fails to understand that medicine offers both the 'right advice' and helpful tablets, it is *medical* advice that those near and dear to the patient are instructed to seek and to reinforce. The role of the patient is emphatically not to have a mind of their own, nor to believe that any efforts of their own are likely to be helpful. Thus, in the following extract, we are reminded of the complaints of Peter Byrne (2000) and Rita Baron-Faust (2000) — discussed earlier — about the way popular film overrates will-power (auto-correction) as a treatment by comparison with medical intervention (alio-correction):

> Extract 18: (from ARAFMI, *Taking the Mystery out of Mental Illness*)
> Unfortunately, just as using your will-power alone won't cure your broken leg or diabetes, will-power alone won't cure mental illness.

To bolster this essentiality of professional intervention and help, certain conditions are actually characterised as involving (having as one of the condition's own 'symptoms') the sufferer's lack of awareness of the condition itself. Indeed this is implicit in Pfizer's advice to 'sufferers' from a condition not usually described as being characterised by lack of 'insight'. Recall that people with 'PD' are told that they 'need' to 'realise that you have a treatable condition'. In such a logically paradoxical situation, it is frequently *only* through another's intervention that the condition can be recognised:

> Extract 19: (from National Mental Health Strategy, *What is Schizophrenia?*)
> Symptoms of Schizophrenia:
> Loss of drive — where often the ability to engage in everyday activities such as washing and cooking is lost. This lack of drive, initiative or motivation is part of the illness and is not laziness.
> Lack of insight or awareness of other conditions — because some experiences such as delusions and hallucinations are so real, it is common for people with schizophrenia to be unaware they are ill. For this and other reasons, such as medication side effects, they may refuse to accept treatment which could be essential for their well-being.

> Extract 20: (from Royal College of Psychiatrists, *Depression*)
> We may not realise how depressed we are if the depression has come on slowly, or if we blame our

selves for being lazy or feeble. Other people may have
to point this out to us and some of us need persuading
that seeking help is not a sign of weakness.

As we have seen, these information pamphlets define 'mental illness'
almost exclusively as an inevitable consequence of some biological
malfunction; likewise, 'cures' are represented as beyond the
individual's control. In all pamphlets, autonomous personhood is
stripped from the diagnosed individual: they are characterised as
being unlikely to understand or accept their 'condition' spontane-
ously, so that the 'only' effective means of dealing with it is external
intervention. And the assumption of a fundamental biological cause
would mean that, even if they did understand or accept their 'illness', sufferers would be unable to make any change in themselves
because they are, by expert definition, insufficiently equipped. Hence:

Extract 21: (from National Mental Health Strategy, *What is*
    Schizophrenia?)
    Regular contact with a doctor or psychiatrist and
    possibly a multidisciplinary team of mental health
    nurses, social workers, occupational therapists and
    psychologists can help a person with schizophrenia
    organise and do the important things in life.

Note that the framing of this statement strongly suggests that what
is important in life is to be decided by those same practitioners, rather
than by the person actually living their life. Or at least: the pamphlet
positions its own discourse such that *that* discourse alone is
authorised to decide what constitute 'the important things in life'.
Control and regulation are framed as benevolence.

    Clearly, the rhetorical point of these pamphlets is that they should
be read as benevolent on all fronts. Their titles convey that we, the
experts, are telling you what you, the consumer, *need* to know, what
you *should* know, for your own good. Their very existence and broad
circulation suggests that they are designed for public persuasion on
two fronts: firstly, and self-consciously, as *marketing exercises* by
pharmaceutical companies, the supposedly voluntary sector
organisations they fund (such as SANE) and collaborating institutional mental health agencies. The drug companies are, clearly, eager to persuade both the public and psy-practitioners of the 'real'
existence of both widely-believed-in 'disorders' as well as invented
diseases such as 'social phobia' or 'social anxiety disorder' (Double,
2002; Healy, 2002b; Moynihan et al., 2002; Moynihan, 1998; Payer,
1992); of the irreducibly biological nature of their 'cause' and of the
desirability of proprietary pharmaceutical solutions. Indeed the essential role of such 'educational' publications as these pamphlets is
clearly acknowledged by the psychopharmaceutical complex itself.

Thus, in the case of 'social phobia' the trade press journal *Pharma-ceutical Marketing,* in its article 'Practical Guide to Medical Educa-tion', noted that Roche's promotion of social phobia was an exem-plary instance of conjoint disorder/drug marketing. In describing how marketers may, practically, 'educate' doctors Cook (2001) wrote:

> You may even need to reinforce the actual existence of a dis-ease and/or the value of treating it. A classic example of this was the need to create recognition in Europe of social phobia as a distinct clinical entity and the potential of antidepressant agents such as moclobemide to treat it .... Social phobia was recognized in the US and so transatlantic opinion leaders were mobilized to participate in advisory activities, meetings, publi-cations, etc. to help influence the overall belief in Europe. (Cited in Moynihan et al., 2002: 888)

Similarly, Moynihan et al. describe the mounting of the parallel cam-paign in Australia:

> When Roche was promoting its antidepressant Aurorix (moclobemide) as a valuable treatment for social phobia in 1997, its public relations company issued a press release, picked up by some of the media, announcing that more than one million Australians had an underdiagnosed psychiatric disorder called social phobia. The release described a 'soul-destroying condi-tion' and quoted a clinical psychologist strongly endorsing the role of antidepressants in its treatment. At that time govern-ment figures suggested the number of people with the disorder might be closer to 370,000. In 1998 a newspaper article, 'Too shy for words' — this time not orchestrated by Roche — sug-gested that two million Australians were affected by the condi-tion. All the media stories seemed to be part of a wider push to change the common perception of shyness, from a personal difficulty to a psychiatric disorder. An important aspect of Roche's marketing for moclobemide involved working with a patient group called the Obsessive Compulsive and Anxiety Disorders Foundation of Victoria .... According to the Foundation's chief at the time, 'Roche is putting a lot of money into promoting social phobia .... Roche funded the conference to help get social phobia known among [general practitioners] and other health professionals .... It was a vehicle to raise aware-ness with the media too'. (Moynihan et al., 2002: 888)[5]

---

5. If we accept these figures, a full 5% of the Australian population has this particular 'psychiatric disorder'. However, as the Roche Australia MD recently noted, there is some latitude in the numbers. As Ray Moynihan has it: 'Using the example of his company's promotion of "social phobia", Fred Nadjarian, ...

'Promoting' invented psychiatric disorders — and underpinning the claimed biological causes of already 'accepted' psychiatric disorders such as 'schizophrenia' or 'depression' — then, is one, entirely self-conscious, purpose for 'patient education' pamphlets (aided and abetted, as we have seen, by practitioners keen to enjoy the benefits accruing) (Healy, 2000b; 2002a; 2002b). Indeed, Healy points out that 'antidepressants and depression were almost unknown outside of mainstream psychiatry 20 years [ago] but we [are] now apparently in an Age of Depression …. The antidepressant market has in fact grown 800% by value in the 1990s and by 2000 had become a $10 billion market' (2002b).

Secondly (and this is by no means an entirely distinct project), these publications (especially when they include whimsical Calman cartoons) can be read as attempting to make the 'mentally ill' appear less frightening and mysterious to a general population that may be (or, at least, this is the assumption) used to associating them with danger and aggression. The naturalisation of personal and social problems *as* biologically caused 'mental illnesses', as essentially a part and parcel of human experience like heart problems, diabetes and the flu, and widely advertising proprietary solutions to these complaints clearly serve to lower the threshold for self-referral and self-medication when times get tough. The immensely effective, and entirely unhelpful, effects of direct to consumer (DTC) advertising of pills to the public are well documented (Mintzes, 2002). Among other items, Mintzes notes the marketing savvy of GlaxoSmithKline, who seized the opportunity of the 11 September WTC attacks to run an ad reminding readers of the *New York Times Magazine* that Paxil® could help 'millions' with their anxiety.

From what we have just seen, what is proclaimed to be myth- and stereotype-debunking is, then, another of the main rhetorical purposes of these texts:

Extract 22: (from National Mental Health Strategy, *What is Schizophrenia?*)
> Myths, misunderstandings and facts. People with schizophrenia are generally not dangerous when receiving appropriate treatment. However, a minority of people with the illness become aggressive when experiencing an untreated acute episode, because of their fears. This is usually expressed to family and friends, rarely to strangers.

… managing director of Roche in Australia, said: "The marketing people always beat [hype] these things up. It's just natural enthusiasm" …. He argues that his experience with that one condition highlights a much wider problem: "If you added up all the statistics, we all must have about 20 diseases. A lot of these things are blown out of all proportion" …. Mr Nadjarian said: "Behind every statistic there is a vested interest … there's a natural human tendency to exaggerate'" (Moynihan, 2002: 867).

Such myth-debunking may be the product of the best of intentions. But it carries with it what may be unforeseen consequences. In Extract 22, for example, professional 'treatment' figures in the narrative as the only barrier standing between the dangerously ill minority and the safely ill majority. This suggests to the supposedly unenlightened reader (the one in need of having their 'myths' and 'misunderstandings' debunked by 'facts') a quite precarious situation: a thin veil of chemicals stands between themselves and dangerously psychotic axe-wielding madmen. This 'treatment' would, indeed, have to be of heroic proportions to carry out such a task! However, that task is then somewhat lessened by the identification of the targets of the aggression in question: family and friends. Much comfort, then, for the general (supposedly uninformed) public who are, by definition, 'strangers' to schizophrenics and schizophrenia. Less so for family and friends who may, we reasonably suppose, also have an interest in reading these publicly available and (in many cases) publicly financed leaflets. All the more, then, for them to come to appreciate and support the heroic work that 'treatment' can do on their behalf. For 'family and friends', the choice is bleak but clear: they can either risk being victims of (routine stereotypical) schizophrenic aggression, or (as encouraged by these pamphlets) recruit themselves into treatment's first line of defence. So the 'myths' and 'misinformation' are debunked, displaced with 'facts', no doubt about it. The question is whether or not these 'facts', intendedly or otherwise, are merely parts of another myth: the myth of the psy-professional as public hero.

The pamphlets use a number of such devices to claim a professional jurisdiction for themselves. The psy-disciplines are promoted as services to be used, with every brochure in our collection recommending a visit to a professional for, at least, further information. Additionally, the pamphlets include routine references to the psy-experts' 'scientific' status and condone their claiming of the domain as part their store of knowledge. As noted earlier, 'mental illness' is presented specifically as an object of knowledge, and the psy-experts figure in these texts as the *only* source of knowledge governing that object. For example, the pamphlets routinely advert to and promote specialist or 'insider' terminology:

Extract 23: (from National Mental Health Strategy, *What is Bipolar Mood Disorder?*)
    Bipolar mood disorder is the new name for what was called manic depressive illness. The new name is used as it better describes the extreme mood swings from depression and sadness to elation and excitement that people with this illness experience.

Extract 24: (from National Mental Health Strategy, *What is Depression?*)

> For some severe forms of depression, electroconvulsive therapy (ECT), or shock treatment as it is some times misnamed, is a safe and effective treatment. It may be life saving for people at high risk of suicide or who, because of the severity of their illness, have stopped eating and drinking and will die as a result.

Why are 'manic-depression' and 'shock-treatment' less than adequate names for what they are applied to? Is it just possible that they have, by now, come so much into common usage, thereby decreasing the distance between lay and expert claims to knowledge? Could it be that the new 'expert' nomenclature is simply deployed here to lend legitimacy to the publications, or to suggest that a new name implies a greater and more valid understanding of how, for example, the administration of electrical currents to a person's brain alleviates suffering?

Techniques of this kind — claiming that the refinement of disorder names somehow makes them more representative of their referent — attest to the apparent progressive scientificity of the psy-disciplines. Nature is said to be — appears to be — described objectively and directly, beyond the distortion, the emotion or bias that apparently bedevil terms such as 'shock-therapy'. This conscious alignment with science and its methods is an explicitly self-conscious attempt to secure a professional jurisdiction, an exercise in discrediting alternative voices, and designed to distinguish so-called scientific psychopathology from the everyday assistance that other possible 'mental health' service providers — such as ordinary people — could offer (Double, 2002; John, 1998). The construction of psychological distress as 'illness', with identifiable 'symptoms', allows psychiatry to claim illicit 'scientific legitimacy' and bogus 'professionalism', simply because of the artificial link it provides to medicine (Kutchins and Kirk, 1999).

We began with various cases of psy-expertise pronouncing critically on the popular media — especially cinema, TV and the press — and their portrayals of 'madness'. Against such supposedly spurious and merely commonsensical accounts and images, the psy-professionals made out their various cases for a more 'scientific' approach to mental illnesses, as specifically bio-locatable diseases and, accordingly, for an end to such negative depictions of the afflicted. There, little concession was made to developments in media analysis, discourse analysis and semiotics which argue for media discourses to be seen as just that: specific sorts of knowledge in their own right which viewers and readers — including children — readily acknowledge as such and recognise as distinct from everyday reality since they are 'active and powerful decoders' of media content (Hodge and

Tripp, 1986: 213). The 'expert' psychological accounts of the media and its misrepresentations appear to be effectively bogged in a now-discredited 'effects' model of media viewership/readership: a model which simply assumes that, for example, all audiences are vulnerable and will (mis)take screen images as models of correct, real and proper conduct (Nightingale, 1997).

Or perhaps these experts merely reapply the infantilisation of their own clientele across the board, so that cinema-goers, TV audiences, newspaper readers and pamphlet recipients are viewed as cultural dopes. Of course, producing people as cultural dopes is made that much easier by using the sorts of tactics we have examined here, and which Lynne Payer, Ray Moynihan and David Healy have documented on a broader canvas. In an online article, Healy has suggested with respect to the entire biological-pharmacological-psychiatric project:

> If our drugs really worked, we shouldn't have three times the number of patients detained now compared with before, 15 times the number of admissions and lengthier service bed stays for mood and other disorders that we have now. This isn't what happened in the case of a treatment that works, such as penicillin for GPI. Aside from the inadequacy of our clinical trial methods, professors of psychiatry are now in jail for inventing patients. A significant proportion of the scientific literature is now ghost written. A large number of clinical trials done are not reported if the results don't suit the companies' sponsoring [the] study .... Trials are multiply reported so that anyone trying to meta-analyse the findings can have a real problem trying to work out how many trials there have been. Within the studies that are reported, data such as quality of life scale results on antidepressants have been almost uniformly suppressed. To call this science is misleading.
>
> One of the other aspects of the new medical arena is that the most vigorous and hostile patient groups of the antipsychiatry period have been penetrated by the pharmaceutical industry. Other patient groups have been set up *de novo* by companies. Part of the market development plans for many drugs these days include the creation of patient groups to lobby on behalf of a new treatment. (Healy, 2002b)

Put simply: not only do the 'experts' not accept that there is expertise in misery and madness anywhere else but, where their preferred account is unsupported by the facts, they fabricate the figures, hide the results, set up front organisations and — as we have seen here — provide widely disseminated 'patient education' materials that can be straightforwardly misleading. Trading on the widely culturally shared trust in doctors, the psy-professions set out a deceptive case that demonstrates a complete contempt for the intelligence of their 'consumers'. The other evident assumption is that when the popular media present a perspective different from psychodoxy, then pretty much anyone in the psy-professions who has opinions about highly specific discourses (here, the discourses of cinema, television and the press) is presented as, actually, much better than they (filmmakers, broadcasters, journalists, for example) at telling it for how it 'really' is. This ought to have alerted us, right from the start, to the peculiarity of this kind of self-professed 'expertise'. It has all the hallmarks of the monolithic, hegemonic and the exclusionary.

But, when we started to turn the tables and to apply even a mildly critical discourse analysis to the sanctioned public face of psy-expertise itself — to, if there is such a thing, the psy-complex's *own* 'mass media' — we found a whole range of problems with its explicit and implicit characterisations of the 'mentally ill', of specific 'conditions', of drug (and other) 'treatments' and, finally, of itself as the final arbiter in all such matters. And this is before the frank admission by the industry itself that these so-called, self-proclaimed, public 'education' pamphlets are, at root, more about maximising pharmaceutical companies' market share than they are about anything else. Even the World Health Organisation has recognised — and warned of — what it describes as an inherent conflict of interest between the business goals of the psychopharmaceutical complex and those of the public who are encouraged to consume their products (WHO, 1993). What we have shown here is that conflict of interest *in action*, in publications purporting to be 'educational health guides', produced by purportedly benevolent authorities. We can only hope that, as potential consumers of psy-expertise, our readers might be encouraged to develop a healthy scepticism, at the very least, if not an industrial-strength bullshit detector. But what happens when the psy-knowledges are themselves transplanted into mass-media forms? How do they fare in, to take just one case, the genre of the popular magazine?

Inter ... media ... ries — tales of ordinary madness

The popular media are awash with stories about misery, madness and the best ways to cope with them. The media are also full of helpful 'experts', be they psychologists and doctors mentioned by name, anonymous counsellors, or merely staff reporters. As readers, we are offered helpful advice on everything from schizophrenia to surviving teenagers; from postnatal depression to performing cunnilingus; from shopping addiction to 'shopping for a therapist' (McNamara, 2001). These are topics on which, it seems, we have developed an 'appetite' for expert guidance and reassurance. And, increasingly, the mass consumption publications carrying these stories too appear to be in the service of transforming personal misery, mundane woes, and everyday problems, if not into specifically named psychiatric disorders, then almost certainly into a 'problem' which needs a counsellor/psychologist/doctor/therapist to pronounce upon and to assist with. That is, many of these pieces serve to problematise experience while purporting to 'explain' it. By this ubiquitous device — which we have seen at work in chapter three — psychology appears to give with one hand while taking with the other. Take our knowledge — but find yourself left wanting.

Thus, in between accounts of Brad Pitt's wedding and the latest breakthrough in eye-shadow technology, we are offered 'advice' which routinely claims psychology's warrant and which naturalises the turn to professionals for assistance with everything from your boyfriend's relationship with his ex, to 'getting over' your father. Equally routinely, these publications suggest the need for medications and, like the so-called 'educational' pamphlets we have just examined, equally rarely draw attention to their risks. However, and paradoxically, these advice columns also 'help' to imbue our lives with everyday risks, for which (it is suggested) expert advice on preventative self-maintenance — or, increasingly, self-improvement — should be sought.

A random selection from a range of easily available publications gives a flavour of what we are dealing with here. Our selection is anything but scientific. We have not conducted a rigorous survey, nor have we methodically sampled the market. In fact, what we have done is simply to turn to magazines readily to hand — of the doctor's waiting-room variety — *Woman's Own*, *New Idea*, *Reader's Digest*, *Cleo*, *Cosmopolitan* and so on, and extracted what we have found. The very fact that we have *not* gone looking for the stories we discuss here is, paradoxically, a testament to their representativeness: in fact there is simply no need to search for them. These popular media are, massively, sites for the dissemination of psychological truths. They are, in essence, one of the descendants of Samuel Smiles: they are new, glossy, textbooks of the self.

The extracts we examine range from the relatively innocuous to the chillingly sinister. At the relatively innocuous end of the scale we find stories which simply tell their readers what any competent cultural member already knows, but which — by being packaged as specifically *technical* advice — serves to call into question precisely that everyday mundane competence which might be resistant to the 'psychologisation' of experience. As we say, this is only *relatively* innocuous: such stories (and they are legion) relentlessly respecify what it is that people can trust themselves to know as citizens (Illich, 1976). It is precisely the *generation* of this alienation from everyday (personal, relational, social) mundane competence, that is such an essential part of the project of the psy-professions. If persons cannot trust their own experience, cannot trust their family members or their neighbours to have the requisite expertise — then where are they to turn?

Coming to recognise the conditions under which we might require professional assistance — rather than expert advice — appears part and parcel of our duty as good consumers. As we have seen, the psy-professions are particularly keen to support our right to access information — so that we may evaluate and selectively apply psychology's 'practical truths' to our everyday lives, and so that we are empowered to make 'informed' choices, should we choose to go 'shopping for a therapist'. So, how are our everyday, humdrum, lives problematised by these 'helpful' and 'educational' advice columns?

As we noted in chapter three, the professional psychological associations distinguish 'public advice' from 'therapeutic advice' by its 'educational' or 'skills-based' nature. This is a neat way of avoiding the (once unethical) activity of giving personal advice outside a professional relationship — and of presenting psychology as entertainment. The idea of 'advice', as educational rather than prescriptive, is congruent with the practices of modern behavioural — or 'skills-based' — therapies, where the consumer can expect to acquire a set of practical skills for overcoming particular problems, or for enhancing certain aspects of ourselves or our relationships.

The first articles we examine are drawn from the kind of magazine that tends to be purchased by women concerned with the arts of family management. Psychology has long provided expert advice on such matters. Nikolas Rose (1999: 134) notes that 'It has become the will of the mother to govern her own children according to psychological norms, and in partnership with psychological experts'. As early as 1914, *Good Housekeeping* magazine produced an article titled 'Mothercraft: A New Profession for Women'. This asserted that the 'amateur mother of yesterday would soon be replaced by the professional mother of tomorrow' (Dineen, 1998: 1). Writing in 1934, psychologist Leslie Weatherhead noted in *Psychology and Life* that 'The intelligent and well-read mother of a family today understands nearly as much about the hygiene of the body as did the doctor of a hundred years ago, and in some directions more. The result is that physical fitness has improved' (Weatherhead, 1934: 6). The appearance of such 'practical psychological truths' in women's magazines is, in part, one of the legacies of the mental hygiene movement which stressed the responsibility of ordinary women to be attentive to, and to care for, their mental health and that of their families:

> The concern for the health and welfare of children in the early twentieth century ... sought to utilize the family and the relations within it as a kind of social or socializing machine ... but this was to be done not through the coercive enforcement of control under threat or sanction, but through the production of mothers who would want hygienic homes and healthy children. The promotion of hygiene could only be successful to the extent that it managed to solicit the active engagement of individuals in the promotion of their own bodily efficiency. (Rose, 1999: 132)

So, through this new kind of responsible family — one which voluntarily undertakes to look after the physical and psychological wellbeing of its members — a number of social objectives, once met through coercive means, are achieved. Why, then, would such self-governing and responsible families choose to seek the advice of psychologists — either in problem pages or in person? For starters, it is more difficult than we might assume to produce a 'normal' family. As we will see, normality is something that *itself* is increasingly defined by experts, and used by ordinary people, to evaluate their families. A 'normal' healthy family is something to which we should aspire. It is the inevitable gap between our psy-sustained aspirations and what our families actually look like that produces a need for expert information, help and guidance.

Here, we don't wish to characterise people as the obedient and passive stooges of manipulative media forces, predatory practitioners and professional bodies. We are not talking here of the widespread adoption of false beliefs, ideologies or the implantation of monolithic aspirations — despite the hopes of early professionals for the dissemination and adoption, by society at large, of a 'simplified' set of 'practical psychological truths'. Technologies of consumption are far more complex than such an Orwellian conspiracy theory might suggest. Indeed, our account of psychology's generosity within the field of advertising (in chapter three) attests to the increasingly complex technologies involved in 'consumer engineering' — or manufacturing and motivating particular kinds of consumer. As Rose argues:

> what is involved here is the delicate construction of a complex and hybrid assemblage, in which the processes and desires that are imagined to lie in the psychological interior of persons of particular genders, ages, classes or typifications are connected up to the promises and pleasures that can be invested in representations of styles of existence and their associated artifacts, and located within sets of everyday routines for the conduct of life. (Rose, 1999: 271)

As we noted in chapter one, we style our lives through manifold acts of choice and consumption. Again, it is dissatisfaction, or the engineered 'gap' between our aspirations and the promises of self-actualisation that psy-commodities can never deliver, that leaves us *wanting*. We have seen that the psy-professions claim a unique ability to clarify such unfocused dissatisfaction — by rendering it as suddenly both intelligible and problematic: 'It might ... happen that you simply feel vaguely dissatisfied with your life, but you can't get a clear sense of what the problem is. In this case you might consult a psychologist to help define the problem' (Interdependence, 2002). Again we are reminded of the helpful SANE pamphlet which we examined earlier in this chapter — *Something is Not Quite Right* — which offers precise diagnostic certainties to replace vague, unfocused, worries.

We now look at three articles published in magazines for 'family managers' i.e. those women whose responsibility it is to ensure the health and wellbeing of the family, and to take care of themselves. In the 'Relationships' section of *Woman's Day* for 11 February 2002, is a two-page story called 'Teenagers! All they Need is Love' (52–53). Although this article has, in common with the next, a focus on 'unruly' children, it is concerned to normalise such worrying 'teenage' behaviour, and to provide some practical tips for managing your teenager. Thus, the reader is informed that: 'teens learn by taking risks and making mistakes'. Taking risks is to be encouraged. We all want our children to learn, but inevitably 'mistakes' will be made. What to do then? Dr Rosie King goes on to supply a practical suggestion: 'When they do, don't lecture about how they've failed'. Why not? By such ineffective parental lectures, we may risk further alienating our teenagers from the family. However, should our teenager not respond to responsible parental encouragement of risk-taking, their behaviour may well prove pathological. Through no fault of our own, we may come to require the expert assistance of an accredited professional to return our family to 'normal'. The next article we examine is concerned with just such an eventuality.

This is the 5 February 2001 edition of *Woman's Day* ('Life gets better every Day') on the 'Help Me Doctor' pages. The magazine this week is dominated by three stories: Irritable Bowel Syndrome, a worry about the flu vaccine from 'Feeling Low', Coolup, WA, and, in a bright red text box under a smiling head and shoulders head shot of Dr David Worth (Write to me if you're worried about a health problem. I'm here to help you every week), the headline: *What is Schizophrenia?* This story is a straight, if simplified, recycle of the type of materials we have seen earlier distributed by SANE and the National Mental Health Strategy. This placement of 'schizophrenia', alongside stomach problems and the flu is, in a variant on the direct analogies with asthma and diabetes made in the pamphlets examined earlier, in the service of strengthening the notion that 'schizophrenia is just everyday medicine', and the medical/biological promotion that is to come. After all, these are common health concerns that every 'family manager' should take an active interest in — and, depending on her assessment, may go on to seek further, expert, 'help' with.

Dr David Worth 'says':

Schizophrenia, the most stigmatised and distressing of all diseases, can strike at any family. It is a biological brain disease that usually appears in teenage years, altering the way the brain functions and causing a wide range of symptoms, including hallucinations, delusions, strange behaviour and alienation from the family. Affecting one per cent of all people, schizophrenia is the biggest single cause of lifelong disability and suicide in youth. The cause is not known. Although a family history of schizophrenia increases risk, most cases occur in families with no known history of the illness. Current research is trying to find a way to identify children at risk before symptoms appear .... The biggest problem is non-compliance, when patients deny they have the illness and refuse medication. Current anti-psychotic drugs adjust brain chemistry to diminish symptoms. Recent research indicates that chances of recovery are much improved if treatment begins during or soon after onset. My thanks to the Neuroscience Institute of Schizophrenia and Allied Disorders for the information in this article.[6]

While sighing with relief that those who contract AIDS, Ebola or Creutzfeldt-Jakob Disease will not be nearly as 'distressed' or 'stigmatised' as we naively thought they might be, we note the agency attributed to the 'disease' which can 'strike' at random. We also note that, as the 'biggest problem in treatment' is said to be the blasé response of the stricken to their brain disease, the 'distress' and 'stigma' must actually be somebody *else's* problem. Aside from the explicit use of these 'marketing of fear' tactics (Moynihan et al., 2002) we are struck by the strength of the claims to factuality made here. With the use of strong expressions like 'research *indicates*', we see none of the hedging, modalising or qualification of claims typical of the pamphlets examined earlier. That is, there is a striking absence of constructions like: 'PD *may* be caused by'; 'serotonin is *thought* to be involved in'; 'research *suggests* a genetic link'. Rather here the address to the reader is at once direct, simple and characterised by facticity-enhancing redundancy. Schizophrenia is, we are *told*, 'a biological brain disease'. (Can we have non-biological brain diseases?) It is, we note, not '*thought* to be a brain disease'. The now unambiguous 'brain disease' is, equally, not 'thought' to do anything. Dr Worth tells us straightforwardly that the 'disease' is *responsible for* 'altering the way the brain functions and causing a wide range of symptoms, including hallucinations, delusions, strange behaviour and alienation from the family'. There is no suggestion here that we are dealing with anything but well-established scientific facts.

We are then apprised of the frightening 'fact' that 'most cases occur in families with no known history of the illness'. Here, the symptoms described — including 'strange behaviour' and 'alienation from the family' — are signs that the responsible family manager

6. The NISAD website (www.nisad.org.au/about/supporters.htm) records that: 'Important donations and support have also been received from Tyrrell's Vineyards, Janssen-Cilag, Eli Lilly, Pfizer, Novartis, Lundbeck, AstraZeneca, Sydney Airport, Rothmans Holdings, News Corporation, the ANZ Trust, the Eastern Suburbs Leagues Club, the Construction Forestry Mining Energy Union, the NSW Labor Council, and Chubb Insurance'.

should be wary of, as schizophrenia is described as an unpredictable illness that may 'strike at any family'. These symptoms bear a remarkable resemblance to the description of 'normal' teenage behaviour as described by Dr Rosie King, when understood as 'learning through risk-taking'. Worth's article, however, goes on to describe the virtues of 'early intervention'. Heroic psy-researchers (URLs provided) are, apparently, now attempting to diagnose children who show absolutely no signs at all of having anything wrong with them (yet). Lest this prospect be too alarming, Worth reassures us that, because 'anti-psychotic drugs adjust brain chemistry to diminish symptoms', 'recovery' is more likely if the brain-diseased are chemically adjusted as early as possible. The repeated invocation of 'recent research', and the note of thanks to the highly prestigious sounding Neuroscience Institute of Schizophrenia and Allied Disorders for the information, put the matter to rest. Schizophrenia, at least for *Woman's Day* then, is a well-understood, if scary and randomly-occurring brain disease — to which your teenager may be vulnerable, and for which expert assistance should be sought. Thankfully, this can be treated with life-saving medicines. Dr Worth clearly doesn't feel the need to trouble the reader with any mention *at all* that anti-psychotic drugs have ghastly side effects: perhaps knowing this isn't the sort of information that his column is 'here to help you with every week'. But what is the Neuroscience Institute of Schizophrenia and Allied Disorders (NISAD) that has so generously provided this 'information'? In the interests of 'informed' consumption, we digress to dig out our industrial-strength bullshit detector.

NISAD is an 'independent' body which sponsors neurobiological research on 'schizophrenia'. It runs (by its own admission) a poorly subscribed register of 'schizophrenics' who have agreed to make themselves available for research purposes, and engages in an extensive PR operation on behalf of biological psychiatry. The close relationship between the media, pharmaceutical marketing and a very specific, biological, view of madness is exemplified in another of NISAD's helpful information dissemination exercises. In the April issue of *NISAD News*, the appointment of Jackie Crossman as the new Executive Director is announced. The story notes that she is well suited to the task of heading up what is supposed to be a biomedical research unit, by virtue of her experience of 'over 20 years of high level management in the marketing, communications and service industries. She was responsible for initiating and developing New Zealand's leading PR agency, and has won a number of global PR awards. Her career has encompassed many campaigns for non-profit organisations such as Royal NZ Foundation for the Blind, Guide Dogs, RSPCA, and for health-related marketing efforts such as the New Zealand launch of a new antipsychotic medication'.

The same issue features a story about NISAD's recent promotional activities around the release of *A Beautiful Mind*.

'BEAUTIFUL MIND' WINS MEDIA ATTENTION FOR SCHIZO-
PHRENIA
The new Russell Crowe movie *A Beautiful Mind* is without doubt
the most powerful public awareness media event schizophrenia
has ever had, and NISAD speakers have been much in demand
to provide information and comment. Orchestrated by Executive Director Jackie Crossman and leading PR firm Porter Novelli,
Scientific Director Philip Ward, Director Don McDonald, and 'Gift
of Hope' Patron and consumer advocate Marilyn Mitchell were
interviewed by major radio stations, newspapers and magazines
during the pre-premiere period. NISAD also offered sponsors
and other organisations tickets to the movie, making a commission on each one sold through bulk purchasing from Greater
Union. The biggest order of 200 came from Bristol Myers Squibb
Pharmaceuticals in Melbourne. The BT Financial Group
organised a great night at the movie for staff, and made a collection for NISAD in the cinema foyer. (NISAD, 2002)

Given Dr Worth's informative column in *Woman's Day*, one can imagine what NISAD speakers have had to say when asked to provide
'information and comment'. 'A great night at the movies': Hollywood,
the drug companies, the 'big end of town', 'leading PR firms' ... and
'independent' 'neuroscientific' research.

Our third 'family manager' magazine piece comes from the UK
magazine *Woman's Own*. Here, in the 'Your Health' section, under the
banner headline 'Giving Birth Ruined My Life', Annette Wright (2002)
offers the story of Louise Jones, 43, from Ilkley in Yorkshire. Right from
the start, the headline trades on its own incongruity — giving birth is,
conventionally, supposed to be life-enhancing, a joyous event, etc., etc.
— to suggest that something is not quite right.[7] And indeed, Louise
Jones, 43, is here to inform us about her experience of postnatal depression in a piece which resolutely pushes the similarly paradoxical
line that human despair is never about human relationships.

GIVING BIRTH RUINED MY LIFE
After giving birth to her third baby, Louise Jones, 43, spiralled
into an intense cycle of postnatal depression, which robbed
her of her husband, her home and her children ....
In 1987, after giving birth to her youngest daughter, Hannah,
Louise was diagnosed with postnatal depression. Within months,
she'd lost everything. 'My world collapsed', Louise says sadly.
'Mainly because I — together with those people closest to me —
had no understanding of mental distress. I felt isolated and alone,
and I had no one to talk to'.

---

7. Newspaper headlines frequently trade on precisely this incongruity: our
favourite is 'Killer Nuns!'

'I loved being a mother', Louise explains, 'so I was overjoyed when I became pregnant again in 1987.' But this time there was a problem. Louise's labour was fraught with complications. 'Giving birth to Hannah was a painful process which I found humiliating and disturbing', she recalls. 'Lying in that maternity ward afterwards I realised I couldn't cope any more'.

Three weeks later, at home, Louise became desolate, and started to harm herself. 'I wasn't thinking rationally', she explains. 'I had a baby, a toddler and a severely disabled child to care for and I just couldn't cope with the responsibility. Attacking my arms and legs with a razor blade distracted me from my immediate problems'.

Discovered in a pool of blood by Derek [her husband] in 1987, she was sectioned under The Mental Health Act at their local psychiatric hospital, Scalebor Park, and diagnosed with postnatal depression. 'I was given tranquillisers and Derek authorised a course of electric shock treatment, but none of the medication improved my condition ...'

... 'It's been an uphill struggle to recover', says Louise. 'And even now I have days when I'm affected by depression'.

Immediately below the story is a highlighted text box titled 'Postnatal depression' which assures the reader that 'postnatal depression affects one in ten women ... treatment includes practical and psychological support, as well as antidepressants. Puerperal psychosis is a rare but serious form ... sufferers always have to be hospitalised. Treatment is with drugs and psychotherapy. Electro-convulsive therapy (ECT) may be considered. For more information, advice and support call The Association for Postnatal Illness'. While there is much that could be said about this story, we simply wish to note here the overwhelming causal agency attributed (in both the 'fact box' and the main text) to depression *qua* illness/disease. The piece accounts for Louise's appalling distress and suicidality not in terms of pain, humiliation, despair, desolation, unmanageable demands, spousal abandonment to psychiatric brutality (and, it transpires, his infidelity while Louise was incarcerated and his subsequent abandonment of her upon her release), but rather as simply what happens when *illness* strikes.

Thus in phrases such as 'postnatal depression, which robbed her of her husband, her home and her children' it is *depression* (rather than her husband, as the narrative actually makes clear) which is said to have 'robbed' Louise. Similarly, Louise's voice is pressed into service to attribute the cause of her despair to the agency of illness and (as per the propaganda leaflets we studied earlier) her failure to recognise depression *as illness*. Thus her entirely realistic appreciation of a harrowing birth, overwhelming child care demands and Derek's refusal to offer adequate support are ascribed to not 'thinking rationally' and to having 'no understanding of mental distress'. In the same way that one might say 'even now I'm affected by hayfever', Louise tells us at the end of the piece that: 'even now I have days when I'm affected by depression'.

By contrast, the *Reader's Digest* (masthead — 25 million copies in 19 languages) in June 2000, while relentless in its psycho-peda-gogy and keen to offer more explicitly technical advice to a more general — indeed global — audience than the British *Woman's Own* or the Australian *Woman's Day*, is more circumspect in its endorse-ment of psy *per se*. The image of a pretty, swimsuited, woman on the cover is nearly obliterated by the trailers (all, interestingly, phrased in the imperative) for the stories inside. 'The Health Test You Mustn't Ignore'; 'Revamp Your Life — How to Worry Less' and 'New Rules for Landing A Job'. *Reader's Digest* offers both an 'Art of Living' section and a 'Better You' section. The former offers 'real life' stories, about love, marriage and families. The articles in the 'Better You' section — on employment, health, mental health and parenting — offer more practical and applicable skills, suggestions and other tips for self-improvement.

In the 'Art of Living' section we 'Meet the Bickerson's: They fight dirty and they love it', a 'true-life' piece by Mary Roach, reprinted from the November/December issue of *Health*, which explains in simple terms how to have an argument with your spouse. Notably, after opening with the observation that 'psychologists have long said it's possible to predict whether a couple will stay happily married simply by looking at how they fight', and offering a series of sugges-tions for practical application, the article is ultimately *dismissive* of the utility of professional psychologists' advice. The psy-techniques of 'validation' (I can see why you feel x when I do y), 'I-statements' (When you a I feel b), and 'active listening' ('what I hear you saying is z') are described as being a hindrance to the conduct of 'normal' domestic arguments: 'When you talk like this I feel like throwing up'.

Indeed, nowhere in *Reader's Digest* do we find a recommenda-tion for engaging the services of a psy-professional. Rather — in keep-ing with its demographic — it is the trusty general practitioner who is wheeled in where expert advice is suggested. Practical skills for tack-ling certain problems, or for enhancing particular aspects of our-selves or our relationships, are presented as somehow more 'genu-ine' than the advice offered by psy-professionals. Thus, Paul Kropp's 'Is Your Child Addicted to Praise? Ego polishing can get in the way of real life planning' starts by lamenting the burgeoning self-esteem movement, and the related 'advice' of child counsellors before help-fully — and with no apparent sense of irony — providing parents with five tips on how to go about 'building your child's self-confi-dence'. Attempts to boost 'self-esteem', through unwarranted paren-tal praise, are described as posing a threat to our children's 'self-confidence' and, ultimately, as a route to insecurity via an unhealthy reliance on praise from others. In order to raise children who are genuinely self-reliant, and who have a 'realistic sense of self-worth', we should 'remember that activity and success build the self, not phoney praise'.

The 'Better You' section features the promised 'New Rules for Landing A Job — Interview skills that give you the edge', offering readers 'new principles for successful job hunting' and a number of other self-improvement pieces. We also have Edward Hallowell MD on 'When Worries Go Haywire: Practical suggestions to ease your mind': 'Excessive worry, *toxic* worry, is unnecessary and unproductive'. However, as Hallowell reassures the reader, 'not all worry is bad. Effective planning depends on anticipating trouble. You need to plan.' He goes on to provide a series of 'practical suggestions' for 'taking control' of excessive worry. These include a DIY guide to 'cognitive therapy', or how to 'retrain your habits of thought' by monitoring and interrogating your thoughts and by reflecting on 'how you look at life and yourself .... You will have to practise, but if you keep at it, it will almost always help'. Other tips include keeping a list, exercising, breathing techniques, prayer, limiting the amount of 'news' you consume, adding structure to your life, drinking in moderation and having a good cry.[8]

If self-reliance and the concerted application of these practical skills for self-improvement fail to satisfy, then maybe therapy will help. The May 2002 edition of *Cleo* includes 'Travelling Light', a guide to 'ditching your emotional baggage', along with recommendations for further self-help reading, 'cathartic' films to watch (*Star Wars*; *Sliding Doors*; and *The Breakfast Club* are suggested) and DIY tips. Anne Hollands, CEO of Relationships Australia, and David Baldwin, psychologist and managing director of Life Connect, offer a set of 'questions to ask yourself' to 'heal pain from the past', with the proviso that, should these practical suggestions prove ineffective, the services of a professional 'baggage handler' should be sought:

> Think about it — we have no trouble seeking a professional's help when we want to get well, eat right, buy a vehicle, manage our cash better, or even colour our hair. So, why suddenly get all DIY when it comes to one of the toughest tasks there is — keeping our hearts and minds healthy? 'It's like a car', explains Hollands. 'You can get from A to B with the rattles, and after a while you simply adjust to the fact that it's not performing at its peak. But get a pro to give it a tune-up, and you'll be amazed at the difference.' (Cleo, May 2002: 121)

8. As if this were not enough psy-technology for one issue, this *Reader's Digest* also features an exceptionally practical piece by Tim Rayment for those who frequent beauty spots like Beachy Head, detailing precisely 'What do you say to someone who might be about to kill herself?' in his piece, 'Life on the Edge'.

If the neophyte entrepreneurial self is puzzled about where to turn for a tune-up, further information on the marketplace for professional psychological expertise may be found in Sarah McNamara's 'The Shrink Rap: shopping for a therapist' in *Cleo* (March 2001: 72-74). This piece provides another 'consumers' guide' for its readers — with the universally appealing subtitle 'We're all headcases, but only some of us choose to seek professional help'. McNamara's article helpfully starts by bringing her readers up to speed on the dramatic progress in science over the last hundred years.

> We've come a long way since psychiatrists at the end of the nineteenth century believed peddle-powered [*sic*] sewing machines provoked lesbianism. If you'd like to tackle therapy and don't know where to begin, start here. It might be the Age of Aquarius but an increasing number of young women are seeking answers from their shrink rather than their stars. It's the twenty-first century and not only is there no longer a stigma involved in sharing your problems with a professional, but in some social circles, think *Ally McBeal*, trading notes about your therapy sessions has become almost as fashionable and competitive as comparing handbags over dinner.
> So who you gonna go to when the strain begins to show? While most of us will consult a GP to guide us in the right direction, the mind is an infinitely complex phenomenon so choosing the right person to help you is, not surprisingly, a pretty complicated business .... To help you understand your choices we've put together a short guide to shopping for a shrink, but if you have any other questions consult your doctor. (McNamara, 2001: 73)

The presentation is tongue-in-cheek, upbeat, funny and positive. It also presumes that which it sets out to 'analyse': that therapy is a consumer product like any other and, moreover, one which fashionable young women ('think *Ally McBeal*') may want to try. One can easily imagine an entire œuvre of articles: 'if you'd like to tackle (delete as applicable) therapy/hang-gliding/scuba-diving/motorsport/swinging/meditation/gardening/etc./etc./etc. and don't know where to begin, start here'. In a glorious preview of the tactic employed by psychology textbooks (discussed in the next chapter), here a commercial TV sitcom — (the 'charmingly neurotic') *Ally McBeal* — is held up as the 'fashionable' warrant for 'sharing your problems with a professional'.[9]

The second presumption is that there *will* (inevitably) come a time 'when the strain begins to show', that as the (tongue-in-cheek)

---

9. This is an increasingly common trope in the 'fashion' popular magazine market. *Cleo*, in May 2002, features 'Crazy for You ... meet the women suffering from *Fatal Attraction* syndrome'.

subtitle insists, 'we're all headcases' — we are all, that is, essentially flawed beings for whom it is only a matter of time before the inevitable psychological disorder begins 'to show'. The third presumption? That we, the reader, may be a bit of a klutz — or new to independent living — but that we are keen to take on our responsibility for 'looking after ourselves' because we're 'worth it' (à la Lean Cuisine and L'Oréal). Just as we are, as 'psychological selves', uniquely flawed — not to mention the 'infinite complexity of [our] mind[s]' — so, too, 'choosing the right person to help *you* is … a pretty complicated business'. Should we want to 'tackle therapy', we may need 'help' to choose the right professional for our unique needs, in the shape of *Cleo's* 'short guide' to our 'choices'. Here, it's clear that not just any old psychologist will do. 'Shopping for a Therapist' advises the reader on how to secure a psy-professional tailored to their needs — and how to work out what these needs are. This article, then, belongs to a wider genre, common to *Cleo*, and its demographic — containing such titles as 'How to find Mr Right'; 'How to find the perfect handbag' — all of which can become topics for 'competitive' dinner party conversations.

We note a fourth presumption: that, routinely, it is *medical practitioners* to whom we will turn first for expert guidance. Not friends, not family, not other community members, but GPs who are, after all, in a position to steer us in the right direction given their extensive understanding of that 'infinitely complex phenomenon', the mind. And of course, if *Cleo's* short consumer's guide fails to satisfy, it is again to medicine ('please consult your doctor') that we are to turn. This may, however, not be necessary: for online shoppers, the Australian Psychological Society's website address is usefully placed at the foot of the second page of the article ('shop for a shrink at www.aps.psychsociety.com.au').

However, it is possible that the tempting menu of 'professionals' *Cleo* provides ('GP, psychologist — e.g. cognitive behavioural, counselor, therapist, family therapist, relationship psychologist, psychiatrist, Freudian psychoanalyst, Jungian psychoanalyst, neuro-psychologist, social worker/youth worker') for a smorgasbord of difficulties ('depression, anxiety, panic attacks, obsessive-compulsive disorder, life events, PTSD, relationship or career difficulties, self-actualisation/personal development/family problems, personal problems, manic depression, mental illness with a genetic component, schizophrenia, psychosexual difficulties, phobias, fixations, insight into your unconscious, organic brain disorder, brain damage, neural damage, financial difficulties, legal difficulties, family difficulties, problems with drugs') is a little overwhelming. So much to choose from! Thus, some direct advice is given on how to tell if we need professional help:

But how do you know when you need professional help? If you've been experiencing distress in a way that disrupts your life and is stopping you from fulfilling your potential, seek a professional opinion. Your GP may advise you to wait some time before seeing a specialist, to see if things improve on their own. Alternatively, they may recognize from your symptoms that you would benefit from seeing a professional. There are now standard criteria for diagnosing different mental conditions. For example to be 'depressed' you need to experience a range of feelings, thoughts and behaviours for at least two weeks consistently. Labelling the condition is helpful in that it can give you a clearer idea about what's going on and offer you ways to approach the problem. Seeing a psychologist can be useful ....

So, it is as simple as that: all it takes to establish a genuine need for professional assistance is to be 'experiencing distress in a way that disrupts your life and is stopping you from fulfilling your potential'. Quite what aspect of everyday unhappiness or frustration could *not* potentially come under this rubric is opaque. Professional help with our — now *symptomatic* — disrupted lifestyle or thwarted potential offers a route to transformation. The idea that being told that one's unfulfilled potential is, actually, a 'mental condition' might end up being anything other than positive does not seem to have occurred to *Cleo*. Acquiring a diagnostic 'label' can only be empowering for the consumer — who will also acquire a raft of new approaches for gaining a 'clearer idea' of herself.

Psychology has long promised us a 'clearer view of ourselves', so long as we 'give its directions practical application'. In the 1930s, popular psychologist Eleanor Montgomery explained that:

Psychology is that branch of knowledge which shows us how mental growth may become possible for us if we are sufficiently concerned about the quality of our living to make voluntary efforts to improve it; but neither psychology nor any other kind of knowledge can relieve us of the necessity to give its directions practical application if we are to derive the benefits they confer. (Montgomery, 1938: 2)

However, these 'benefits' are also contingent upon 'setting certain goals' for ourselves:

As soon as we begin to see the wisdom of setting before us a goal of freedom and conscious self-government, then we are at least on the way to an important point of vantage from which there is a truer and more wholesome form of self-expression, based on clearer self-understanding. (Montgomery, 1938: 85)

Cleo could not have put it more clearly, albeit in more contemporary terms. But even *Cleo* has competition in the straight-talking psy-stakes. Our next article on 'therapy' is drawn from the May 2000 edition of *B*, subheaded with a straightforward endorsement of consumerism, 'B indulgent'. *B* is a newly established, handbag-sized, competitor for the 'twenty-something' *Cleo* demographic. Here, in 'Secret Confessions', the *'real-life* confession' (our emphasis) of a therapist is sandwiched between those of a music publicist, a strip club doorman, a transsexual brothel owner, a parliamentary press secretary, a journalist, a concierge, a hospital nurse, and a beautician. Interesting company. In what is described as this 'shocking real-life special', we 'enter the world of vengeful women, insider information, teenage prostitution and sex shops'. The first page of the 18-page 'real-life special' is addressed to the reader: 'Shhhhh! You are now entering the confessional. Bow your head and try not to gasp as the revelations pour forth .... BE WARNED: it's not pretty' (*B*, May 2000: 66). All 'confessions' are about 600 words long, all 'spoken' in the first person, and all presented as 'factual accounts' that reveal 'what goes on behind the scenes'. So what does *B* tell its readers 'goes on behind the scenes' in the therapy professions?

CONFESSIONS OF A THERAPIST

I've been a therapist for ten years and in that time I've treated people with schizophrenia, manic depression, panic disorders, personality problems, marital, sexual and relationship problems and alcohol and drug addicts.

I've had lots of psychotic patients with bizarre delusions. One man believed his mother snuck into his room at night and felt his testicles. Another man believed he lived on the moon and that his parents were dogs. I've treated people with bizarre cultural beliefs such as an Italian lady who was a psychic in her community. If a woman wanted to marry a certain man, she told her to put her menstrual blood in his coffee.

The worst part of my job is the sadness when people don't get better. The saddest case I had was a beautiful lesbian girl who was dumped by her girlfriend. Over the next five years she deteriorated and became psychotic. She tried suicide by sticking coat hangers in her uterus, slicing her arteries and overdosing on pills. She got so obese she could barely sit in her seat and she ended up killing herself ....

Patients often fall in love with their therapist. One woman told me she dreamed she was riding a horse naked with me. Another lady propositioned me to have an affair with her. After I stopped treating a homosexual patient, he admitted that he'd been in love with me. I tell them that I respect their view that they're in love, but it's a fantasy.

Let's assume that this is not intended as a factual account of therapy from the inside. Rather let's examine this 'confession' as a piece of seductive fiction. As entertainment, 'Confessions of a Therapist' can tell us much about the way in which the popular media construct therapy, and the prevailing cultural common sense about the psy-professions and their clientele. Indeed without the existence of just such a cultural common sense, an article such as this would not — could not — make sense. So, what is going on here?

The unnamed therapist establishes their *bona fides* at the out-set of the piece by claiming not only a specific number (ten) of years of experience, but also to have treated people with a wide range of immediately recognisable 'disorders'. In the same way that the pa-tient information pamphlets we looked at earlier sweep 'conditions' like 'schizophrenia' and 'manic depression' into the same category of 'psychological problems amenable to therapy' as 'relationship prob-lems' and 'drug addictions', so too here. We immediately segue into the 'hard data' to warrant these claims: 'I've had lots of psychotic patients with bizarre delusions. One man believed his mother snuck into his room at night and felt his testicles' does exactly this. Need-less to say, such 'bizarre delusions' may provide a cheap frisson for the reader. So what are we to make of the next 'confession', detailing the 'weird cultural beliefs' of the Italian psychic? This kind of 'weird-ness' acts as a straw-person counterpoint to the (silent) claims that therapy can make a real difference. Unless it is the patient's fault that therapy doesn't make people better (in this 'true confession' it is never the therapist's). We would argue that the 'patent' weirdness of believing that menstrual blood in coffee might make a difference in a seduction is, actually, no more odd than believing that psychotherapy can 'cure' anything, that shyness is a psychiatric disease, or that neuroleptic medication is good for people.

The 'true confession' ends where it starts, with a nod to the commonsensical notion of psychotherapy, that dealing with 'fantasy' and 'transference' — specifically knowing better than the patient about what is and is not real — are essentials of the therapist's stock in trade. So we read that 'after I stopped treating a homosexual patient, he *admitted* that he'd been in love with me. I tell them that I respect their view that they're in love, but it's a fantasy'. The therapist is then presented as both entirely exculpable when patients 'fail to get bet-ter', but simultaneously as omniscient when it comes to matters of fantasy. We are reminded here of Freud's (cynical?) observation in the *Introductory Lectures* that it doesn't much matter whether the patient uncovers repressed memories or not, so long as they believe the analyst's story. 'Confessions of a Therapist' is another part of the project of naturalising therapy as everyday life — and psychology as entertainment. One of the more illicit aspects of this confession is notable by its absence: according to the code of ethics of Australian psychologists, it remains unethical to 'bring the profession into dis-repute' by providing 'any statement which is vulgar [or] sensational' (Australian Psychological Society, 1995: 9).

Cleo's August 2000 issue splashes a range of pedagogic head-lines across the cover — 'Best friend bust-ups: Why it hurts more than losing him'; 'Chicks with dicks and the straight men who love them'; and 'Are you dating your Dad?'. In Patricia Skalkos's article, 'Are you dating your Dad?' 'psychologist Toby Green' offers a helpful 'diagnostic' guide designed to enable the reader to 'recognize' whether their father (and boyfriend) is one of the 'five basic negative types that might lead you into less-than-satisfying future romantic rela-tionships'. This article is, again, an instance of the wider 'How to' relationships genre. Here, a cyclical series offers practical sugges-tions on how to find the right man — and how to know whether he is 'right' as a longer term partner (if so, how to 'keep him'; if not, how to 'fix' or 'dump' him). If dumped — or dumpee — how to get over him. If (still) single, how to value your self/dump your emotional bag-gage/flirt effectively (repeat as applicable!).

Green is quoted, directly and indirectly, at the start of the piece, as saying:

> Your father can set the pattern for all the men you date. Of course this can be positive if the relationship between you and your father was nurturing and loving. But if there were problems, there's a chance of repeating them in your relation-ships with other men. 'I believe that we often recreate rela-tionships of struggle because we didn't master them the first time around', she [Green] says. 'In this case, we look for a partner to give us the arena to solve the issues we didn't work out with our fathers'.

Three case studies of women who 'date their Dad' are used to illus-trate the 'negative types'. Thus (as we will see in more detail in chap-ter seven) again the ultimate consumer product, celebrities (here Catherine Zeta-Jones and Michael Douglas, Marilyn Monroe and Arthur Miller, Jill Vanden Berg and Tony Curtis) are recruited to illustrate 'the demanding father', the 'doting dad', the 'dangerous dad', the 'distant dad' and the 'disapproving dad'. Each type comes with a concise 'dilemma' and 'diagnosis' provided by 'psychologist Toby Green'. Needless to say, the 'nurturing and loving' ('doing OK?') dad described in the introduction does not come with a dilemma or diagnosis. Vigilant attention to the warning signs of a putative pat-tern of relationship dysfunction (of our choice) assists in assessing the level of risk associated with a (potentially) 'less than satisfying' relationship. However, dysfunctional relationships are not described in purely negative psychological terms. Rather, they may present a 'training ground' for working through unresolved childhood issues. Here, an awareness of these issues, and of their current significance, is described as being necessary for the health of our current (and future) relationships. Should we be overly concerned about the relevance of these issues to our current relationship, some perspective is provided at the close of the piece. Green tells us that:

> Therapy will help you ... realize that a loving partner has the right to have a few drinks or be obnoxious, or flirt innocently occasionally. It doesn't necessary [sic] mean that he will turn into your father.

The routine recommendation of therapy is continued in what were once known as 'problem pages', a genre that has expanded enormously since the seventeenth century scribe we encountered in chapter three. *B*, for instance, offers advice to its readership about their problematic boyfriends via the feature 'I'd love to have a beer with Duncan .... Let our barman put your troubles on ice'. (December 2001's problems include 'Are guys turned off by girls who are stronger than them, and swear a lot?' 'My boyfriend never gets jealous! Is this a sign he doesn't give a damn?' and 'I keep humiliating myself by coming on to gay guys! How can you tell?'). While Duncan offers practical tips for managing these matters, and resists the temptation to psychopathologise jealousy and repetitive, self-defeating, self-inflicted humiliation, over at *Cleo* Bettina Arndt's 'Q&A' sees things rather differently. The August 2000 issue sees three 'reader's queries' dealt with; two serious matters, one an issue of netiquette. Again, we see the project of the naturalisation of the therapeutic state by association: how to deal with a tricky email is in the same basket as unplanned pregnancy and abject misery. Both 'serious' letters are dealt with via referral to psy-professionals. Under the heading 'Downtime', we read:

> Q: For the last few years I've been depressed. I cry all the time, verbally and physically abuse my partner, get extremely jealous and have even mutilated myself. I don't know why I'm like this. Is there medication I can take? What else can I do?
> A: You say you've talked to people about it, but have you sought professional help? It sounds like you could be suffering from a depressive illness and, in this case, medication could certainly help you. But first you need to find the right person to help you: someone with a medical background, who can prescribe you the correct medication and provide the counseling you need. Ask your GP to refer you to a psychiatrist. At this point you need more than a box of tissues — get counseling.

The first recourse (after what appears to be a reference to an unpublished part of the letter) is to recommend professional help with what is, apparently self-evidently, a diagnosable 'illness'. Crying all the time, verbally and physically abusing one's partner and getting extremely jealous are, obviously, things that are the business of 'people with a medical background'. Talking to people who are not 'professional' clearly does little good. Apart from anything else, they cannot prescribe the medication which can 'certainly help'. Arndt's solution to the second problem falls back on the same advice: see a professional.

> From here to paternity?
> Q: My boyfriend of four years has just dumped me, saying he doesn't want anything more to do with me. Now I've found out I'm pregnant with his child. I don't think I want to keep the baby — I'm only 22. Should I tell him? I don't know if this will change his mind about the relationship.
> A: Your boyfriend shares equal responsibility for this pregnancy and needs to know about it. But don't tell him in the hope of salvaging your relationship. He wanted out, so using the pregnancy to try to hang onto him is bound to end in disaster. You also need to find a counselor ....

Lest we assume that it is just young Australian women who require such guidance, let's look at the problems confronting their British peers. In the 17 June 2002 edition of *Woman*, 'Agony Aunt, Sue Frost' offers 'help when you need it'. This week Sue helps with problems including 'I still love my ex' ('take it slowly, try counselling'); 'I'm having an affair' ('start talking. It will take honesty and it will hurt') and 'I'm scared of giving birth' ('your GP can reassure you'). If you need Sue's help urgently, and/or you just can't wait for the printed version, the 'Ask me anything' page also reveals that 'Sue has recorded some brilliant new helplines based on the most frequently asked questions in her mailbag. Dial at anytime of the day or night. Calls cost 60p per minute and last approximately three minutes each'. Sue's FAQs include 'He's a bully'; 'I can't have an orgasm'; 'He's gone off sex'; 'I've gone off sex'; 'I can't stop myself from worrying'; 'I'm so insecure'; 'He's been unfaithful'; 'Surviving a break-up'; 'I'm so depressed'; 'I'm so lonely'; 'Will I ever meet anyone?'; and 'How can I be more confident?' The entire panoply (indeed progress) of marital misery can, it would seem, be resolved by phone, in sequence, for £21.60, at just 60p a minute.

Similarly, the British edition of *She* (strapline, 'Hearts, Minds and Shopping') trails heartfelt and mindful consumer guides to fulfilment on the glossy cover of the August 2002 edition. 'More energy, less stress in just 48 hours'; 'How embarrassing! 15 very personal sex questions answered'; 'Is a one-night stand ever OK?'; 'Love triangles: Should you be friends with your ex?'; and, in the 'Special Section', 'How to feel happier and look younger'. Should these features fail to satisfy, inside we find the 'emotional wellbeing' pages, penned by 'life strategist, health and fitness professional and author' Pete Cohen, which promise 'positive practical solutions to boost your happiness and success'. August's problems include worries about domestic violence, how to cope with having a strong Liverpool accent, what to do when friends take the mickey and what to say to an 'overprotective' mother about one's new boyfriend. Once more alert to the possibility of having raised expectations that cannot be fulfilled merely by vicarious advice, Pete's page offers the suggestion that, if one is still left wanting: 'for information about his workshops or to book a session with one of Pete's Habit Busting consultants, call 0845 602 1607 or check out his website at www.habitbusting.com'. As we have come to expect from such sites (see chapter five), the website provides glowing celebrity testimonials ('star quotes') from popular GMTV doctor Hilary Jones; 'World Famous Hypnosist' [sic] Paul McKenna; Katie Agnew, editor of the UK edition of *Marie Claire* and Sally Gunnell, OBE, the 'Olympic and World Champion Athelete' [sic] — along with helpful links to 'Pete's new book' at Amazon.co.uk (Amazon's price, £3.99; used price £3.00). Sadly the cost of consultancies is only available on application (but one can sign up for one-day workshops at £99).

Together, these various versions of our problems work to provide the consumer with a range of possibilities for making sense of, and (often commercialised) techniques for acting upon, ourselves, our relationships and our life(style). These assorted descriptions of 'therapy' — as practical professional service, desirable commodity, salacious entertainment, or 'out of touch' and unreliable expertise — along with the forms of practical advice offered by columnists and psy-experts, skills-based tips for self-enhancement, and technologies for solving particular problems, help to make us visible to ourselves in particular ways. That is, many of these pieces serve to make certain aspects of our lives newly worth noticing as (potentially) problematic, and make new ways of approaching these problems, and thinking about ourselves — as wanting something more — possible.

Our final example — on 'shopping addiction' — highlights, by design, the (psycho)pathologies made possible by our contemporary motivation/obligation to consume as means to self-actualisation, and as the exercise of our right to informed choice. Nikolas Rose describes:

> 'an epidemic' of diseases of the will — failures of responsible self-control and self-management, surrender to some baser aspect of the self in compulsive consumption of drink, drugs, gambling, sex. These are the dangers of freedom, illuminated by all these stories, the perils and pitfalls we must avoid in treading the path of the responsible enactment of our all-consuming freedom. (Rose, 1999: 266)

'Nay, big spender: shopaholics can now buy a pill to counter their addiction', a recent article in the *Weekend Australian Magazine* (Aitken, 2001) is both a tongue-in-cheek account of the medicalisation of consumption, and an infomercial for Luvox. The story turns on *both* the explicit grounding of the 'disorder' in popular culture ('sex-and–shopping authors Jackie Collins, Jacqueline Susann and Judith Krantz' and 'hit television show *Sex and the City*' are called upon to illustrate 'shopaholism') *and* the contribution made by an expert psychologist. Dr Michael Kyrios, 'a psychologist at the University of Melbourne', is on hand to lend (in)credibility to what might otherwise be laughed off as another non-problem:[10]

NAY, BIG SPENDER: SHOPAHOLICS CAN NOW BUY A PILL TO COUNTER THEIR ADDICTION
Shopping has taken on a life of its own and become as strong a part of feminine culture as hair or lipstick. Sex-and–shopping authors Jackie Collins, Jacqueline Susann and Judith Krantz exploited this some time ago, but it was during the 1990s that shopping moved from simple hobby to quasi religion.
Hit television show *Sex and the City* might just as well be called 'Shopping and the City' for all its depicted dysfunctional splurging and flashing of plastic. *In Style* magazine, on closer inspection, is a glossy retail guide for women who can't help themselves .... Lurking behind the thrill of buying is a medical problem known as Compulsive Shopping Disorder (CSD). And to illustrate just how far it has taken us, the cure for CSD is a medicine with its own must-have status: a pill called Luvox.
One of a family of similar-acting antidepressants, Luvox is the favoured drug for spender benders, a selective serotonin re-uptake inhibitor (SSRI) which acts on a compulsive shopper's underlying depression by ensuring sustained levels in the brain of the feel-good agent, serotonin. As with its sister drug Prozac, the patient is placed on a course of medication rather than simply taking one when she passes the Hermes window display.
'The typical compulsive shopper', says Dr Michael Kyrios, a psychologist at the University of Melbourne, 'is female, depressed, with her marriage in trouble. You've got the husband out there working and the wife is busy buying things they don't really need .... Shoes are a big one. Everyone needs shoes, but you don't need 45 pairs. Sometimes they never come out of the box'.

Consumption then may be a late-modern imperative, but it can — apparently — easily veer into psychopathology. And while *B* has a

---

10. Dr Michael Kyrios is real. On his webpage at the University of Melbourne School of Psychology (www.psych.unimelb.edu.au/staff/kyrios.html) he lists his research interests as including: Anxiety and mood disorders, Obsessive-compulsive disorder (OCD), Obsessive-compulsive spectrum disorders, Obsessive-compulsive personality disorder, Hoarding, Compulsive buying and shopping and Cognitive therapy.

regular column called 'Retail Therapy', this may be a potentially dangerous 'therapeutic' intervention. Again, as in the patient information pamphlets which opened this chapter, we note that the reader is encouraged to separate conduct from morality: too much consumption (how much is too much? who can we turn to in order to find out?) is a disorder that has an agency all of its own. Thus compulsive shoppers, consumers 'addicted' to 'dysfunctional splurging', are in the grip of something alien to themselves. They are 'women who can't help themselves .... Lurking behind the thrill of buying is a medical problem known as Compulsive Shopping Disorder'. And to complement the paradox that 'must-do consumption' can easily become 'can't help it pathology', 'the cure for CSD is a medicine with its own must-have status: a pill called Luvox'.

The promised infomercial for Luvox® recycles the standard conclusions of (drug company sponsored) research: conduct in the world is not a moral matter. Rather, it is caused by the 'compulsive shopper's underlying depression'. That we should pay no heed to the *meaning* of this fictive 'depression' is cemented by assuring the reader that even this is a matter of no more significance than the concentration of serotonin that can be titrated from the afflicted consumer's cortex. And this bio-babble is, of course, immediately ratified by the citation of a psychologist. Dr Michael Kyrios is produced with a flourish to 'tell' us that not only is owning 45 pairs of shoes a scientifically-established abnormality but also that, whereas Jackie Collins, Jacqueline Susann and Judith Krantz merely wrote racy novels, CSD is now securely in the province of science. However, Kyrios's description of the typical 'patient' as 'female, depressed, with her marriage in trouble ... the husband out there working and the wife is busy buying things they don't really need' — remains (with a chilling appropriateness) little more than a synopsis of *The Valley Of The Dolls*.

Here, psychology's efforts to manufacture and to motivate particular kinds of consumer by 'engineering' new wants, and promising to assuage the inevitable anticlimax that accompanies their disappointment, is the ultimate marketing coup: the *success* of the psy-project guarantees an endless stream of (vaguely) dissatisfied consumers/customers. That is, a new epidemic of *psychological* problems is created out of our wavering self-control, in the face of what is often a bewildering and overwhelming set of 'meaningful' choices — and unfulfilled promises.

However, one crucial thing that we have noted in this chapter is the fact that, contrary to the will of the professional associations, in the popular press psychological advice, and expert assistance, are not always described — or received — in a uniformly positive manner. As we have seen, far from supporting a monolithic account of the effectiveness of psy-techniques, consumers are rather presented with an assortment of (more or less) 'useful' information. Some of this recommends particular strategies, therapies and medications, and some of it ironises, or is otherwise critical of, their utility for dealing with particular problems. A vital way that this is achieved is by describing or implying that the defective psy-technique in question is, in some way, 'inauthentic' — as offering a forced and false strategy for the resolution of (otherwise worthy) problems (for example Pfizer's damning with faint praise of psychological interventions for 'PD'). Thus, 'relationship counselor speak' was dismissed, in *Reader's Digest*, as being a hindrance to 'normal' ways of working out domestic disputes; and unwarranted parental praise — recommended by psy-professionals, as a means to boost the 'self-esteem' of our children — was described as being ultimately damaging to 'realistic assessments of self-worth' and 'genuine self-reliance'.

Rose (1999) suggests that an 'ethic of authenticity' has come to supplant the use of external codes of moral judgment. We no longer examine our behaviour in terms of 'shared' agreements about the boundaries of moral conduct. Instead, we have come to search for the 'inner truth' that corresponds with our 'outer' behaviour — or to adjust our outer behaviour to match our 'inner selves' — and to use psychological terms and methods of judgment to make sense of our lives, work and relationships. This 'ethic of authenticity' comes with a new 'axis of evaluation': authenticity vs. hypocrisy. 'Hypocrisy' — or the lack of correspondence between our inner selves and our outer conduct — provides a new basis for judgments of pathology, and has come to 'motivate' our work on ourselves, whether through self-directed tactics, or by choosing to seek ('shop for'?) professional assistance.

References

Aitken, Andrew (2001) Nay Big Spender: Shopaholics Can Now Buy a Pill to Counter their Addiction. *The Weekend Australian Magazine* (2–3 June) 41

Arscott, Katy (1999) ECT: The Facts Psychiatry Declines to Mention. In: Craig Newnes, Guy Holmes and Cailzie Dunn (eds) *This is Madness: A Critical Look at Psychiatry and the Future of Mental Health Services.* Ross-on-Wye: PCCS Books, 75–96

Australian Psychological Society (1995) *Code of Professional Conduct.* Carlton: The Australian Psychological Society

Baron-Faust, Rita (2000) Me Myself and Irene: Film Review. *British Medical Journal, 321* (23 September) 770

Boyle, Mary (1999) Diagnosis. In: Craig Newnes, Guy Holmes and Cailzie Dunn (eds) *This is Madness: A Critical Look at Psychiatry and the Future of Mental Health Services.* Ross-on-Wye: PCCS Books, 75–96

Breggin, Peter R. (1990) Brain Damage, Dementia and Persistent Cognitive Dysfunction Associated With Neuroleptic Drugs: Evidence, Etiology, Implications. *The Journal of Mind and Behaviour, 11*(3/4) 179–218 and 425–64

Breggin, Peter R. (1996) Should the Use of Neuroleptics be Severely Limited? *Changes, 14,* 62–6

Breggin, Peter R. (2002) Luvox. Retrieved 6 April 2002: (www.breggin.com/luvox)

Britten, Nicky (1998) Psychiatry, Stigma and Resistance. *British Medical Journal, 317* (10 October) 763–4

Byrne, Peter (2000) Some Voices: Film Review. *British Medical Journal, 21*(23 September) 770

Commonwealth of Australia (1999) *Mental Health Promoting Media Strategy — A Positive Approach: A Strategy to Promote the Accurate Reporting and Portrayal of Mental Illnesses.* Canberra: AGPS

Conrad, Peter (2001) Genetic Optimism: Framing Genes and Mental Illness in the News. *Culture, Medicine and Psychiatry, 25*(2) 225–47

Cook, J. (2001) Practical Guide to Medical Education. *Pharmaceutical Marketing,* 6 14–22

Coulter, Jeff (1979) *The Social Construction of Mind: Studies in Ethnomethodology and Linguistic Philosophy.* London: Macmillan

Diefenbach, D. (1997) The Portrayal of Mental Illness on Prime-time Television. *Journal of Community Psychology, 25,* 289–302

Dineen, Tana (1998) *Psychologists and Section 15 (Custody Evaluation) Reports: Illusions of Expertise, Ethics and Objectivity.* Address to the Vancouver Family Law Sections, Canadian Bar Association, 6 May 1998

Dixon-Woods, Mary (2001) Writing Wrongs? An Analysis of Published Discourses about the Use of Patient Information Leaflets. *Social Science and Medicine, 52,* 1417–32

Double, Duncan (2002) Limits to Psychiatry. *British Medical Journal, 324* (13 April) 900–4

Gabbard, Glen O. and Gabbard, Krin (1999) *Psychiatry and the Cinema* (2nd Edition). Washington: American Psychiatric Press Inc.

Granello, Darcy Haag and Pauley, Pamela S. (2000) Television Viewing Habits and Their Relationship to Tolerance Towards People with Mental Illness. *Journal of Mental Health Counseling, 22*(2) 162–75

Hannigan, Ben (1999) Mental Health Care in the Community: An Analysis of Contemporary Public Attitudes Towards, and Public Representations of, Mental Illness. *Journal of Mental Health, 8*(5) 431-40

Hawton, Keith; Simkin, Sue; Deeks, Jonathan J.; O'Connor, Susan; Keen, Allison; Altman, Douglas G.; Philo, Greg and Bulstrode, Christopher (1999) Effects of a Drug Overdose in a Television Drama on Presentations to Hospital for Self-Poisoning: Time Series and Questionnaire Study. *British Medical Journal, 318* (10 April) 972–7

Healy, David (2000a) Antidepressant Induced Suicidality. *Primary Care Psychiatry, 6,* 23–8

Healy, David (2000b) Good Science or Good Business? *Hastings Center Report, 30,* 19–22

Healy, David (2001) The SSRI Suicides. In: Craig Newnes, Guy Holmes and Cailzie Dunn (eds) *This is Madness Too: Critical Perspectives on Mental Health Services.* Ross-on Wye: PCCS Books

Healy, David (2002a) *The Creation of Psychopharmacology.* Cambridge: Harvard University Press

Healy, David (2002b) Psychopharmacology and the Government of the Self. Retrieved 28 May 2002: (www.academyanalyticarts.org.healy.html)

Hodge, Bob and Tripp, David (1986) *Children and Television: A Semiotic Approach.* Cambridge: Polity

Hyler, Steven E.; Gabbard, Glen O. and Schneider, Irving (1991) Homicidal Maniacs and Narcissistic Parasites: Stigmatization of Mentally Ill Persons in the Movies. *Hospital and Community Psychiatry, 42*, 1044–8

Illich, Ivan (1976) *Limits To Medicine*. London: Marion Boyars

Interdependence [Website] (2002) Self-Therapy for People who Enjoy Learning about Themselves. Retrieved 28 May 2002: (www.helpyourselftherapy.com/index.html)

John, Ian (1998) The Scientist-practitioner Model: A Critical Examination. *Australian Psychologist, 33*(1) 24–30

Jorm, Anthony; Korten, Ailsa; Jacomb, Patricia; Christensen, Helen; Rodgers, Bryan and Pollitt, Penelope (1997) 'Mental Health Literacy': A Survey of the Public's Ability to Recognize Mental Disorders and their Beliefs about the Effectiveness of Treatment. *Medical Journal of Australia, 166* (17 February) 182–6

Kerin, John and Hickman, Belinda (2002) PM Orders Inquiry After Drugs Blowout. *The Weekend Australian,* (13–14 April) 6

Kutchins, Herb and Kirk, Stuart (1999) *Making Us Crazy: DSM — The Psychiatric Bible and the Creation of Mental Disorders*. London: Constable

Lazar, Susan G.; Gabbard, Glen O. and Hersh, Elisabeth K. (1993) The Press's Portrayal of Mental Illness. *Nieman Reports, 47*(4) 17–23

Marshall, J. Richard (1988) Psychiatry, Psychology and Social Values. *BPS Psychotherapy Section Newsletter, 3*, 16–25

Martinez, Renee; Johnston-Robledo, Ingrid; Ulsh, Heather M. and Chrisler, Joan C. (2000) Singing 'The Baby Blues': A Content Analysis of Popular Press Articles About Postpartum Affective Disturbances. *Women and Health, 31*(2–3) 37–56

Mayer, A. and Barry, D. (1992) Working with the Media to Destigmatize Mental Illness. *Hospital and Community Psychiatry 43*, 77–8

McCarthy, David and Rapley, M. (2001) Far from the Madding Crowd: Psychiatric Diagnosis as the Management of Moral Accountability. In: Alec McHoul and Mark Rapley (eds) *How to Analyse Talk in Institutional Settings: A Casebook of Methods*. London, Continuum, 159–67

McNamara, Sarah (2001) The Shrink Rap: Shopping for a Therapist. *Cleo* (March) 72–4

MIND (2002) *Shock Treatment: A Survey of People's Experiences of Electro-Convulsive Therapy (ECT)*. London: MIND Publications

Mintzes, Barbara (2002) Direct To Consumer Advertising is Medicalising Normal Human Experience. *British Medical Journal,* 324 (13 April) 908–9

Montgomery, Eleanor (1938) *Can Psychology Help?* London: Rich and Cowan

Moynihan, Ray (1998) *Too Much Medicine?* Sydney: ABC Books

Moynihan, Ray (2002) Drug Firms Hype Disease as Sales Ploy, Industry Chief Claims. *British Medical Journal, 324* (13 April) 867

Moynihan, Ray; Heath, Iona and Henry, David (2002) Selling Sickness: The Pharmaceutical Industry and Disease Mongering. *British Medical Journal, 324* (13 April): 886–91

Nairn, Raymond (1999) Does the Use of Psychiatrists as Sources of Information Improve Media Depictions of Mental Illness? A Pilot Study. *Australian and New Zealand Journal of Psychiatry, 33*, 583–9

Nightingale, Virginia (1997) The Vulnerable Audience: Effects Traditions. In: Stuart Cunningham and Graeme Turner (eds) *The Media in Australia: Industries, Texts, Audiences*. Sydney: Allen and Unwin, 364–80

NISAD (2002) Headlines: March 2002. Retrieved 28 May 2002: (www.nisad.org.au/nisadNews/headlines/march2002.html)

Payer, Lynne (1992) *Disease-Mongers*. New York: John Wiley

Philo, Greg (1994) *Media Representations of Mental Health/Illness: Audience*

Reception Study. Glasgow: Glasgow University Media Group

Potter, Jonathan (1996) *Representing Reality: Discourse, Rhetoric and Social Construction*. London: Sage

Potter, Jonathan and Edwards, Derek (2001) Discursive Psychology. In: Alec McHoul and Mark Rapley (eds) *How to Analyse Talk in Institutional Settings: A Casebook of Methods*. London, Continuum, 12–24

Roach, Jason and Yamey, Gavin (2000) Two Minutes to Change Minds. (Film review). *British Medical Journal, 321* (21 October) 1028

Rose, Diana (1998) Television, Madness and Community Care. *Journal of Community and Applied Social Psychology, 8*, 213–28

Rose, Nikolas (1999) *Governing The Soul: The Shaping of the Private Self.* 2nd edition. London: Free Association Books

Rose, Steven; Lewontin, Richard and Kamin, Leon (1984) *Not in Our Genes: Biology, Ideology and Human Nature*. New York: Pantheon Books

Rosen, Alan and Walter, Garry (2000) Way out of Tune: Lessons from *Shine* and its Exposé. *Australian and New Zealand Journal of Psychiatry, 34*, 237–44

Ryle, Gilbert (1949) *The Concept of Mind.* London: Hutchinson

SANE Australia (2000) Mental Illness: The Facts. (Pamphlet). Melbourne: SANE

Schacht, Thomas (1985) DSM-III and the Politics of Truth. *American Psychologist, 40*(5) 513–21

Smyth, Mary (2001) Fact Making in Psychology: The Voice of the Introductory Textbook. *Theory and Psychology, 11*(5) 609–36

Szasz, Thomas (1961) *The Myth of Mental Illness.* London: Paladin

Szasz, Thomas (1994) *Cruel Compassion: Psychiatric Control of Society's Unwanted.* New York: John Wiley and Sons

Townshend, Pete (1967) Pictures of Lily. London: Fabulous Music Ltd. Recorded by The Who, 5 April 1967. Track Records 604002

Wahl, Otto (1992) Mass Media Images of Mental Illness: A Review of the Literature. *Journal of Community Psychology, 20*, 343–52

Wahl, Otto (1995) *Media Madness: Public Images of Mental Illness*. New Brunswick: Rutgers University Press

Weatherhead, Leslie (1934) *Psychology and Life: Sound Psychology Made Vivid and Practical.* London: Hodder and Stoughton

Wessely, Simon (1997) Mental Illness as Metaphor, Yet Again. *British Medical Journal, 314* (11 January) 153

Wilson, Claire; Nairn, Raymond; Coverdale, John and Panapa, Aroha (1999) Constructing Mental Illness as Dangerous: A Pilot Study. *Australian and New Zealand Journal of Psychiatry, 33*, 240–7

World Health Organisation (1993) *Clinical Pharmacological Evaluation in Drug Control.* Copenhagen: WHO

Wright, Annette (2002) Giving Birth Ruined My Life. *Woman's Own*, (6 May) 20–1

'Here's Johnny!'

The pliability and plausibility of popular pics

The McDonald's Golden Arches symbol — the big yellow M — is now more readily recognised around the world than the Christian cross (Vidal, 1997: 135). In Australia and New Zealand, as in France, governments concerned about the increasing cultural hegemony of the US pass laws to protect the language or to regulate the proportion of foreign content that can be shown on TV. The 'quality' British media routinely deplore the inanity, crass taste and unavoidability of American daytime talk shows on TV, and bemoan the commercial preponderance of Hollywood movies. Yet Disney's centre of operations in Europe is near Paris and, over 15 years since Hollywood was told that 'the British are coming', the Australian popular media are full of celebratory stories about the way in which Aussie actors like 'our Nic' (Kidman) and Russell Crowe are picking up starring role after starring role, and Oscar after Oscar.

In *No Logo* Naomi Klein puts the position clearly: 'logos, by force of ubiquity, have become the closest thing to an international language, recognised and understood in many more places than English' (Klein, 2000: xx). Logos, of course, work precisely because still visual images can carry a weight of reference that is widely culturally shared and virtually instantaneously transmissible — a quality entirely unavailable to longer texts. Such images and, for that matter, stills from movies — with an immediacy that a newspaper article or a magazine piece cannot — can thus not only stand for a singular meaning, but also make immediately available a back-story: an entire body of common sense about whatever it is that happens to be depicted. Hence both product placement and the immense cultural resonance of certain photographs. Because photographs 'flicker between fixed and mobile meanings', pictures are simultaneously both tied to the conditions of their production and can also 'have new and unpredictable meanings in different times and places' (McHoul, 1996: 19). That is, images can tell whole stories on the basis of the momentary scene that they capture: for example, the five marines raising the Stars and Stripes on Iwo Jima and the napalmed girl running naked down the road sum up versions of the totality of America's wars in the Pacific and, later, in Vietnam.

And yet any image can, in other times and places, have entirely different meanings. Indeed one of the key themes of this chapter is precisely this fluidity of meaning. In particular, we are interested in how this fluidity is exploited by the producers of psychology textbooks. We argue that they do this so as to present partisan meanings, even though they, themselves, often trade on a kind of (naive) semiotic realism. This chapter then presents an analysis of the way in which psychology textbooks selectively borrow from the history of art and other image banks. By the judicious application of contemporary captions, they routinely reread medieval, Renaissance and pre-Raphælite images to reveal the follies of the past and, by implication, the resolutely rational and scientifically-sound nature of their own knowledge claims. Or else, they show that, while they could not know what it 'really' was, our ancestors were strangely all too familiar with the 'mental illnesses' of the present. This chapter, then, is a study in fundamental anachronism.

But let's start closer to the present.[1] Images of the hatchet-wielding Jack Nicholson from *The Shining* feature in pedagogic material on 'schizophrenia' (Meyer and Salmon, 1988: 228). Images of a slightly less dishevelled Jack Nicholson dodging cracks in the pavement from *As Good As It Gets* illustrate 'obsessive compulsive disorder' (Schwartz, 2000: 164). And stills of a dishevelled Jack Nicholson in *One Flew Over The Cuckoo's Nest* appear in chapters on the management of both schizophrenia (Davison and Neale, 1990: 400) and depression (Shorter, 1997: 283). These images are the counterpart of increasing references in popular American television to 'psychological' themes, from *The Simpsons*, through *South Park* to *Dr Katz, Professional Therapist*. In this chapter then we examine both the increasing use, by explicitly instructional texts, of popular cultural forms such as cinema, and also the appropriation of historical images, in order to 'naturalise' contemporary psychological stories about misery and madness.

What we are seeing here is effectively how the next generation of commercial-psychological practitioners is being trained via canonical texts which increasingly draw upon both historical and contemporary popular culture in order to buttress their knowledge claims. To see this in action, we looked in detail at four recent, and heavily promoted, abnormal psychology texts (Barlow and Durand, 2001;

---

1. From this point on, we refer for the most part to the world's best-selling textbooks in abnormal psychology. Naturally enough, the examples are American; for just as the American Diagnostic and Statistical Manual of Mental Disorders has all but displaced the European International Classification of Diseases and as McDonalds has displaced Wimpy's hamburgers, so US psychology textbooks now dominate international markets.

Comer, 1998; Kendall and Hammen, 1995; Schwartz, 2000). These textbooks — all originating in the USA — are specifically designed for use in undergraduate psychology courses and are authored by eminent psychologists with degrees from, and/or senior positions at, prestigious universities. Each text is accompanied by an array of up-to-the-minute technological supplements: CD-ROMs, websites, ready-made PowerPoint presentations, full-colour acetate transparencies, pre-scripted examinations for the busy lecturer, and so forth. One textbook goes so far as to describe itself (amusingly in this context) as a 'New media edition' (Barlow and Durand, 2001). All four texts are, moreover, careful to address themselves *directly* to the concerns of late adolescents or young adults at university. Accordingly, *Abnormal Psychology: A Discovery Approach* (Schwartz, 2000) frames the entire field by using teen stories as bookends. The Preface opens with a newspaper story about the suicide of Danielle Wood, a 20-year-old woman, following disappointed career hopes and a break-up with her boyfriend. The first chapter is entirely devoted to this story and, rather than using a dry, theoretical, title like 'Psychopathology and Suicide', it is headlined 'The Death of Danielle Wood'. The similarly snappily titled epilogue, 'Littleton, Colorado, and the Future of Abnormal Psychology', discusses the mass shootings by high school students Dylan Klebold and Eric Harris.[2] Between these bookends of teen despair, then, there are 12 chapters detailing the spectrum of human misery, carefully arranged by the American Psychiatric Association's Diagnostic and Statistical Manual's (DSM-IV) diagnostic category.

By contrast, Barlow and Durand's *Abnormal Psychology: An Integrative Approach* (2001) directly addresses the lecturer setting their book as a course text. In the Preface, they excitedly compare the current state of knowledge in psychopathology to geology's breakthrough understanding of plate tectonics and to the radical rethinking of evolutionary biology afforded by Eldredge and Gould's (1972) concept of 'punctuated equilibria'.[3] They go on:

---

2. One-third of page 599 is taken up by Harris and Klebold's 1998 Yearbook pictures. The caption tells us that they 'look like typical suburban high school students, not young men who would go on a shooting rampage at their school'. Naturally enough, this constructed paradox works to point the reader to the conclusion that there must have been something 'psychologically disordered' about the teenage gunmen. For a more detailed analysis of the sort of work this type of anomalous membership category work can do, see Rapley et al., (in press).

3. Intriguingly, despite their championing of the importance of genetics in abnormal psychology, Barlow and Durand don't expect their colleagues to know anything at all about evolutionary biology. Despite being 30 years old, and one of the most controversial theoretical developments in the biological sciences, the concept of punctuated equilibria is not mentioned as such, rather the university staff member entrusted with teaching abnormal psychology simply needs to know that 'evolution ... happens in fits and starts' (2001: xix).

as colleagues, you are aware that we understand some disorders better than others. But we hope you will share our excitement in conveying to the student ... what we currently know about the causes and treatment of psychopathology .... We include substantial current evidence of the reciprocal influences of biology and behaviour .... Our examples hold students' attention; for example, we discuss genetic contributions to divorce. (2001: xix)

Would the genetics of divorce be the most salient example of what young psychology students enrol in courses on abnormal psychology to hear about? This is highly unlikely. However, given the prevailing divorce rates in the USA and other Anglophone countries, it is a reasonable marketing guess that many students will have experienced their own parents' divorce or that of friends' parents. There is nothing new in showing that the grounding of such notions as 'genetic contributions to divorce' is intellectually thin or that the penchant of these texts towards half-baked biology is both massively present and overwhelmingly denied.[4] It is, however, a great twist to offer a supposedly scientific account of 'psychopathology' which recommends itself to its readership by way of presenting yet another no-fault account of family difficulties. As we will see in more detail later, when such claims are made they are often shored up by recourse to an image.

Naturally enough, then, any concerns about the scientificity of biogenetic accounts of divorce are dispelled by the inclusion of a picture. In the subsection of Barlow and Durand's chapter on 'Research Methods' subtitled 'Studying Genetics', we are shown a photograph of a bare-chested, bearded, black man, with a young girl (possibly his daughter) piggy-back, looking out over the stable door of what appears to be a wooden hut. The picture is carefully placed in the primary visual position, at the top left-hand corner of the facing page. The caption reads: 'Although family members often resemble each other, genetics has to do with far more than what we inherit from our parents' (2001: 103). Quite what genetics has to do with anything other than heredity is unclear here and is not explicated in the surrounding text. Given the well-documented evidence of racism in psychological theory, research and practice from the moment of the discipline's inception (Browne, 1995; Fernando, 1990; Littlewood and Lipsedge, 1989; Rose et al., 1984), and the preponderance of biologically-based explanations for both the achievements and the supposed pathologies of dark-skinned peoples, the use of an image of black people in a section on genetics suggests a degree of insensi-

---

4. David Barlow was a member of the American Psychiatric Association task force which invented the DSM-IV. In a note on the criticism of the DSM-IV — that it is as much a political as a 'scientific' document — he disingenuously describes the experience of sitting on the task force as 'interesting' (2001: xx).

tivity that is hard to comprehend. Perhaps a picture of a white, middle-class, woman and a blond boy toddler would have been incapable of illustrating the point that families have DNA in common?

Barlow and Durand helpfully include case studies in almost all chapters. (In their Preface they note that the popularity of their book 'indicates that students appreciate the humanization of data' (2001: xxi)). This approach is further described as being designed to reinforce the fact that psychological disorders affect 'real people'. The 'disorder' chapters underpin this point by including 'a compassionate review of a first-person memoir by someone who survived or is living with a challenging psychological condition .... They complement the research-based text without pretending to be scientific .... A "real" voice can be heard as a counterpoint to our objective discussion' (2001: xxi). Presumably people 'living with a challenging psychological condition' are only marginally 'real', and certainly they are incapable of saying anything 'objective' about their 'condition'. If this is indeed the case, then it is somewhat puzzling that, throughout the text, brightly lit, and unfailingly unflattering, video-captured colour mugshots of people 'living with a challenging psychological condition' are presented in text boxes. These anonymous faces are presented on a black background with the edges rounded so that they look like faces on a TV screen. And indeed the instructor's kit CD-ROM helpfully includes short clips of the 'challenged' being interviewed by preppy young researchers to elicit their 'real' (but non-objective) 'stories'. Unidentified faces, black background, white type in Courier Typewriter font, direct reported speech as a device for persuasion, what are presented as direct quotations from 'sufferers', do indeed 'complement the research-based text'.

By complete contrast with the questionably 'real' voices of patients, when actual names *are* used with images, they accompany either colour pictures of celebrity 'cases' (Jeffrey Dahmer, Ted Kaczynski, Loreena Bobbitt and David Helfgott are favourites), dignified black and white images of well-known literary figures (such as Virginia Woolf or Sylvia Plath) or portrait style photographs of eminent psychological researchers. And, accordingly, there is often an implicit theoretical axe to grind. For instance, Barlow and Durand's discussion of the effectiveness of lithium as a treatment for 'bipolar disorder' is illustrated with a pensive shot of one Kay Redfield Jamison. She is, we are told in the accompanying caption, 'an internationally respected authority on bipolar disorder [who] has suffered from the disease since adolescence' (Barlow and Durand, 2001: 212). This Kay Redfield Jamison is not shot in washed-out but brightly-lit colour. She is not full face to camera. She is not just a head shot: we can see her black polo-neck sweater. She appears as a portrait inset into the text, not on a black background with 'quotes' of her 'voice'. Rather the use of Jamison's words is much more subtle, and much more effective. She is recruited here (and also in the other three texts under examination) by name, to 'say' that 'bipolar' disorder is indeed a 'disease'. She is, after all, not just an anonymous 'real person' complementing the hard science with an understandable, but non-objective, human interest story to which we need give little credence. Rather she is 'an internationally respected authority' on the topic. Her suffering is, by comparison, incidental, but also apparently direct evidence of psychology's capacity to match 'scientific' theory with 'actual' experience.

Given that we are encouraged not to trust the objectivity of the nameless faces whose words are quoted directly to us, it seems a little incongruous to say the least that Jamison is *another* 'person living with a challenging condition', but whose identification (and the studious, serene appearance she wears) is there to do nothing but vouchsafe the veracity of her account. We learn later, in a glowing review of her memoirs (*An Unquiet Mind: A Memoir of Moods and Madness*), that she 'combines a scientist's detachment with a novelist's involvement in the dual subject of herself and the disorder that is part of her .... We come to the end where we find Kay Jamison happily married, adjusted to the lifesaving lithium, and continuing her active professional life' (Barlow and Durand, 2001: 223). That this Mills-and-Boonery just happens to support the position of the American Psychiatric Association that 'bipolar disorder' is a life-threatening 'disease' requiring medication to guarantee happy marriages and active lives is, one imagines, purely coincidental.

Kendall and Hammen's *Abnormal Psychology* (1995) also suggests that their intended aim is not only to naturalise 'psychological problems' as inescapable and universal, but also to push this message by deliberately focusing on matters likely to be highly salient for young adults at university. They are also explicit in their support for biological accounts of misery and madness. They proudly state in their Preface that they:

> include more biological research information than other books do because such approaches have commanded considerable research attention in the past decade and because we believe that they play a key role in understanding certain disorders — among them schizophrenia, Alzheimer's dementia, some forms of mood disorders and many others. (Kendall and Hammen, 1995: x)

We note in passing that their list of 'certain disorders' nicely packages a genuine brain disease along with everyday misery and the hypothetical construct 'schizophrenia'. We further note that the highly underspecified phrase, 'and many others', leaves the conceptual doors wide open for 'biological research' approaches to be said to 'play a key role' in 'understanding' almost any form of unwanted conduct. However, just because something has commanded 'considerable research attention' in the past decade is absolutely no warrant for conferring credibility on it by inclusion in a basic text. Such a strategy is merely to throw open the doors to pseudo-science. In the intellectual disability literature the notion of 'facilitated communication' commanded considerable research attention in the past decade: it is now known to be an entirely bogus 'therapy'. Equally, the idea that people could 'recover' memories under hypnosis received massive research and media attention in the past decade: again 'recovered memory' therapy is now known to be sheer (iatrogenic) charlatanism.

But what is the upshot of this 'belief' in the biological? Kendall and Hammen go on to state that they:

> strove to produce a book that would be relevant to students' lives. After all, psychological problems are part of life, and no person or family escapes untouched .... We include numerous actual cases, from both our clinical practice and teaching experience as well as some of the more famous cases. The well-known cases feature famous individuals who have managed their experiences with psychopathology and have adjusted, and others whose fame was a result of the pathology .... These cases illustrate how the various symptoms hold together in a real case, and they communicate the experience of abnormal behavior patterns. (Kendall and Hammen, 1995: xx–xxiii)

What are Kendall and Hammen telling their readers here? That 'psychopathology' is a central, probably biological, but certainly unavoidable, part of human nature: it is as much a part of being human as families themselves. It is also something morally separable from persons, something which one 'experiences' — like a flat tyre, a poor meal or a lousy hairdo. It is, sadly, just one of those things that happens to people. This, it is claimed, is true even for those (like Jeffrey Dahmer, Charles Manson or Ted Kaczynski) who had 'experiences with psychopathology' that made them famous. We are then being told that, if you are lucky, your madness can even make you a celebrity (the ultimate consumer fantasy) — whether you 'adjust' or not. Effectively, this is only a small step short of telling us that we are all lunatics now.

That these texts are very well aware of the explicitly *pedagogical* use they make of *images* is shown by their own reflexive address to them. On the front cover of Barlow and Durand's *Abnormal Psychology* (2001), then, we are presented with a grainy, black-and-white close-up photo of a middle-aged, bearded, Caucasian man wearing the kind of round specs made famous by John Lennon. Aside from a passing resemblance to Freud, it would be difficult not to pick the subject as a typical American WASP. The plain black back cover features a smaller reproduction of the same image in a text box, accompanied by the following note: 'About the cover: people are larger than their disorders. The cover photo is designed to be emblematic of *all* people, regardless of their specific psychological disorder or their age, race gender or culture'. Quite how this man is supposed to be emblematic of, say, young black women, whether or not 'psychologically disordered', is left entirely unaddressed. For all this, Barlow and Durand go on to stress the innovativeness of their 'special photo feature' which means that, throughout the text, pictures of 'actual clients who were diagnosed with psychological disorders' (2001: xx) are used to illustrate these respective 'disorders'. The pedagogic rationale for this 'special' feature is described in the following way:

> by showing these faces, which represent both genders and most races, cultures and stages of development, we hope to convey the hardship imposed by psychological disorders and help reduce the stigma, anxiety and isolation that add to the burden of people who struggle with them. (Barlow and Durand, 2001: xx)[5]

One can well imagine how much less stigmatised, less anxious and more closely in touch with their fellow beings these 'faces' now feel. We can almost hear echoes of the public display of Bedlam, the freakshow and the zoological exhibit.

Here's Johnny — recruiting Hollywood

All four texts recruit celebrity figures in order to bolster their arguments. This device takes two broad forms. In the first of these, images of famous people are used as 'case studies' of specific disorders, or to reinforce possibly contentious points. Of course, in late modernity, the cult of celebrity means that, often enough, the gory details of the lifestyles of the rich and famous are sufficiently familiar, so that a simple portrait alone can suggest the requisite behavioural details. The mere depiction of a Michael Hutchence (Schwartz, 2000: 354) or a Kurt Cobain (Barlow and Durand, 2001: 220) is, in and of itself, enough to call up an entire biography of rock 'n' roll excess, existential angst and problematic conduct, thereby laying the groundwork for a psycho(bio)logised account of the putative 'disorder' that leads to suicide. In the second form of this device, stills from films are reproduced, so that images can *stand for* the disorder in question, or for the treatment of the 'mentally ill' more generally. (That feature films are creative fictional works, not supposedly 'objective'

---

5. On page 79, in the chapter on 'Assessment and Diagnosis', a charming chocolate-box image is used to illustrate the point that 'despite their wide physical variation, all dogs belong to the same class of animals'. Yet it seems to have escaped Barlow and Durand that, despite *their* wide physical variation, all people belong to the same, human, race.

documentaries, is never explicitly mentioned.) In a number of cases, there is no obvious and compelling connection between the still and the text it supposedly illustrates. Here film is used merely to claim vicarious street-cred, to show students how hip psychology can be, how engaged it is with things that matter in popular culture. Other instances simply 'cite' Hollywood to shore up a specialist disciplinary claim against everyday common sense. For example, Schwartz reproduces a still from *Good Will Hunting* in his chapter 'Psychological Assessment, Classification, and Clinical Decision Making'. This colour shot, in the top right-hand corner of the facing page, shows Robin Williams placing a hand on Matt Damon's shoulder. The caption tells us that:

> Rapport is essential in a client-therapist relationship. In *Good Will Hunting*, Dr Maguire (Robin Williams) is able to break through to Will Hunting (Matt Damon) *in part* because they both come from the same Irish-American blue-collar neighborhood in Boston. (Schwartz, 2000: 97; our emphasis)

If we thought that a shared background, common humanity, and respect for persons was enough, we may have been mistaken. The image, via its caption, now tells us something else: all that may be *part* of it, but we now know that it is actually a specialist disciplinary technique called 'rapport' that makes the real difference.

In a few, quite rare, instances, film stills are used for the reverse effect: to show how wrong popular accounts can be, rather than to mobilise them on behalf of science. Here they are reproduced in order to dismiss the case that they are (very loosely) interpreted as making. For example Comer (1998: 504) uses the film poster from Pink Floyd's *The Wall* to illustrate how the counter-culture and 'the arts' unscientifically (and therefore, we must infer, irresponsibly) 'romanticize' the theories of R.D. Laing.[6] In another intriguing instance — and in what one would have thought was a heaven-sent opportunity to illustrate sociopathy — a grinning image of Alex (Roddy McDowell) from Stanley Kubrick's *A Clockwork Orange* is actually employed to show how irresponsible cinematic portrayals of psychological themes can somehow derail therapeutic research. Images of Alex's aversion therapy in the film, we are informed in the painfully punning caption, 'left a bad taste in the mouths of movie-goers, making it difficult for behaviorists to further develop and apply aversion therapy' (Comer, 1998: 68). Kubrick has been accused of many things,

---

6. Strangely, Laing is identified as a 'clinical theorist [who] combined sociocultural principles with the existential philosophy that was his hallmark, and argued that schizophrenia is actually a constructive process' (Comer, 1998: 504). This description is interestingly nuanced, given that Laing was a practising (empirical) psychiatrist.

but this is the first and only time we have seen him credited with single-handedly putting a stop to aversion therapy — and by, somehow, using a very similar technique on his audiences!

Comer states in his Preface to *Abnormal Psychology* (1998) that the text deliberately employs: 'stimulating illustrations'. He amplifies this: 'Chapters illustrate concepts, disorders, treatment and applications with many photographs, diagrams and graphs. I supply detailed captions, to make the point of illustrations clear, interesting and self-contained' (Comer, 1998: xvii). Here, the page is dominated by a self-referential image of another page from the textbook advertising the similarly stimulating extra feature of each chapter — the 'Thought and Afterthought' section. This section is, we are told, 'a fresh look at events in the world around us .... Each chapter's "Thought and Afterthought" opens with stories from today's headlines' (Comer, 1998: xvii). Accompanied by a picture of the pianist clutching a battered score with his eyes screwed shut, and looking to be in extreme pain, the Preface rehearses the book's later discussion of 'Clinical Assessment, Diagnosis and Treatment' with a review of *Shine* ('The David Helfgott Story: When Labels Fail'). Here, we are informed that 'everyone who has seen *Shine* is familiar with Helfgott's symptoms'. And although we are told that (at least in this case) 'labels fail', at no point is it suggested to the student reader that such failure in any way invalidates, or even raises questions about, the labelling of odd conduct as 'disease'. Rather, Helfgott's psychiatrist is approvingly quoted as saying: 'He's not autistic, not schizophrenic, and may be manic only in the colloquial rather than the clinical sense'.[7] What this, in turn, accomplishes is to allow the next claim, that: 'the absence of a clear diagnostic label does not seem to trouble anyone, however. If anything, it adds to Helfgott's charm and to the public's fascination with him' (1998: xvii and 153). Helfgott is thus held up as a quirky, odd-looking and amusing puzzle for good-hearted psychiatrists whose proper business is to be concerned about 'clear' diagnostic labels. A 'clear' diagnostic label might not be forthcoming, but the supposed encouragement this segment is said to offer to students to 'think critically about what they have learned' (Comer, 1998: xvii, 153) is neatly aborted — not only by Helfgott's inclusion as a thinkpiece in the first place, but also by the clear implication that he is (albeit unclearly) actually diagnosable and the suggestion that his 'mania' may, in fact, be real in a 'clinical' as opposed to a 'colloquial' sense. Had *Shine* not been a huge box-office success what, we wonder, could have illustrated the question of 'When labels fail'?

In Comer's chapter on 'Generalized Anxiety Disorder and Phobias', we are presented with a colour picture of a masked Hannibal

---

7. Comer's reference is '(Chang and Gates, 1997, p. 62)'. Chang and Gates, however, fail to make it as far as the Bibliography.

Lecter in a face-off with an intense-looking male FBI operative.[8] The caption reads:

> Cognitive researchers have found that people respond less fear-fully to negative events when they can predict and control their onset. In fact, many people enjoy the feeling of fear as long as it occurs under controlled circumstances, as when they are safely viewing the sinister plots of Hannibal Lecter or other movie villains. (Comer, 1998: 169)

The picture is, at best, only tangentially related to the text which it supposedly illustrates: a discussion of rational emotive therapy techniques. The image of Lecter appears simply to add a degree of pop credibility to the all but banal observation that horror movies tend to be popular at the box office, *ergo* we can confidently suggest that people 'enjoy' being scared by them. Of course, when this fundamentally self-evident noticing is recycled in Comer's textbook, we are not asked to read this for what it is: blindingly obvious. Rather we are enjoined to take it as a penetrating insight into human nature discovered by impressive-sounding (but unnamed) 'cognitive researchers'.

Captioning continuity, by-lining biology

A key device for the management of persuasion in these texts is the construction of the impression that they do not deal in conjecture, speculation or opinion, but in facts derived from the progress of various sciences. A related task is to establish that the facts presented are accurate descriptions of the way things really stand in the world. And a crucial tactic towards this end is to persuade the reader that 'it was ever thus': that historically observed phenomena are *identical with* those described in the DSM-IV. So what these texts seek to do is to cement their authority by saying, in effect, 'at first it was thought *x*, now we know *y*'. Just as one might strengthen a knowledge claim in conversation by expressing initial scepticism about the position you now advance, so too these texts hold up (often for ridicule) historical and/or non-western accounts of phenomena which appear to bear (or which can be bludgeoned into bearing) a resemblance to contemporary unwanted conduct and then claim that a putative correspondence proves the case that they are making.[9]

In our first instance of this anachronistic strategy, a full-colour

---

8. The image is so well known, it appears, that the film source, *Silence of the Lambs*, does not even need to be mentioned.
9. This is a tactic routinely used by advertisers of soap powder in TV commercials: 'I used to believe nothing could wash whiter than Ariel, until I tried the new cold wash formula!'

photographic image takes up one-third of the facing page. A heterogeneous group of people appear to be dancing in rows of seating, or sitting in what appear to be pews. One man clasps his hands in a prayer-like gesture; a large woman in a baggy dress gazes at the roof, her mouth wide open. The caption reads: 'speaking in tongues in some churches today *may be* similar to the "dancing manias" of Europe in the Middle Ages, like St Vitus' dance and tarantism' (Schwartz, 2000: 19; our emphasis). Of course, 'speaking in tongues in some churches today' may *not* be in any way similar, or even bear the slightest resemblance to, so-called dancing manias or St Vitus' dance. It is enough that the text accompanying the photograph should assure us that the term 'St Vitus' dance' 'is still in use today to describe the odd muscle movements that accompany some forms of brain disorder, especially brain damage caused by some high fevers' (Schwartz, 2000: 18). The implications are clear enough: specific odd behaviours have historically continuous identifiable forms and, in all probability, they are caused by 'brain disorder'.

In the next example, monochrome head-and-shoulder portraits of Ernest and Margaux Hemingway, both smiling, both turning to look over their right shoulder to camera, fill half the page. The caption reads:

> Depression and suicide are unusually common in some families, suggesting that heredity plays a role. Ernest Hemingway's father, brother, and a sister committed suicide, as did his granddaughter Margaux. Hemingway and his father probably suffered from manic-depression; Margaux, once a model and movie actress, had suffered from depression and bulimia. (Schwartz, 2000: 46)

Models, movie actresses and Nobel prize-winning novelists, it seems, can't escape the clutches of biology: again we see the recruitment of celebrity to sell the biological story. The lesson between the lines is clear enough. This is the flip-side of the 'American Dream': if it can happen to them — people with money, fame, wealth, beauty, everything to live for — it *must* be biological. Like a 'complete the sentence to win' promotion for a package holiday, the caption works by being careful to include enough detail to let the story speak for itself, while leaving a line of dots where the correct answer is to be inserted: 'Hemingway and his father probably suffered from manic-depression'.... (which is why they committed suicide). 'Margaux, once a model and movie actress, had suffered from depression and bulimia'.... (showing evidence of the inherited mental disorder which caused her suicide).

We also note the judicious use here of *maybe*'s close relative, *probably*. 'Hemingway and his father *probably* suffered from manic-depression': Hemingway and his father also *probably* travelled by train, *probably* had lots of recreational sex, *probably* wore red socks, and so forth. What Hemingway and his father 'probably suffered' from (or did not) can, quite obviously, be little more than speculation. But the structure of the caption works to mask this by the immediate presentation of the 'bald fact' that Margaux '*had*' suffered from depression and bulimia. Equally, Ernest Hemingway's father, brother, and a sister all had American accents, as did his granddaughter Margaux, but are we to believe that 'heredity plays a role' in this too? Being middle class runs in families too, as does voting one way or the other. Are we to presume that these forms of conduct are equally genetically determined?

If the Hemingways are insufficient to convince the reader that depression and suicide must be biological simply because they are observed in rich families, then the message is spelt out in simple terms in Kendall and Hammen's chapter on 'Suicide' (1995: 270). Filling the lower third of the page, Marilyn Monroe appears in a black-and-white shot. In furs and framed by the rear window of her limousine, she looks up past the camera, lips parted and smiling. Two police officers escorting the car are reflected in the window glass immediately behind her. The back of a man in a herringbone jacket is visible squatting in the back of the limo in front of her, talking to the driver. What is the reader to make of this image? Kendall and Hammen's caption dismisses soft-headed, existentialist understandings of self-killing. Marilyn's image, they suggest, is hard evidence of the overwhelming, and context-independent, agency of 'psychological problems' in determining human action. They state that:

> Suicide is usually seen, tragically, as a solution to unbearable misery — but most often it is a baffling and 'irrational solution'. For example, Marilyn Monroe was one of the most beautiful and famous women in the world, with all the wealth and adoration one could ever want, but her psychological problems prevented her from finding solace in her good fortune. (Kendall and Hammen, 1995: 270)

In another of our texts, Comer reproduces a black-and-white photograph taken a matter of moments later. Here Marilyn is standing beside the limo behind one of the two police officers who had been approaching the car in Kendall and Hammen's image. Surrounded by a crowd of onlookers, fur falling around her bare shoulders, she smiles past the camera. What does Monroe's smiling image show here? The caption once again instructs the reader not to trust their everyday experience:

> Some people mask their depression by smiling and looking happy most of the time. The movie star Marilyn Monroe was such a person. Emotion researcher Paul Ekman and his colleagues ... claim that certain facial and behavioural clues dis-

tinguish genuine happiness from masked depression, but that 'we learn to ignore them, not wanting the burden of knowing the truth'. (Comer, 1998: 241)

Again, we see Marilyn's image recruited to *stand for* the theoretical claims that depression is a thing inside persons and, moreover, a thing that requires carefully trained 'emotion researchers' (but not, it appears, ordinary folk) to detect leaking out via 'certain facial and behavioural clues'. What Ekman and his colleagues have to say (the real 'message' of the image) is, however, not a fact, but a conjecture, a 'claim'. In a massively used device in these texts, what may be seen to be a flimsy or partisan proposal (here, that there is a real disorder called 'masked depression') is prefaced by factual claims immune to refutation. Whether Marilyn Monroe 'really' 'suffered' from 'masked depression', whether Marilyn Monroe was such a person, is absolutely irrelevant to the rhetorical point being made here. It can be asserted as fact, safe in the knowledge that she is, sadly, unable to answer back. (Though we can well imagine the gobful she could have delivered in response.)

Two scruffy-looking bearded men stare out of a full-colour photo on the page facing Barlow and Durand's discussion of 'cultural factors in schizophrenia' (2001: 417). Their argument is that a well-known (and, for biological psychiatry, deeply inconvenient) World Health Organisation study (Leff et al., 1992) which demonstrated large cross-cultural variations in the 'course and outcome of schizophrenia', along with the raft of research which demonstrates race-dependent diagnosis, has been misunderstood. They state that: 'differing rates of schizophrenia, therefore, appear to be due to misdiagnosis rather than to any real cultural distinctions' (Barlow and Durand, 2001: 416–17). If readers are unconvinced, they can refer back to the two scruffy men in beards, whose photo appears immediately above the words '… due to misdiagnosis rather than to cultural distinctions'. What does the picture caption tell us? That supposedly 'mentally ill' hoboes in New York, Ulan Bator and Wagga Wagga all look bedraggled? No. The picture represents the fact that: 'schizophrenia has been known throughout the ages all over the world. In this scene, Shakespeare's King Lear descends into "madness"' (2001: 417). It seems that Shakespeare, aside from being a handy thespian and poet, was, without even knowing it (which is what Barlow and Durand's scare quotes are there to tell us), the direct seventeenth-century ancestor of Kraepelin, Bleuler and the American Psychiatric Association. It's schizophrenia, Will, but not as we know it.

Side by side, a colour reproduction of Francisco de Goya's (1812–14) *The Madhouse* and a black-and-white still from *One Flew Over the Cuckoo's Nest* occupy the top third of the second page of Comer's discussion of the use of token economies for the treatment of schizophrenia. In both images, the background figures are grouped on the left-hand side of the image, with a leading figure apparently holding back the others. Slightly offset to the right of centre, the main figure (in the *Cuckoo's Nest* still, of course, Randall McMurphy/Jack Nicholson) stands with outstretched arms. Comer (1998: 514) writes in the caption:

> Francisco de Goya's early nineteenth-century painting *The Madhouse*, depicting a typical mental hospital of his day, is strikingly similar to the portrayal in Ken Kesey's 1950s novel (later a play and a film), *One Flew over the Cuckoo's Nest*. Institutions of both the distant and the recent past were overcrowded, often negligent, and concerned primarily with keeping order.

It is indeed remarkable, is it not, that two *works of art* so far apart in historical time should represent, with such accuracy, just how bad conditions used to be? We are encouraged to read these images then, again, as monologic: as forms of actual historical documentation. The caption is telling us that it could only be because that is what it was *really* like, that two such convergent representations could have come about. The similarity is, we are told, 'striking'. Perhaps that is why the picture editor chose them? Or perhaps Milos Forman knew of Goya's work and incorporated it into his direction of this shot? But these are not questions germane to the work this pair of images is doing. Once again, the reproduction of these images is all about the progress of science. They are mobilised in the service of setting up, rhetorically, what comes next: Francisco de Goya and Jack Nicholson are not there simply to show the reader how bad things were way back when; they are there precisely to establish *as factual* a putative historical continuity with the past, which is then used as a contrast case to celebrate the supposedly humane, enlightened treatment that 'schizophrenics' are now said, in the text, to receive. In other words, we can read Goya's and Kesey/Forman/Nicholson's images as being there precisely to 'show', to offer historical 'evidence' for, the claimed overcrowding, negligence and control which the next subsection of the text ('Antipsychotic Drugs') is specifically concerned to deny plays any part in contemporary 'treatment'.[10]

Artful uses of art and artifice

The four textbooks examined in this chapter not only draw upon contemporary images from popular culture, but also freely use his-

---

10. The uneasy relationship of abnormal psychology textbooks to so-called non-'objective' texts — such as the 'testimony' of people 'living with challenging conditions' as Barlow and Durand (2001: xxi) have it — is also highlighted in this instance. Why do we need to be told that *One Flew Over The Cuckoo's Nest* was a novel, a play and a film? Are T-Shirts available too?

torical artworks. Only Schwartz (2000: 17) uses art (Hieronymus Bosch's *The Ship of Fools*, c. 1490–1500) to caution *against* the historicist fallacy (which he terms 'presentism') — into which trap all four authors fall. As a 'deviant case', then, Schwartz's use of the Bosch is particularly illuminating. A full-colour reproduction of the painting is a key feature of a 'highlight' box in the first chapter of his book. The highlight box device is supposed to elucidate in greater detail a core conceptual point of the chapter. 'Why we should never judge the past by the present' (which is the main caption) is thus intended to reinforce the point that imaginative reconstruction of the past in today's terms, and using current concepts (the historicist fallacy), is intellectually incoherent. Schwartz writes that: 'by assuming our current theories and practices are always wise and that previous generations and ancient cultures were ignorant we are succumbing to what historians call presentism — imposing the standards of one civilization on another. Presentism colors most published histories of abnormal psychology' (2000: 16). While Schwartz is to be commended for explicitly drawing students' attention to the problem, he lapses directly into the closely related fallacy of disciplinary imperialism and, subsequently, into a version of 'presentism' itself. As we shall see, his own text draws freely upon 'current theories and practices' and the standards of one culture to account for another.

But to return to the 'Ship of Fools': Schwartz's stalking horse, in this example, is Michel Foucault and, specifically, his arguments in the first chapter of *Madness and Civilization: A History of Insanity in the Age of Reason* entitled 'Stultifera Navis'. The argument runs that Foucault has made a fundamental mistake about an artistic representation (the Bosch painting); he has taken it for a literal figuration of an historical practice and, worse, has gone on to equate such cruel and unusual treatment of the insane in the fifteenth century with today's methods.[11] But if we go to Foucault's text and look closely, we find that Foucault is primarily interested in one overwhelming event occurring in the fifteenth and early sixteenth centuries throughout Europe. That event is no less than the first appearance of ur-insanity itself — as 'folly', *la folie*, and a host of similar terms in the various European tongues. This is nothing less than an explosion of interest in insanity on all sorts of fronts: in literature, in painting, in religious thinking, in philosophy and so on. Foucault is trying to show how the whole of what we would now call 'European culture' was suffused with an entirely new phenomenon: the possibility of delineating persons and populations as insane or otherwise. And what interests him about this 'pre-classical' (or Renaissance) period is that it was not until a good deal *later* that this new 'madness' could be counterposed against reason, rationality or science. Madness, that

---

11. In this respect, a better stalking horse for Schwartz's argument would be Comer's 'presentist' equation between Goya and *Cuckoo's Nest*, discussed above.

Hieronymus Bosch, *The Ship of Fools* (c. 1490–1500). Oil on wood, 58 x 33cm.
Musée du Louvre: Paris.

is, emerges *before* and separately from its later (seventeenth century) binary juxtaposition with reason. And the techniques for its production and management are, he shows, largely taken over from the earlier techniques for handling leprosy:

> Poor vagabonds, criminals, and 'deranged minds' would take the part played by the leper, and we shall see what salvation was expected from this exclusion, for them and for those who excluded them as well. With an altogether new meaning and in a very different culture, the forms would remain — essentially that major form of a rigorous division which is *social exclusion but spiritual reintegration*. (1967: 7; our emphasis)

This sets the theme then: the double *form* of 'social exclusion but spiritual reintegration' is maintained, while the cultural context shifts dramatically. Accordingly, Foucault is extremely interested in the shift in cultural context. And so he does not confine himself simply to contemporary paintings (let alone to a single work by Bosch). If one is interested in critical cultural changes, one needs to be much broader than this and, where possible, identify general dominant cultural associations common to multifarious representations. There is one such association that Foucault locates throughout the graphic, literary, religious and philosophical works of the time. This is actually quite simple, but also new (for the time) and devastating. It is also so strange to us today as to throw into *contrast* our current means of handling madness. The association is this (as José Barchilon MD puts it in his Introduction): 'folly, water, and sea, as everyone "knew", had an affinity for each other' (1967: vi–vii).

To this extent, the literary and artistic allegory of the 'Ship of Fools' (as a general cultural mythos and not just in the Bosch) is precisely that: a literary and artistic allegory — and Foucault explicitly tells us as much. But it is not *just* an allegory for all that. It is one that expresses a whole new cultural 'mentality' with regard to the displacement of the leper by the madman. In the following passage, for example, we can witness Foucault distinguishing the 'Ship of Fools' allegory from its near neighbours; namely, those that *were* mere allegories with no possible basis in social and political fact:

> The *Narrenschiff* [Ship of Fools], of course, is a literary composition, probably borrowed from the old Argonaut cycle, one of the great mythic themes recently revived and rejuvenated, acquiring an institutional aspect in the Burgundy Estates. Fashion favored the composition of these Ships, whose crew of imaginary heroes, ethical models, or social types embarked on a great symbolic voyage which would bring them, if not fortune, then at least the figure of their destiny or their truth. The Symphorien Champier composes a *Ship of Princes and Battles of Nobility* in 1502, then a

Ship of Virtuous Ladies in 1503; there is also a *Ship of Health*,
alongside the *Blauwe Schute* of Jacob von Oestvoren in 1413;
Sebastian Brant's *Narrenschiff* (1494), and the work of Josef Bade:
Stultiferae naviculae scaphae fatuarum mulierum (1498). Bosch's
painting, of course, belongs to this dream fleet. (1967: 7–8)

Note several points here. Firstly: the Bosch painting is just *one* instance (albeit a particularly emblematic one) of a widespread popular allegorical tradition that associates the sea voyage with social
distanciation in (for us, perhaps, paradoxical) harmony with the saving of the soul.[12] Foucault has not simply mistaken a single painting
for 'historical fact' and been led astray in amateur schoolboy fashion.
He is far too astute an historian for that. Secondly: Foucault is explicit about the literary and allegorical nature of the material he is
dealing with. He tells us directly that the 'Ship of Fools' is a literary
composition, and one in a whole panoply of contemporary composi-
tions concerning the meaning of the sea voyage throughout Renaissance cultures. Foucault, who was later to take the title 'Professor of
the History of Systems of Thought', is interested in precisely that: the
general system of thought operating at the time on a whole range of
fronts and specifically its means of *imagining* the new phenomenon
of folly. But thirdly, and even though this may not in fact be germane
to an argument about a *mentality* (perhaps even about a 'spirit of the
time'), it turns out that the 'Ship of Fools' allegory distinguishes itself
from the others by having at least some possible basis in fact. And,
ever the accurate historian, Foucault gives us the evental (Foucault,
1981) details and the few remaining facts and figures to back this
up. Continuing directly from the passage quoted above:

But of all these romantic or satiric vessels, the *Narrenschiff* is
the only one that had a real existence — for they did exist,
these boats that conveyed their insane cargo from town to town.
Madmen then led an easy wandering existence. The towns drove
them outside their limits; they were allowed to wander the open
countryside, when not entrusted to a group of merchants and
pilgrims. The custom was especially frequent in Germany; in
Nuremberg, in the first half of the fifteenth century, the presence of 63 madmen had been registered; 31 were driven away;
in the 50 years that followed, there are records of 21 more

---

12. Of course, Schwartz — along with all other abnormal psychology textbook
writers — in fact specifies social distanciation as not only a documented historical form of treatment of 'the mentally ill' (for example in discussions of the
reasons for the placement of Victorian asylums well away from centres of population), but also in their descriptions of 'diagnostic criteria' for such 'illnesses'
as 'schizophrenia', 'agoraphobia' or 'depression' where, in the present-day in-
version of this association, the shunning of social contact becomes a pathognomic
indicator of madness.

obligatory departures; and those are only the madmen arrested by the municipal authorities. Frequently they were handed over to boatmen: in Frankfort, in 1399, seamen were instructed to rid the city of a madman who walked about the streets naked; in the first years of the fifteenth century, a criminal madman was expelled in the same manner from Mainz. Sometimes the sailors disembarked these bothersome passengers sooner than they had promised; witness a blacksmith of Frankfort twice expelled and twice returning before being taken to Kreuznach for good. Often the cities of Europe must have seen these 'ships of fools' approaching their harbours. (1967: 8)

The point of Foucault's work is absolutely and clearly not then to show some kind of direct continuity (or even parallel) between the cruelties of yesteryear and those of today in matters of managing the insane. Quite the contrary: the point is to get to the very different and unique system of thought of the Renaissance. How could we think, today, of madness — in and as its very social exclusion — as being a kind of journey to spiritual salvation, R.D. Laing notwithstanding? How would it be possible for us to re-associate madness primarily with the sea and with water, rather than with, for example, brain dysfunction or a whole range of other quasi-medical correlates?

These are all but impossibilities today and require remarkable leaps of the historical imagination. The sheer impossibility of thinking *that* (as Foucault once put it in another context): this is what can set off our thinking about the unique and particular strangeness of our own psychologisation of the insane and the sane alike. And that strangeness is all the more poignant specifically because it is *not* strictly continuous with the Renaissance myth of travel-as-salvation. Indeed, then, as Schwartz tells us, the past must not be judged in terms of the present and this is precisely Foucault's point as an historian of evental specificity. Our current arrangements, as Foucault shows in *Madness and Civilization*, may well be the very distant descendants of the Renaissance when, after all, ur-forms of madness and insanity made their European debut. And they may contain vestiges of those remote ancestors — the mad *are* still sometimes confined; therapy *is* still very occasionally respecified as the soul's salvation — but it is the discontinuities that set into relief our own very specific regimes of governing, today, not just the certifiably insane but also the normally anxious citizen.

For all this, the Bosch's painting is used by Schwartz, in conjunction with the citation of a paper by Maher and Maher (1982), to illustrate Foucault's own supposed follies. The caption reads:

Presentism can distort psychological research. For example, as this fifteenth-century painting by Hieronymus Bosch exemplifies, the 'ship of fools' was a popular allegorical device used in the early Renaissance to ridicule aspects of society. It was not a method for dealing with the mentally ill, as Michel Foucault has claimed.

In the surrounding text Schwartz suggests that:

> Michel Foucault, in his influential history of abnormal psychology, *Madness and Civilization* (1967), claimed that in the middle ages people with mental disorders were loaded onto boats and sent out to sea. These 'ships of fools' were often denied permission to dock, so they sailed from one port to another or simply drifted on the ocean. (2000: 17)

It is a neat move to recruit your critics, neater still to present a fifteenth-century painting as self-evident warrant for your up-to-the-minute analysis. How Bosch's painting 'exemplifies' the 'fact' that the 'Ship of Fools' was an 'allegorical device' is at no point stated: it is simply presented as fact. (Compare Foucault himself who offers, as we have seen, a historically-grounded discussion of its generic status.) In conjunction with this presentist reading of Bosch, Foucault is enlisted as a historian of *psychology* by fiat. One notes that *Madness and Civilization* is, in fact, neither 'psychological research' nor is it a 'history of abnormal psychology', but rather (as the subtitle of the English translation actually has it) 'a history of insanity in the age of reason' which, in its first chapter, is discussing the emergence of 'folly' prior to the said age. Presentism, it seems, can blind even those who warn of it: we simply can't *have* a history of abnormal psychology as such in the fifteenth-century, because there was no such thing as psychology in the fifteenth-century, 'abnormal' or otherwise. Equally, it would be very difficult for the 'Ship of Fools' to have been a method for dealing with 'people with mental disorders' or the 'mentally ill' in late medieval Europe, again precisely because such persons did not exist in the 1400s.[13]

Ironically then, Schwartz's efforts to debunk work critical of the standard psy-complex Whig history of itself falls into precisely the trap (of unthinking literalism) that he claims renders Foucault unreliable.[14] As Green (1998) has noted:

---

13. Foucault never actually describes ships of fools as mobile 'concentration camps' as Schwartz claims. Perhaps this is the sort of historical inaccuracy that psychology can live with? Interestingly enough, Rosenhan and Seligman, in their textbook *Abnormal Psychology* (1984), reproduce a woodcut of a *Narrenschiff* on page 33, and accurately describe Foucault's conclusions on the prior page.

14. The 'scientific' scorn for 'historically unreliable' sources such as literature and art is selective. In his chapter on 'Sexual Dysfunctions', Schwartz's highlight box, complete with a period woodcut portrait, introduces an apparently entirely serious discussion of 'sex addiction' as follows: 'Don Juan, the ...

Madness and Civilization ... is [similarly] a history of a *concept*: 'madness'. What Foucault aimed to show was that efforts of traditional histories of psychiatry to link the modern concept of 'mental illness' with the various concepts of 'madness' as they were understood during the Renaissance, the Enlightenment and the nineteenth-century are misguided in exactly the same way as is the effort to locate the modern concept of 'reflex' in the work of Descartes. To do so confuses the description of a phenomenon with its explanation and location in the conceptual network of a period, and is, in part, the result of similar terms being used to express different understandings in different times.

Such concerns, however, do not appear to trouble either Barlow and Durand, Comer or Kendall and Hammen. Comer's (1998) first chapter, discussing 'Abnormal Psychology: Past and Present', thus opens with a half-page, full-colour reproduction of *The Surgeon* by van Hemessen (c. 1555). As shown in the figure overleaf, *The Surgeon* depicts a man bound to a chair in the process of having an object excised from the centre of his bloodied forehead. A wimpled older woman holds the patient's head while the bespectacled surgeon wields his scalpel. Behind the old woman, another, younger, woman holds a bowl and approaches a table on which sit retorts, jars, rags and a manuscript. Suspended between the women's heads are a series of objects such as that being removed from the patient. At the bottom right-hand corner of the painting another man, head thrown back, eyes closed, appears to crack his knuckles in the air above his head. In the background, we can discern a canal-side scene with a large building and, on the canal bank, figures stand and talk.

So, what are we to make of this complex image? Comer makes it clear and simple. The caption states straightforwardly that:

> *The Surgeon*, by Jan Saunders [sic] van Hemessen, reminds us that demonological beliefs dominated the study and treatment of abnormal behaviour until recent times. As far back as the Stone Age, people viewed abnormality as the work of evil spirits, and 'practitioners' sometimes opened a person's skull to release the spirits. (1998: 1)

As with all other instances of the use of historic images in these texts, the device here is simple enough. The use of this image is designed to accomplish the 'documentation' of a historic continuity in the phenomena under question (abnormal behaviour *qua* mental

---

... legendary profligate immortalized in poems, novels, and operas was supposed to have made love to hundreds or even thousands of women before being dragged off to a fiery hell. Was he addicted to sex?' (Schwartz, 2000: 580).

Jan Sanders van Hemessen, *The Surgeon* (c. 1555). Oil on wood, 100 x 141 cm. Museo del Prado: Madrid.

illness) from the 'Stone Age' to the present, with the rider that we nowadays have a more sophisticated understanding of these matters.[15] What work does the simple term 'reminds' do here? It suggests that, of course, we *already knew* that our forebears reliably identified as abnormal the same forms of conduct that we do — even if they resorted to primitive beliefs to account for them. The term 'beliefs' is also carefully chosen: not 'theories', 'accounts' or 'explanations', but 'beliefs' — opinions held in the absence of evidence. The caption furthers its project of ridicule by suggesting that the benighted cavemen who opened skulls on the basis of their 'demonological' beliefs were not *really* practitioners (hence the scare quotes). Until recently then, and unlike the lobotomists of today who base their openings of the skull on hard science, our ancestors treated 'abnormality' on the basis of unsubstantiated fantasy.

Barlow and Durand's use of *The Surgeon* is similarly straightforward. In their chapter on schizophrenia, in the subsection on 'treatment', they reproduce a heavily cropped version of the same image, framed by a helpful explanatory text:

15. Sadly, as the Stone Age written record appears to be unavailable, we have to resort to conjecture to establish how Stone Age peoples viewed 'normality' and 'abnormality'. But why let the facts (or their absence) get in the way of a good story?

The search for help [for someone who has delusions, hears his dead uncle's voice, or can't communicate complete thoughts] has taken many paths, sometimes down some very disturbing roads; for example in the 1500s primitive surgery was conducted to remove the 'stone of madness', which was thought to cause disturbed behaviour. As barbaric as it may seem today, it is not very different from the prefrontal lobotomies performed on people with schizophrenia as late as the 1950s .... Even today, some societies use crude surgical procedures to eliminate the symptoms of schizophrenia. In Kenya, for instance, Kisii tribal doctors listen to their patients to find the location of noises in their heads (hallucinations), then get them drunk, cut out a piece of scalp, and scrape the skull in the area of the voices (Mustafa, 1990). In the Western world today, treatment usually begins with one of the neuroleptic drugs that are invaluable in reducing the symptoms of schizophrenia. (Barlow and Durand, 2001: 428)

The Surgeon appears, in colour, immediately adjacent to this text. It is captioned 'An early sixteenth-century painting of psychosurgery, in which part of the brain is removed to treat mental illness'. Let's look at what Barlow and Durand are doing here. The image is visually striking and is carefully positioned in the right-hand column of the verso page. One cannot but glance from the description of 'primitive surgery' in medieval Europe and 'crude surgical procedures' among today's 'tribal' Africans to the gory image of a clearly conscious man, his head cut open and a scalpel buried in his forehead. So that's what it looks like! It is just as well that 'in the Western world today' science has advanced enough to realise that such 'barbaric' practices are (and always have been) misguided. The text works to elide historical phenomena with today's orthodoxy, and simultaneously to demonstrate the superiority of 'Western' science over the primitive beliefs of crude tribespeople. (Was van Hemesen's surgeon perhaps helping his client overcome hearing the voice of his dead uncle, or to communicate complete thoughts?) Whether 'noises in the head' and the notion of 'hallucination' are, in practice, referents for the same phenomenon is simply not a question which can be asked in this context. In a simple, yet profound, parenthesis the world view of the Kisii is wiped out. They are no better informed than superstitious medieval Europeans. If only they knew it, like all the rest of the schizophrenics throughout history, their 'hallucinations' are really symptoms of schizophrenia-as-disease.

To show concession to the errors of the past, the brief mention of 'prefrontal lobotomies' carried out 'as late as the 1950s', in itself, does some careful work here. This is a plea in mitigation: a 'that was then, but this is now' device which sets up the segue into the wonders of today's shiny new product, the 'invaluable neuroleptic drugs'.

The device is remarkably similar to that routinely used by people who have weird, baffling or supernatural experiences to report. Robin Wooffitt (1992) has shown how such accounts typically start with a claim to utter banality — 'I was just doing the washing up' — as a grounding for the sanity and ordinariness of the speaker, immediately followed by the possibly suspect claim, 'When a UFO landed on the lawn'. Here we see an analogue, with a pre-admission of culpability followed by a claim to reform. 'I used to beat my wife when I drank, but now I'm on the wagon and cook dinner for her'. 'We used to give schizophrenics prefrontal lobotomies (as some tribal savages still do) but now we give them invaluable drugs (being the up-to-date, humane and enlightened scientists that we are).' The device then works, paradoxically, to establish the unquestionable *bona fides* of the subsequent claim by virtue of an admission of past error.

As well as falling straight into the historicist fallacy, both Comer's and Barlow and Durand's captions play fast and loose with the actual historical record. For Comer, that van Hemessen painted *The Surgeon* in the late 1550s (and that the figures appear to be wearing the dress of that period rather than 'Stone Age' skins — not to mention the fact that the man with the scalpel appears to be wearing glasses) is, apparently, not relevant to our understanding of what the picture means. While Comer may be upbraided for merely misunderstanding medieval theories of the 'falling sickness' and what were then thought to be the relations between the presence of stones in the head and the production of gibberish, Barlow and Durand's caption is more blatantly deceptive. *The Surgeon* is anything but a 'painting of psychosurgery' (and not least because 'psycho' surgery only became possible after Descartes). Neither does the painting depict the removal of 'part of the brain' — as even a cursory examination of the image reveals — to treat 'mental illness'. Rather, *The Surgeon* is a satirical painting of a phenomenon that was widespread in pre-Renaissance Europe (and we shall see another example shortly). That is, it depicts a 'Stone Cutter' operating at a fair. It is not a 'part of the brain' that is being removed, but rather a 'stone' (held since Galen to be the cause of 'falling sickness') and the removal thereof, denounced as charlatanism since the time of Rhazes of Persia in 900 (Epilepsy Museum, 2002). Of course, in this case, there actually *is* a documentable historical continuity in the condition which has also been called 'epilepsy' since at least the twelfth-century — for instance the British Museum's Sloane Manuscripts Collection features a twelfth-century artwork depicting cranial surgery titled *Epilepticus sic curabitur* ('The way to cure an epileptic'). Unfortunately for the case that Barlow and Durand, and the other textbook writers, wish to make, epilepsy is widely accepted to be a *neurological condition*, *not* a 'mental illness', *not* a 'mental disorder' and absolutely *not* a 'psychological problem'.

Stone cutting also features in Hieronymus Bosch's (c. 1475-80)

Hieronymus Bosch, *The Cure of Folly* ('Extraction of the Stone of Madness') (c. 1475–80). Oil on board, 48 x 35 cm. Museo del Prado: Madrid.

The Cure of Folly ('Extraction of the Stone of Madness') reproduced in both Barlow and Durand (2001: 11) and Kendall and Hammen (1995: 9). *The Cure of Folly* shows a central image, with Gothic text above and below a circular graphic. The text reads 'Master cuts out the stone — my name is Lubert Das' while the figure depicts an elderly, rotund man sprawled in a chair in the middle of a field. Behind him stands a robed figure with a steel funnel on his head, carefully cutting an object out of the top of the seated man's head. A Dominican friar stands beside the seated figure gesturing with his right hand, while holding a flagon in his left. A bored looking woman is to the right of the friar, leaning on a table with a book balanced on her head.[16]

Kendall and Hammen's first chapter is called 'Abnormal Behavior in Context'. *The Cure of Folly* appears in the subsection, 'Changing historical views of psychological abnormality' which starts with what, it seems, is to be understood as a 'case vignette', and then launches straight into the project of confecting an historical continuity between unwanted, odd or unusual conduct in the ancient world and in contemporary California.

> The old woman can be seen at night, wandering the dark streets of her village, muttering meaningless phrases. Her clothes are torn and she is dirty. Sometimes she'll cry out as if she's being attacked, commanding the unseen intruders to go away.
> This scene recurs throughout civilization. Such people — men or women — could be found in Greece a thousand years before Jesus, in ancient India, or in tribal Africa. They could be seen walking the streets of medieval England or imperial China — or colonial Salem, Massachusetts, or today's Venice Beach, California ... Ancient texts from most cultures contained clear descriptions of major psychological disorders that we would recognize today: depression, manic-depression, schizophrenia, senile dementia, anxiety states and more. (Kendall and Hammen, 1995: 9).

The half page (facing page, as we have come to expect) below this text is entirely taken up with two images. On the left, a full-colour reproduction of Bosch's (c. 1475–80) *The Cure of Folly*. To the

---

16. Lubert Das (little gelded man) had the sense of 'simpleton' in fifteenth-century Flemish (Epilepsy Museum, 2002). Bosch's caption to his own painting (needless to say untranslated and unexplicated in any of the texts examined here where it appears) thus makes it entirely clear that the painting is not a realist representation of psychosurgery, not a technical manual for Hippocratic brain surgery and certainly not a 'piece of the brain' being removed. It is nothing of the sort. It is, in fact, a satire on quackery and the gullibility of those who will believe anything that doctors (and the church) tell them. It is, in that sense, an unintentionally apt illustration.

right, a smaller black and white photograph of a skull, taken from the left side with a round hole just above and behind the temple. Again, text and image designedly work in harmony, with the caption, immediately below the skull, reinforcing the point. How are these utterly diverse images joined? The caption reads:

Stone Age skulls display the earliest evidence of a surgical attempt to alter abnormal behaviour. Scholars presume that the holes were made to release demons suspected by ancient societies of causing madness. The process, called *trephining*, was a forerunner of the views of Hippocrates who, centuries later, taught that mental illness is caused by the brain — a view that continued in the Middle Ages and that continues to be prominent in modern explanations of disorder.

All three elements, text, images and caption, work in concert.[17] The piece of fiction about the 'old woman' (some of whose 'meaningless phrases' apparently mean that 'unseen intruders' should 'go away'?) is immediately followed by a breathtaking truth claim that sweeps the entire history of humanity into *Abnormal Psychology*'s remit. How what is clearly marked as a fictionalised generalisation of clinical experience, and which reads as much like a stage direction or script instruction as it does anything else, furthers the project of repudiating the difficulties supposedly caused by 'clinical experience or talk-show exposure often pass[ing] for truth about psychological problems' (Kendall and Hammen, 1995: ix) is far from clear. But what is immediately apparent is that this claim to near-universal relevance is itself followed at once by the highly dubious claim that 'ancient texts from most cultures contained clear descriptions of major psychological disorders that we would recognize today'. Would not the exact opposite bring us closer to the truth?: *no* ancient text from *any* culture contains a 'clear description' of any 'major psychological disorder' quite simply because 'major psychological disorders' are the invention of our own times. Indeed, we *are* told that Socrates heard the voice of his dæmon and Achilles spoke with Zeus (Leudar and Thomas, 2000) 'in Greece a thousand years before Jesus', but the texts of Ancient Greece (none of which, of course, are identified by the 'relentlessly research-focused' Kendall and Hammen) do not describe *any* 'major psychological disorder' afflicting Socrates or Achilles: they describe the hearing of the voice of a dæmon, or of the Gods.

One of the nicer ways in which undergraduate students can be

---

17. This careful piece of elision of fictionalised vignette, explicit truth claim, speculation and simple falsehood comes just eight pages after the Preface states that: 'this book is relentlessly research-focused ... to help students develop scientific attitudes to counteract the influence of an era in which clinical experience or talk-show exposure often pass for truth about psychological problems' (Kendall and Hammen, 1995: ix).

persuaded is by simply presenting dubious statements as *facts*. Don't cite sources for your claims: Which ancient texts? From which cultures? Who wrote them? Who translated them? Don't tell your reader the name of the painting you reproduce; don't even mention it explicitly in the text or the caption. Just put it in a visually salient place on the page and let it carry the weight of implication. Allow it to 'speak for itself'. And, if at all possible, preface statements which might imply scientific incompleteness, uncertainty (or speculation) with ones that simply make bald assertions. So if one must concede that 'scholars *presume* that the holes were made...', ensure that this concession to presumption (a knowledge claim made in the absence of knowledge) is preceded by a claim such as 'skulls *display* the earliest *evidence* of a surgical attempt to alter abnormal behaviour'. This shifting of voice is exquisite: it is now not Phillip C. Kendall and Constance Hammen *claiming* that cave dwellers attempted to 'alter abnormal behaviour' by surgery, it is a Stone Age skull *displaying* it. That the display and the 'truth' are to be treated as identical with each other is cemented by the careful use of the term 'evidence'. Surely the upcoming 'presumptions' of 'scholars' (again a careful lexical choice: not 'researchers', not 'palæontologists', but 'scholars') grammatically invites 'suggestion' as the most one might expect holes in old bones to afford as a knowledge claim. But no: we aren't told 'because we find skulls with holes in them, some researchers imagine that holes were made to release demons'. Instead, by very careful use of language, the student is assured that one archæological theory is, in fact, fact. The *skull* shows *evidence*. The rest of the case is built upon this. The Bosch painting is there to add a further layer of 'truth' — that the same procedures used by Stone Age people were employed in medieval Europe — affording the supposition (reinforced in the caption) that the same practices demand, *ipso facto*, the same interiorised understandings to guide them, regardless of cultural or historical context. As such, this section of this text explicitly undermines its own earlier rhetorical commitments to 'truth', and also its purported efforts to suggest that there have been 'changing views of psychological abnormality' (1995: 9). Again, what the student is being told is that the preferred DSM-IV view of misery is timeless and unchanging truth, the pinnacle of modernity's understanding of the (present and historical) self.

Barlow and Durand's use of *The Cure of Folly* occurs in their first chapter, 'Abnormal Behavior in Historical Context', in the subsection addressing 'The biological tradition'. They caption the image thus: 'bloodletting, the extraction of blood from patients, was intended to restore the balance of humours in the body' (2001: 11). A charitable reading of this caption is that Barlow and Durand were simply careless in their research. A less charitable reading would be that this is a deliberately false reading of the painting constructed to complement the discussion of the Galenic theory of humours into which it is embedded.[18] Readers unschooled in medieval art may be excused for failing to notice that *The Cure of Folly* is not a realist image of brain surgery, but rather a picture of a tulip being removed from a man's head. Slipshod research, carelessness or cavalier use of data are surely not the scientific qualities that abnormal psychology texts claim so assiduously for the discipline?

The Cure of Folly also makes an appearance in Schwartz (2000: 597) in his final chapter 'Littleton, Colorado and the Future of Abnormal Psychology'. Here, forgetting the errors of 'presentism' shown by such apparently careless researchers as Foucault, the (facing-page, full-colour, quarter-page) image is captioned:

> Our understanding and treatment of mental disorders has progressed since the fifteenth-century. In *The Extraction of the Stone of Madness* (*The Cure of Folly*), a satirical work painted in 1475-1480, Hieronymous Bosch depicts one of the common treatments of his day.

This represents one of the very few instances in these texts where both artist and title are given for an historical work.[19] It is, however, for the same reasons that we have seen before that the work is reproduced. Here too Bosch is reproduced to bolster the notion that there is an unbroken historical continuity between 'mental disorders' as they are understood and treated today and as they were understood and treated in the fifteenth-century. Where the 'satire' comes in is, unfortunately, left unexplained.

The 'relentlessly research-focused' approach adopted by Kendall and Hammen continues in their chapter on 'Schizophrenia'. In the subsection titled 'Perceptual disturbances', we are presented (on the facing page, again) with a full-colour quarter-page reproduction of an untitled painting showing a man in Elizabethan dress on a lush lawn. Leaning forward towards a translucent green 'angel' surrounded by ghostly, green, bug-eyed, demonic-looking figures, he cups his ears in a pose of attentive listening. The caption is unambiguous.

---

18. The carelessness of the 2001 edition is confirmed by the fact that, in the 2002 edition, *The Cure of Folly* is replaced with an unidentified lithograph entitled *Breathing a Vein*.

19. In what seems to be an oversight in all four textbooks, the artworks reproduced in the text are not routinely identified in terms of their titles, dates or provenances. Similarly film credits are rarely complete, if used at all. Kendall and Hammen (1995) for example, provide no attribution of artworks in the text, reserving them all for an appendix where picture credits appear. Comer is better than the others in this regard, but it seems that — universally — even supplying the likely dates of a painting reproduced in the text can be bypassed. Of course, without a title, often without an ascription, and with only a caption to go on, a less than diligent student may be forgiven for failing to discover that *The Surgeon* is not a documentary image of a medieval lobotomy.

Kendall and Hammen state, in an explicit claim to fact immediately below the image, that:

> Hearing voices — auditory hallucinations — is one of the defining symptoms of schizophrenia, although not all schizophrenic persons experience these hallucinations. (Kendall and Hammen, 1995: 297)

Quite apart from the fact that this boldly asserted 'factual' claim is strange, to say the least — could we imagine a genuinely biological science saying 'fractured tibia are one of the defining symptoms of broken legs, although not all people with broken legs experience these fractures'? — there is another problem here. It is, again, the misleading use of the image. The man in tights is not, sadly, a genuine (Elizabethan?) documentation of the 'auditory hallucinations' of schizophrenia as the text works to imply. Rather he is the late Mr F.G. Stephens, the model for a work in the mid-Victorian fairy-painting genre, commissioned by art dealer William Wethered from Sir John Everett Millais in one of his early pre-Raphælite paintings, *Ferdinand Lured by Ariel* (1849). The subject of the piece comes from Shakespeare's play *The Tempest*, and shows the sprite Ariel, along with a company of other sprites, leading Ferdinand to his master Prospero. The painting, and its period dress, thus demonstrates not the historical veracity of Kendall and Hammen's claims about the timelessness of schizophrenia and its symptoms, but rather the excellence of Victorian imaginative reproduction of Shakespearean conceits, in costume, in a genre extremely popular in the 1840s. So what is Kendall and Hammen's pretence that Millais 'shows' auditory hallucinations in aid of? Why deliberately include a pre-Raphælite painting of a scene from Shakespeare's arguably most fantastical play and pass it off as a picture of a late medieval 'hallucination'? Perhaps in order to foster the highly problematic impression (as has been accomplished via the use of art throughout these texts) that what is depicted is *not* whatever was the case, at that time and in that place, but what psychology now wishes to claim is represented. That is, these anachronistic respecifications are carefully designed to appropriate the art of the past to package the orthodoxy of the present, to repackage in period clothes what is now claimed to be 'truth'.

One is reminded of the thin, but scathing, criticism made in Maher and Maher's (1982) paper — on which Schwartz's dismissal of Foucault partly relies — which claimed to show that Foucault could not be trusted because of the small number of documented cases he provides in his account of the 'Ship of Fools' in *Madness and Civilization*, and the conclusions drawn there about the 'ideological axe' that writers such as Foucault had to grind, supposedly against the psychologisation of 'madness'. Kendall and Hammen — 'relentlessly research-focused' as they claim to be — resort to unsubstantiated claims, and the misleading use of Victorian art. Who is deluding whom? Whose ideological axe is now being ground?

We are not alone in finding coercive psychological consumption, and its wholesale use of misleading marketing; for that is what hijacking celebrity and the logo-isation of art and Hollywood in these supposedly 'scientific' texts amounts to — an affliction in its own right. Even the *New Scientist* has tired of this. In the editorial, 'An end to this madness', dated 17 November 2000, the journal notes that 'the human condition is now so thoroughly medicalised that few people can claim to be normal', and pleads with psychiatry/psychology to develop a sense of irony, to forego its historicist fallacy and, above all, to stop inventing new 'diseases'.

References

Barlow, David and Durand, Mark (2001) *Abnormal Psychology: An Integrative Approach.* 2nd edition. Belmont, CA.: Wadsworth

Browne, Deryck (1995) Sectioning: The Black Experience. In: Suman Fernando (ed.) *Mental Health in a Multi-ethnic Society: A Multi-disciplinary Handbook.* London: Routledge, 62–72

Comer, Ronald (1998) *Abnormal Psychology.* 3rd edition. New York: W.H. Freeman

Davison, Gerald and Neale, John (1990) *Abnormal Psychology.* 5th edition. New York: Wiley

Eldredge, Niles and Gould, Stephen Jay (1972) Punctuated Equilibria: An Alternative to Phyletic Gradualism. In: Thomas Schopf (ed.) *Models in Palæobiology.* San Francisco: Freeman, Cooper, 82–115

Epilepsy Museum, The (2002) Curing Folly. Retrieved 31 March 2002: (www.epilepsiemuseum.de/alt/boschen.html)

Fernando, Suman (1990) *Race and Culture in Psychiatry.* London: Routledge

Foucault, Michel (1967) [1961]. *Madness and Civilization: A History of Insanity in the Age of Reason.* Trans. Richard Howard. London: Tavistock

Foucault, Michel (1981) Questions of Method: An Interview with Michel Foucault. *Ideology and Consciousness, 8,* 3–14

Green, Christopher (1998) Digging Archaeology: Sources of Foucault's Historiography. Retrieved 31 March 2002: (www.yorku.ca/christo/papers/digarch2.htm)

Kendall, Phillip and Hammen, Constance (1995) *Abnormal Psychology.* Boston: Houghton Mifflin

Klein, Naomi (2000) *No Logo.* London: Flamingo

Leff, Julian; Sartorius, Norman; Jablensky, Aaron; Korten, A. and Ernberg, G. (1992) The International Pilot Study of Schizophrenia: Five-year Follow-up. *Psychological Medicine, 22,* 131–45

Leudar, Ivan and Thomas, Phillip (2000) *Voices of Reason: Voices of Insanity: Studies of Verbal Hallucinations.* London: Routledge

Littlewood, Ronald and Lipsedge, Maurice (1989) *Aliens and Alienists: Ethnic Minorities and Psychiatry.* London: Unwin Hyman

Maher, Winifred and Maher, Brian (1982) The Ship of Fools: *Stultifera Navis* or *Ignis Fatuus? American Psychologist, 37,* 756–61

McHoul, Alec (1996) *Semiotic Investigations: Towards an Effective Semiotics.* Lincoln: University of Nebraska Press

Meyer, Robert and Salmon, Paul (1988) *Abnormal Psychology*. Boston: Allyn and Bacon
Mustafa, G. (1990) Delivery Systems for the Care of Schizophrenic Patients in Africa — Sub-Sahara. In: A Kales, C. Stefanis and J. Talbot (eds) *Recent Advances in Schizophrenia*. New York: Springer Verlag, 353–71
New Scientist (2000) 'An End to this Madness' (17 November) 3
Rapley, Mark; McCarthy, David and McHoul, Alec (In press) Mentality or Morality? Membership, Multiple Meanings and Mass Murder. *British Journal of Social Psychology*
Rose, Steven; Lewontin, Richard and Kamin, Leon (1984) *Not In Our Genes: Biology, Ideology and Human Nature*. London: Penguin
Rosenhan, David and Seligman, Martin (1984) *Abnormal Psychology*. New York: W.W. Norton
Schwartz, Stephen (2000) *Abnormal Psychology: A Discovery Approach*. Mountain View, CA: Mayfield
Shorter, Edward (1997) *A History of Psychiatry: From the Era of the Asylum to the Age of Prozac*. New York: Wiley
Vidal, John (1997) *McLibel: Burger Culture on Trial*. London: Pan
Wooffitt, Robin (1992) *Telling Tales of the Unexpected*. Hemel Hempstead: Harvester Wheatsheaf

Art works

Bosch, Hieronymus, *The Cure of Folly* ('Extraction of the Stone of Madness') (c. 1475–80). Oil on board, 48 x 35 cm. Museo del Prado: Madrid
Bosch, Hieronymus, *The Ship of Fools* (c. 1490-1500). Oil on wood, 58 x 33 cm. Musée du Louvre: Paris
Goya, Francisco de, *The Madhouse* (c. 1812–14). Oil on panel, 45 x 72 cm. Royal Academy of San Fernando: Madrid
Millais, Sir John Everett (1849-50). *Ferdinand Lured by Ariel*. Oil on panel, 64.8 x 50.8 cm. Private Collection
van Hemessen, Jan Sanders, *The Surgeon* (c. 1555). Oil on wood, 100 x 141 cm. Museo del Prado: Madrid

Beyond Help?

... Or beyond the science and æsthetics of 'man'?

We wonder: why is it that physicists, economists and biologists are frequently encouraged (sometimes even required) to have a working knowledge of the history of their disciplines as part and parcel of their training — while no psychology degree we know of *mandates* the history of psychology and its broader allegiances to various other systems of thought? Is this, perhaps, because something murky lurks in the dark unopened closet of psychology's history, something that, if let out, might undermine the scientificity and the social respectability of psychological (and related) practice today? Empirically, this might mean, for example, tracing the connections between psychology, fascism, eugenics, drug pushing, and the sterling assistance of German psychiatry to racial hygiene (Masson, 1988). On another front, one which we explore here, it might have to do with psychology's increasingly delimited conceptual base when it comes to thinking, at root, just what it is that 'the self' could *be*, whether 'normal' or 'abnormal', 'healthy' or 'sick', 'sane' or 'mad'. If so, then to rehistoricise psy-practice (rather than, as psychology textbooks so relentlessly do, romanticise a pseudo-history of madness) would be, in itself, at least a way *to start to unhinge* psy-dominance over all matters of 'being human' today, and *to get a brief glimpse* of some possible alternatives. So, in tentatively asking what such an alternative project might involve, we by no means want to propose a quick-and-easy alternative to psychodoxy. To do that would be to turn this book into no more than yet another self-help treatise. Instead, and to repeat, we want to *start* to unhinge psychodoxy and to briefly *glimpse* one of many possible other ways of conceiving the human condition. If you like, having destroyed some of the weeds, we want to at least sketch out what the new garden would look like.

It would seem that, by the end of this book, wherever we look at psychology's commerce in the self today — on the net, in the self-help book industry, in the media, and so forth — we find pretty much the same story about ourselves. That is, we are continually informed that contemporary woes and miseries are a result of the kind of *being* that we fundamentally are: a being eternally divided within itself; divided between cognition and behaviour, inner desires and outer pleasures, spirit and matter, mind and body, imagination and toil, sanity and madness .... And the list could easily continue to include an indefinite number of doubles, binaries, divisions and separations. And the role of the commercial therapies in all of this is, as we have seen, to hold out an effectively impossible hope of re-uniting these supposed 'sides' of the human character. As we saw, psy-commerce (in whichever particular medium) fundamentally depends on and trades in this 'dividual' self, even as it continually promises to restore a state of ideal in-dividuality, wholeness and completeness; to return us to an original (and utterly mythical) 'well-tempered' state (Miller, 1993). It's like playing a piano that, as soon as it's touched, goes out of tune. And so it needs retuning. And, of course, only an expert can advise on how best this may be accomplished.

But this division of the self is only one possible story about ourselves and, historically speaking, it is very a recent one. In fact, it is a story that is confined to the period of modernity itself. The philosopher and scientist, Descartes, in the first half of the seventeenth-century, is routinely credited — possibly unfairly (Gaukroger, 1995) — with this separation of the self into mind-stuff and corporeal machine. His picture of the problem of human knowledge (that is, how a mind-body double can know anything at all about the world it inhabits) runs something like this:

> The world is essentially physical in a specifically restricted sense of that term, but the human mind is transcendental. The human body is a feature of the physical world, is a *res extensa*, but the human mind is cut from non-physical cloth, and is a *res cogitans*, lacking mass and having no spatio-temporal coordinates. One of the most important functions of the *res cogitans* is to endow the otherwise colourless, tasteless, odourless and silent world with its actually experienced colours, tastes, odours, sounds and so on. It accomplishes this astounding feat by integrating the input from the sensorium and presenting us with a rich *internal* representation utterly unlike the 'real' material world whose causal forces acting upon us help to generate this *illusion* of itself, an illusion which, apparently, only a scientifically grounded philosophy can show to be such. (Button et al., 1995: 39)

For us, the most interesting feature of this account of what we are is that, in separating out two distinct realms of being, the material and the mental (or the extensional and the intensional), it leaves the first utterly unknowable *in itself*, and the latter confined to mere *illusion*.

As a picture of the self, then, this is, from the start, a recipe for disaster. We can see, already in the early glimmerings of modernity, the 'science' of the self that was to become psychology; and we can see why it necessarily takes up the model of the divided self in terms of 'problem' and hypothetical 'cure'.

It is sometimes claimed that, more than a century later, Kant solved the Cartesian antinomy of the self by arguing for a balance or harmonisation of the bodily senses (the sensibility) and the mind's reasoning capacities (the understanding) by posing the existence of a prior and overarching faculty (the imagination).[1] In a late work, he summarises his view of this putative harmonisation in a way that is uncannily redolent of today's therapeutic discourses:

> The two kinds of good, the physical and the moral, cannot be mixed together, because they would then neutralize each other and have no effect on the purpose of true bliss. Rather, inclination to pleasurable living and inclination to virtue are in conflict with each other, and the restriction of the principle of physical good by the principle of moral good constitute[s] *through their very conflict* the whole purpose of a well-bred, partly sensuous and partly ethico-intellectual human being. (Kant, 1978/1798: 185; our emphasis)

Note here: a scene of conflict (cf. therapy) has to be gone through where we (cf. the patient) come to realise our impossibly divided condition and to see that this picture of ourselves can be respecified. This is a kind of talking cure in which division promises to become balance (through mutual 'restriction'), as each side (the physical and the interior), as it were, takes care of the excesses of the other. And of course we have become accustomed to hearing that misery, distress, despair are but the consequence of an interior (chemical) 'imbalance' in the brain, which the psychological and pharmacological professions promise to restore to a fictive, truly blissful, equilibrium. Whichever way we go then, psychotherapy or pharmacotherapy, the intended result is precisely the elusive 'healthy' self of modern psychology: 'a well-bred, partly sensuous [behavioural] and partly ethico-intellectual [cognitive] human being'.

It is reasonable, then, to describe this as an *æsthetic* picture of the self; that is, one in which the work we do on ourselves is akin to a work of art. For example, we are reminded of Mondrian's technique of deliberately dividing his canvases in unbalanced and disproportionate ways, so that he could then rebalance or reharmonise them by adding specifically 'weighted' colours to each separate area. And the term 'æsthetic', in this context, is

---

1. An early (c.1810) account of Kant's philosophy by Germaine de Staël (1987) makes this tripartite 'system' the central plank of Kant's new philosophy of the self.

not used lightly; for it was the post-Kantian romantics (especially Schiller) who diagnosed the ills of the late eighteenth- and early nineteenth-centuries in specifically æsthetic terms. In effect, Schiller is the founder of modern æsthetics — based, importantly for us, on a divided æsthetics of the self. His *Æsthetic Education* (1794) explicitly announces the problems of the self in modernity. We are, he tells us, split between two contesting and irreconcilable instincts or drives: the sense drive and the form drive. The first describes our attention to our physical, sensuous existence and needs. If we had this drive alone, we would be pure bundles of behaviour, mere biological organisms. The second drive, however, describes our attention to our rational nature; to the fact that we have mental as well as material existence. If we had this drive alone, we would be pure bundles of immaterial, mental and spiritual energy. But the fundamental assumption behind the æsthetic conception of the self is that each drive, as it were, is to keep an eye on the other via a third and overriding function: the inclination to *play* and *beauty*. Our æsthetic capacities, if — and this is important — they are *politically* allowed to take form individually and collectively, by state support for proper cultural education, will overcome the miseries of being an eternally divided self. Magic idealism!

Lest it be thought, then, that romanticism was (and still is) an abstruse form of mere art-for-art's-sake, we must take serious note of Schiller's explicit *politics* of the modern self. He tells us that it is, effectively, modern times and the modern divisions of labour and ideas — increased specialisation — that have led to forms of society which favour one drive over the other and pay little attention to healthy techniques for their reharmonisation. Interestingly, he calls this state-sponsored insistence on division (over harmony), a 'wound':

> It was civilization itself which inflicted this wound upon modern man. Once the increase of empirical knowledge, and more exact modes of thought, made sharper divisions between the sciences, and once the increasingly complex machinery of State necessitated a more rigorous separation of ranks and occupations, then the inner unity of human nature was severed too, and a disastrous conflict set its harmonious powers at variance. (Schiller, 1967/1794: 130)[2]

Remember, this is a story from 1794. But its legacy is with us everywhere today. It forms the basis of the psychologised picture of the self, always at odds with itself, always seeking a magic recipe for a return to its mythical wholeness and, significantly, confined to a

---

2. On the, often neglected, centrality of Schiller and romanticism for contemporary Marxism, see Hunter (1993).

modern society whose politics continually frustrate our 'natural' æsthetic impulses. How remarkable that, even in some socially critical and politically resistive works today, we can find almost exactly the same 'model of man': one whose inner harmony of drives or instincts has become dislodged by capitalist forms of social organisation. Here's Andrew Howard writing in the progressive culture-jamming magazine *Adbusters*, in 2001, about the problems of being a designer:[3]

> The division of our needs and desires fragments our conscious-ness. We are kept from being complete. Social activity, includ-ing thought, is subject to specialization and compartmental-ization. We are encouraged to concentrate on the details of our activity — to develop its internal logic. This is what it means to be a good professional. Thus we lose track of how things fit together. In our allocated areas of professional concern there is little time for the wider picture. (Howard, 2001: np)

With minor adjustments, this could well have been Schiller himself referring to the late eighteenth-century.

And bringing this up to date in other ways, we have seen (espe-cially in chapter six) how the manufacturers of neuroleptic/psycho-tropic drugs and the 'community groups' they sponsor, such as SANE and NISAD, are attempting to 'de-stigmatise' mental illness by dis-placing supposed 'prejudices' with a biomedical model. As it were, when the mind is a problem, it can be metaphorically converted into the nearest available bodily organ (currently the brain) and, so the story goes, that organ can then be 'treated'. (Genetics, presumably, is the 'next big step'; cf. eugenics with a friendly and probably smiley face.) Or else, moving from the boardroom to the dungeon, when we listen to the words of 'sufferers' themselves who are — despite their supposedly representative 'community organisations' — frequently suspicious of biological reductionist accounts of their 'suffering', we often find accounts based on social problems. In one account, Sean locates the 'problem' as ('recreational') drug use and his consequent dependence on (prescribed) drugs for continued income.[4]

> They put me on Modecate. I gotta get an injection today too. I'm in a bad hurry really. They said it was schizophrenia. They said if I don't take drugs it will go away and it has … almost.

---

3. Our thanks to Nicholas Pratt for finding the following example.
4. The following two accounts are from one of the few publications we have seen that has bothered to extensively consult sufferers themselves: *Colors* (2001/ 2002). Two more: 'My illness is the medicine I need' — Jorge, 37, René Vallejo Psychiatric Hospital, Camaguey, Cuba (*Colors*, 2001/2002: 33). 'Q: What's your illness? A: Four white pills and one green pill every day' — Didier, 22, also in René Vallejo (*Colors*, 2001/2002: 23).

Once they give you an injection instantly you stop hearing voices. It goes straight up into your mind and stops the voices straight away. It lasts for about a week. I'm not real well when I don't take the medication. It's the drugs ... you don't do that. They do that much damage. I wouldn't take them if I had my life again. I wouldn't fall for that. No way .... I gotta get there and get my injection now .... If I don't get there now they won't give me my pension'. — Sean, 37, Edgar Eager Lodge, Sydney. (Colors, 2001/2002: 81)

In a second account, Phil, a 'consumer-consultant' at a Sydney hospital, is more sceptical about the dominant biological discourse of the psy-professions:

'Often mental health professionals may have the knowledge but not the experience to help people. I don't think anyone has come up with a satisfactory explanation for what madness is. There's an overemphasis on biological theories of almost everything. Any ailment is seen as a biological misfunction. I think it's social as well.' — Phil, 47, Rozelle Hospital, Sydney. (Colors, 2001/2002: 81)

All the stories we have seen in this book then, despite surface variations, concur on a general narrative structure: today we live in a world that is so divided in itself, and on every front, that it requires us, as its constituents, to embody (en-mind?) that division. We are structurally required to be 'dividuals' and, in consequence, to pursue an endless and impossible search for individuality, wholeness, completion, perfection. How often have we heard this story — whether from the right or the left of politics; whether from card-carrying philosophers or drunks in bars; whether from the popular press or from psychology textbooks; whether from drug companies, charities 'helping people affected by mental illness' or, indeed, from sufferers? Accepting such a divided version of ourselves, and conceding that this state of being carries with it, indeed constitutes us as, a problem is, effectively by definition, already to be on the cusp of madness — or beyond? — leaving psy-commerce in particular to work its miracles. This is our new consumerist theology.

This narrative of the self (mad or sane), as we have seen throughout this book, is widespread and popular today; and the psy-professions have the strongest possible ethical investment in it, regardless of whether they offer New Age talking cures, self-help books or Prozac™. So how is it possible, given that even standard leftist discourses rely on variations of the same story (hoping perhaps that magic socialism will usher in a new possibility) to think otherwise?

Thinking otherwise?

We can at least make a beginning towards a counter-politics of the self by reminding ourselves that this very limited and limiting story about ourselves is historically contingent. It comes about with the early scientific thinking of the seventeenth-century, is transformed after the Enlightenment into an æsthetic technique and, more recently, has come to underpin both 'scientific' and mass popular understandings of the misery-happiness roundabout. That is, on the broader historical canvas, it is extremely recent. And there are, despite their comparative obscurity today, alternative ways of picturing the self which could, as it turns out, underpin a counter-psychologistic turn.

One such alternative can be glimpsed in the responses to Descartes of his near contemporary, Benedict de Spinoza (1632–1677). Spinoza warns us against grounding our view of the self on the abstract mind — Descartes' 'cogito' — in separation from sheer substance (that is, 'Nature' or, for Spinoza, 'God'). As Scruton puts it in a neat summary:

> [Spinoza] did not seek to found his system in the single indubitable premise of the 'cogito'. The proposition 'I think' has two features which rendered it useless to Spinoza. First, it expresses a merely contingent truth, whereas for Spinoza all certainty must ultimately be founded on necessities. Secondly, it contains an ineliminable reference to a first person, while for Spinoza access to philosophical truth comes only when we rise above preoccupation with our own limited experience and mentality, and learn to see things from the impartial point of view of the rational observer to whom things appear 'under the aspect of eternity' (*sub specie æternitatis*). (Scruton, 1984: 51)

Although we would rarely pose the question in such seemingly theological terms today, it is nevertheless important because it leads Spinoza to positing the fundamental idea that, ultimately, there is only a single substance. In fact, he defines 'substance' as: 'what is in itself and is conceived through itself, that is, that whose concept does not require the concept of another thing, from which it must be formed' (1996: 1). That is, at a *fundamental* level, nothing, including ourselves, comes divided. And this effectively displaces Descartes' starting point, the Cartesian mind-body binary for which resolution to singularity is required.

Without going into the philosophical complexities of Spinoza's arguments concerning substance and individuals (see Scruton, 1984: 55–7), we can note that this position does, at least, give greater centrality and complexity to the body as such. Even if, ultimately, 'under the aspect of eternity', there is only one substance ('Nature', 'God'), actual bodies, including ourselves, are constructed as multi-complexes of possible bodies which have indefinite ways of interacting with other bodies in (or as) their environment. He writes: 'The human body is composed of a great many individuals of different natures, each of which is highly composite' (1996: 44). It is important at this point to stress that nothing in this suggestion could be further from the currently popular and peculiar idea of multiple *personalities*, let alone 'multiple personality disorder'. Spinoza's body is neither a mere vehicle for a Cartesian mind, nor a mechanical (biomedical) entity in its own right. His thought is more radical than either. And so, what happens in human affairs can be understood in terms of multiple and composite bodies and their *affects* without recourse to psychologism, to accounts of experience which rely entirely on the ghostly 'occult qualities of things' (1996: 79).

Instead of 'mind' in Descartes' sense of the *res cogitans* as the primordial stuff of 'being human', we can speak of an *already* complex body and its affects: what it can do, what it is capable of.[5] Here the self is reconfigured as a body, or bodies, relegating the idea of the primacy of the 'psyche', at the centre of Cartesian thinking, to relative unimportance and obscurity. In fact, reading the self cognitively *or* as a mere physical presence are, for Spinoza, simply different ways of conceiving of one thing under two different *attributes* (thought and extension): 'the mind and the body are one and the same individual, which is conceived now under the attribute of thought, now under the attribute of extension' (Spinoza, 1996: 48).

A number of feminist scholars have recently — in the light of corporeal feminism's re-insistence on the body and its complexity as a philosophical and political site — taken up this aspect of Spinoza's thinking, precisely in an effort to locate a de-psychologised understanding of the self. Moira Gatens, for example, refers to the Spinozan self as:[6]

> a relatively complex individual, made up of a number of other bodies. Its identity can never be viewed as a final or finished product as in the case of the Cartesian automaton, since it is a body that is in constant interchange with its environment. (Gatens, 1996: 110)

One step towards a dissolution of the Cartesian picture, then, is to *complexify* the individual *as bodies*, rather than to *simplify* it into a binary ('dividual') on a hopeless quest for resolution, finality, singularity. As a start such an understanding would, once and for all, do

---

5. This question of affects is crucial to our respecification of selfhood. It is taken up again in more detail towards the end of this chapter.
6. Our thanks to Danielle Gallegos for assistance with some considerations of Spinoza and feminism.

away with the possibility of our current propensity to torture our-selves with unanswerable questions (even via therapy) like if I do *x*, will I still be "me"?', 'I've just done *y*, how can I live with myself?'; or to torment ourselves with illusory inquiries about 'what I *really* am': if we are always already multiple bodies, such questions — and the so-called mental disorders that they spawn, viz. gender identity dis-order, ego dystonic homophilia and the like — become nonsensical. Such 'mental disorders' (and this is also the case for all other dis-eases of the self like depression, anxiety, etc., etc.) become viewable immediately as moral questions about the singular 'right way to be' a self engendered by, and sensible only within, Cartesian understand-ings of ourselves — which posit the possibility of a final resolution of these matters. This could at least begin a new kind of thinking to-wards a displacement of the modern idea of the self as a temporally continuous body-psyche which requires constant self-monitoring and internal and external regimes of correction. It would displace what Foucault calls the 'reasonable soul' which

> has a dual role to play: it needs to assign a regimen for the body that is actually determined by the latter's nature, its ten-sions, the conditions and circumstances in which it finds itself. But it will be able to assign this regimen correctly only provided it has done a good deal of work on itself: eliminated the errors, reduced the imaginings, mastered the desires, that cause it to misconstrue the sober law of the body. (Foucault, 1990: 133)

It takes very little effort to read this spurious 'misconstrual' back into Descartes' very own problematics of the psyche as the space of a necessary 'illusion'. And it takes only slightly more effort to see that today's psy-complex (especially in its popular commercial varieties) is still doing booming business because — and *only* because — the 'reasonable soul' is construed as one that can be 'cured' of its depen-dence on just such a non-existent illusion.

Descartes' mistake, in the end (an end inherited by psychology), was to think of humanity as governed by rules and laws separate from nature, and then to find and extract those new rules and laws (of the 'psyche') in order to explain human conduct — even if via a supposedly scientific method. Spinoza's lesson is that we are bodies — and complex bodies at that — which are co-extensive with nature. And this makes a massive, if forgotten, difference. Spinoza could, then, in the following passage, be writing as much about the thera-peutic promises of the psy-professions today, their classificatory schemes such as the DSM, and their consequential status as our contemporary priesthood, as he was about Descartes:

> Most of those who have written about the affects, and of men's way of living, seem to treat, not of natural things, which follow

the common laws of Nature, but of things which are outside Nature. Indeed they seem to conceive man in Nature as a dominion within a dominion. For they believe that man disturbs, rather than follows, the order of Nature, that he has absolute power over his actions, and that he is determined only by himself. And they attribute the cause of human impotence and inconstancy, not to the common power of Nature, but to I know not what vice of human nature, which they therefore bewail or laugh at, or disdain, or (as usually happens) curse. And he who knows how to censure more eloquently and cunningly the weakness of the human mind is held to be godly .... I know, of course, that the celebrated Descartes, although he too believed that the mind has absolute power over its own actions, nevertheless sought to explain human affects through their first causes and, at the same time, to show the way by which the mind can have absolute dominion over its affects. But in my opinion, he showed nothing but the cleverness of his own understanding. (Spinoza, 1996: 68–9)

So what may underpin and warrant the extremely high popularity of the psy-complex is its trading on a relatively recent Cartesian version of what it is to be human. But psy is itself divided in the story that it tells us about ourselves: 'human impotence and inconstancy', along with distress, madness and despair, are increasingly asserted to be nothing but part of our (biochemical) nature, determined by the laws of Nature — while it is simultaneously suggested that the solutions to the essential divisions within ourselves may (with appropriate professional assistance) be determined only by ourselves, by our *acquisition* of absolute power over our actions. Thus we are condemned, like Sisyphus, to be ever engaged in a fruitless search for a psychological primordiality, of one's own 'reasonable soul', via corrective techniques aiming to reduce all of the soul's natural multiplicities to one final, completely rounded in-dividual.

For us, then, the crucial political strategy is, at least initially, a discursive and rhetorical one: the search for a discourse to dislodge this dominant picture of the self; to rethink it along roughly Spinozan lines; to respecify the self as a complex 'made up of a number of other bodies', and as a complexity without need of resolution to a singularity and without, more importantly today, the in-built anxiety of duality. The political slogan for this existentialist position could be: the self is only ever complex and multiple; it has no fundamental (and especially not a cognitive) essence. *This* self is, thus, essentially without need of therapy. And following this Spinozan line of thought about the self-as-body (or bodies), we can arrive at a version of the *power* of the self over itself.

To see this we need to turn to Deleuze's (1988) reading of Spinoza's ethics. This is because, as we have seen constantly throughout this book, the psy-complex is continually pressed into service both to define and to expunge *unwanted conduct*. Whatever the official and semi-official pamphlets may say about the 'ordinariness' of schizophrenia, depression and the rest (see chapters two and six), the agenda is quite clearly one of remediation: the expungement of bodily powers (or affects) that are deemed morally negative. And here we arrive squarely in the domain of the ethics of the psy-complex itself. That is, it not only tells us what we fundamentally are, it also tells us what, within that limited range of being, is acceptable and what is not. It is, in this sense, a form of moral regulation or policing.[7]

Traditionally then, ethics is the field of distinctions between good and evil — and quite often this is posed in terms of absolutes: the absolute good vs. the absolute evil.[8] But, according to Deleuze, for Spinoza, what traditional ethics calls the 'absolute good' is not in fact *ethical* at all in the strict sense. Rather, it is mere moral judgment. By contrast, the ethical, for Spinoza, is instead *utterly confined* to relative judgments. Ethics, in this respecified sense, can *replace* and overcome mere judgment:

> Ethics, which is to say, a typology of immanent modes of existence [an 'ethology'], replaces Morality, which always refers existence to transcendent values. Morality is the judgment of God, the *system of judgment*. But Ethics overthrows the system of judgment. The opposition of values (Good-Evil) is supplanted by the qualitative difference of modes of existence (good-bad). (Deleuze, 1988: 23)

Along these lines, Deleuze-Spinoza would therefore say that any identification of the ethical with absolutes would mean that it actually works on a *moral* distinction between Good and Evil. And by contrast, the alternative position would be that ethics is (and should be) what discerns the relative differences between the good and the bad, in the space of the body itself — which is to say, between bodies.

So Spinoza would agree with, for example, Wittgenstein (1965) that absolute statements (for example, statements about Good as opposed to Evil) are nonsensical. (We can sensibly say 'He is a good footballer' but not 'This man led a good life'.) But he would not agree that they were *ethical* as such. Instead, the ethical would be, in and of itself, a bodily matter: almost like a basic physical or chemical test. It would be a direct test of a body: a question of whether some body

---

7. This is why, perhaps, throughout *Discipline and Punish* (1977), Foucault refers to the modern disciplines of control (including psychology) as 'moral orthopædics'.

8. Parts of this discussion of Spinoza's ethics are based on a section of Alec McHoul's *Culture and Representation: A Critique and Renewal of Cultural Thinking Today* (in preparation).

interacting with it were either good or bad for it. This is, then, an ethics of bodies, and not necessarily just human biological bodies, but also bodies of ideas, chemical bodies, *just* bodies. It is for this reason that Deleuze calls Spinoza's ethics an 'ethology' (1988: 27, 125).[9]

According to this 'practical philosophy', the bodies in question are constituted by what they can affect, their affects, their powers, what they can do in relation to other bodies:

> Children know how to do this: Little Hans, in the case reported by Freud, makes a list of affects of a draft horse pulling a cart in a city (to be proud, to have blinders, to go fast, to pull a heavy load, to collapse, to be whipped, to kick up a racket, etc.). For example: there are greater differences between a plow horse or draft horse and a racehorse than between an ox and a plow horse. This is because the racehorse and the plow horse do not have the same affects nor the same capacity for being affected; the plow horse has affects in common rather with the ox. (Deleuze, 1988: 124)

If the affects increase a body's power, if the relations it engages in with another body 'agree' with it (*convenientia*) then they are good; if they diminish the body's power, if they 'disagree' with it, then they are bad (*disconvenientia*) (1988: 33). And the decision, in any case, is properly ethical. Accordingly, we can say that auto-immune responses are *ethically* good because they enhance a body's powers in the presence of another (Deleuze, 1988: 42) and that, contrastively, a genuine poison — one of Spinoza's favourite cases — is *ethically* bad because it decreases the powers (the affects) of the body it interacts with. As such, substances like the 'antipsychotics' which designedly decrease the body's power to act would, for Spinoza as for Breggin, be a genuine poison.

This puts us in a position to be able to say that the absolute judgments we find marbled (perhaps even crazed) through the contemporary psy-complex and its popular commercial branches are nothing but matters of sheer morality — even (perhaps especially) where they are disguised in medico-scientific discourse. The work that they do, *in actual concrete cases* — including sending electrical currents through people's brains, rendering bodies docile to the point of utter passivity or death with neuroleptic chemicals, dividing bodies into those that are and are not 'disabled' by an ever-increasing list of spurious syndromes and disorders, and so forth — this actual

---

9. Here 'ethology' is not the name of a quasi-anthropological discipline. Indeed, it is not the name of *any* social science. It points us to the fact that 'ethics' derives from 'ethos' and that ethics, as a questioning relation to our own ethos — *opening up* as against *closing off* possibilities of human being — is critical to the contemporary politics of the self.

bodily work can be nothing other than pure *disconvenientia*. Accordingly, in the strict ethical (and not the merely moralistic) sense, it is bad and needs to be continually exposed as such.

But until what point? Here the question is harder. Writers such as David Smail can point us in a useful direction. Smail suggests that

> Perhaps if we were shaken out of our bewitched fascination with imagination and 'virtuality', the wishful invention of interior worlds which have no embodied substance, we might come to see that paying sober attention to the realities of social structure and of our relations with each other as public, not simply private, beings is an option. A difficult one certainly — not so easy as dreaming and wishing — but at least a real one. What this would entail is a recognition that maybe prevention is more possible than cure; a down-grading of psychology in favour of an up-grading of politics. (Smail, 1999: np)

But in order for there to be genuine and effective political resistance to the massive psychologisation of the self, a self-consciously *political* movement which engages in the 'up-grading' of the politics of madness, experience, of life itself, there has to be, first and foremost, a reconstruction and respecification of who and what we fundamentally *are*.

This is no simple task and, in this chapter, we have merely suggested some starting points for such a de-psychologisation. But, in the end, whatever end there is, this can only be completed by the dissemination of a genuine alternative to the Cartesian-Kantian-Romantic binary self which Foucault (1970: 303–87) calls the 'empirico-transcendental doublet', or else the 'man' of modernity itself. Significantly, Foucault attributes this now dominant (though utterly limited) construction of the self to the ongoing work of the human sciences themselves. These disciplines (and, for us, especially, the psy-complex) are not mere abstractions confined by the walls of remote academies. They claim to have a definitive answer to Spinoza's famous and still-to-be-answered question: 'Who knows what a body can do?'[10] They are in our lives at the most fundamental level, continually and very cleverly reiterating a version of us — telling us who we are and why we are necessarily bad or incomplete — that serves no other interests than those of the (psychological) sciences themselves and their allies in the powerful drug nexus. Still all of this is, factually, recent and, at least potentially, *fragile*. Psychologised 'man' is, Foucault tells us — echoing Spinoza — nothing more than an 'invention', a set of 'arrangements', and:

---

10. This is Deleuze's gloss. Spinoza writes: 'no one has yet determined what the body can do' (1996: 71).

If those arrangements were to disappear as they appeared, if some event of which we can at the moment do no more than sense the possibility — without knowing either what its form will be or what it promises — were to cause them to crumble ... then one can certainly wager that man would be erased, like a face drawn in sand at the edge of the sea. (1970: 387)

Come in Spinoza!

At this point we must speculate. We cannot know whether or not psychologised 'man' — that extraordinary creature always caught between cognition and behaviour, thought and action, mind and body — will ever disappear, let alone when. But we can predict, with confidence, the ferocity of the resistance to this disappearance by those with a direct investment in the richly recompensed trade in the self that constitutes our present. The form of counter-mythological rethinking of ourselves that we propose here is, we suspect, likely both to offend the credulous and to attract the derision of psy-professional subscribers to our contemporary theology. But while we cannot predict what life after modernity might look like for us — if 'us' makes any sense in this counter-factual context — we can be certain of the reception that heresy has historically attracted. But supposing this great disappearance were actually to occur one day, still less do we have any idea of what form of subject would take the place of this 'man'. All we can do is speculate: and one form of speculation would be to try to imagine how things would be, especially with regard to matters now covered by the industry of psychology, were Cartesian *'man'* (singular, but always doubled) to be displaced by Spinozan *bodies* (multiple, but always much the same everywhere) as the dominant way of being human. What would this look like?

To begin with, we can remember that the main target of Spinoza's attack in his own times was organised religion. The priesthood in the seventeenth-century effectively held a similar position to our own psy-police. And Spinoza thought that this was both ill-informed and dangerous. Religious thought, he argued, went wrong precisely because it was too anthropocentric, perhaps even humanistic! Its mistake was to conceive of Nature/God as serving the affairs of mortal men instead of (as it was for him) a great mystery to be unravelled by dispassionate inquiry separated from faith and superstition. What he writes in the *Ethics* about this priesthood, then, might (albeit with some modifications) apply equally well to the 'man'-centredness of psy-business today. The whole of the appendix to the first part of the *Ethics* ('On God') ought to be consulted at this point (1996: 25–31) but the following passage is at least indicative:

But while they sought to show that Nature does nothing in vain (i.e. nothing not of use to men), they seem to have shown only that Nature and the gods are as mad as men. See, I ask you, how the matter has turned out! Among so many conveniences in Nature they had to find many inconveniences: storms, earthquakes, diseases, and the like. These, they maintain, happen because the gods (whom they judge to be of the same nature as themselves) are angry on account of wrongs done to them by men, *or* on account of sins committed in their worship. And though their daily experience contradicted this, and though infinitely many examples showed that conveniences and inconveniences happen indiscriminately to the pious and the impious alike, they did not on that account give up their long-standing prejudice. It was easier for them to put this among the other unknown things, whose use they were ignorant of, and so remain in the state of ignorance in which they had been born, than to destroy that whole construction, and think up a new one. (1996: 27)

The parallels between religious orthodoxy and psychodoxy are striking. Both attempt to explain ordinary, if indiscriminate, actions, events and circumstances as necessary effects of a supposed natural order of things. In doing so, they make this supposed nature as mad as the very madnesses they are trying to explain — Mary Boyle's apt title, *Schizophrenia: A Scientific Delusion?* comes to mind (1990). In doing so, they focus on the abnormal in life's rich tapestry of conveniences and inconveniences and try to explain such abnormalities (inconveniences) in terms of occult processes (in the brain, for example). When such accounts are shown to be nothing but the self-serving myth-making that they are, the response from the orthodox now, as in the seventeenth-century, is and was to insist upon the unreason of the disbelievers: all that has changed is that the heretic has become at best a victim of 'unscientific subjectivity', at worst 'mentally disordered'. This confers enormous power on both the priesthood (then) and psy-biz (now), since both can appear to appease (or 'cure') these non-existent occult causes of disconvenience (abnormality). Therapy, on this account, is on a par with the laying on of hands, the sale of indulgences, atonement and absolution.

By contrast, Spinoza's account of just some of the affects of the human body suggests that its powers are sufficient to deal with the various conveniences and disconveniences that occur, again indiscriminately, to it and to others like it. Against the current psychodoxy, he would clearly say that the body can indeed help itself — and others like it. So a Spinozan anti-psy 'science' might begin by questioning whether the various 'symptoms' of so-called mental illnesses (or the various kinds of apparent misery that may easily fall into anyone's life) were necessarily *disconvenientia*. For example, a Spinozan might ask whether or not 'hearing voices' (the classical indication of schizophrenia) was in fact an instance of *disconvenientia*. Might there not be positive aspects to it? — just as small doses of poison can be positive for a body, enhancing its powers of resistance to larger doses? Could 'hearing voices' be just an experience, or even be a kind of *gift* (no pun intended for German speakers)?

The question cannot be answered here. Yet it could be pondered were psychodoxy to release its monopoly on such matters. So let us suppose (since this is but a thought experiment) that there were bodily states, caused by the interaction between one's own body and an other or others, that were indeed 'inconvenient' (cf. abnormal, and the rest). A Spinozan might say that, in such cases, the body would revert to its primary affect: persevering in its being: 'Each thing, as far as it can by its own power, strives to persevere in its being' (1996: 75). The conditional, 'as far as it can by its own powers', could then be imagined to be broken. Here, the body would come into a new (and quite terrible) condition where its powers for self-perseverance had failed. At this point, it might come to approach another body (not suffering such a condition) for help.

In Spinoza's own extremely plain terms, this might mean that, for the first body, joy has become sadness, so that it comes to depend upon the second for a restoration of its possibilities of joy. Here are Spinoza's definitions:

> By *joy*, therefore, I shall understand ... that *passion by which the mind passes to a greater perfection*. And by *sadness*, that *passion by which it passes to a lesser perfection*. The *affect of joy which is related to the mind and body at once* I call *pleasure* or *cheerfulness*, and that of *sadness, pain or melancholy*. (1996: 77)

What is a second (helping) body to do under such circumstances? Spinoza would say that its fundamental perseverance in its own being might be sufficient to affect the first (suffering) body with positive affects. That is, as Spinoza says, one body can be an external cause of joy or sadness in another. The 'receiving' body then takes the 'sending' body as either a source of love (joy) or hate (sadness):

> *Love is* nothing but *joy with the accompanying idea of an external cause*, and *hate is* nothing but *sadness with the accompanying idea of an external cause*. We see, then, that one who loves necessarily strives to have present and preserve the thing he loves; and on the other hand, one who hates strives to remove and destroy the thing he hates. (1996: 78)

What causes sadness (misery) in a body that we love becomes, for us, an object of hate. We have a natural, bodily affect that wishes to destroy such a thing. And vice versa: what causes joy (wellbeing) in a body that we love becomes, for us, an object of love in its own right. These are among the very simple things that we know a body can do. And they lead to what is, today, a much scorned affect: pity. But pity, in its Spinozan sense, is extremely positive: 'We cannot hate a thing that we pity from the fact that its suffering affects us with sadness'. So, 'As far as we can, we strive to free a thing we pity from its suffering' (1996: 84). That is, we *cannot but*, as human bodies, try to destroy the cause of another's suffering, not because there is a professional or industrial mandate to do so, but because our bodies are built that way. Pity, then, is not a terrible form of condescension. For Spinoza, it 'is a sadness, accompanied by the idea of an evil which has happened to another whom we imagine to be *like us*' (1996: 107; our emphasis). And should this affect — which we all have as embodied beings — become a general disposition of a particular body (perhaps, then, of a 'psychologist' of the future), it might then become something both seemingly rare today and yet quite ordinary for any body in our imaginary scenario: compassion.

> There seems to be no difference between pity and compassion, except perhaps that pity concerns the singular affect, whereas compassion concerns the habitual disposition of this affect. (1996: 107)

Ending where we began: it's possible that pity and compassion have as bad a name today as scientific management. But it might be time to make a choice: psy-biz as against what a body (for all we know — given that there is no Spinozan 'science' in our world today) might do.

One of the first readers of this book (in manuscript) asked us, on behalf of the publishers, two questions: 'What would "distress" look like in Spinoza's version of the person, how would we alleviate suffering?' We have seen that the answer to this question is relatively straightforward: distress, or *disconvenientia*, for Spinoza, is at root an effect of bodies on bodies that diminishes their capacity to act, or which nullifies their perseverance in their being. As such we can see that, as Phillip Larkin (1993: 180) so famously put it — and as industrialised psy is so assiduous in denying — 'They fuck you up, your mum and dad .... Man hands on misery to man'. The reinstatement of this recognition into our everyday conduct towards each other is at the heart of our project. And, of course, we can also see that the effect of psy (as body of knowledge) on our (corporeal) bodies is but straightforwardly *disconvenientia* — it is productive of distress. Via information pamphlets, textbooks, the world wide web, problem pages and magazine articles, the DSM and the formalisation/ industrialisation of pity, psy alienates us from our bodily affects; seeks to disqualify our perseverance in our being — except upon its own increasingly limited terms; inflicts corporeal damage in the name of concern; and sequestrates compassion by telling us that the distressed bodies it is energetic in producing are *not like us*. Being unlike us, our capacity for everyday pity, for the destruction of the causes of the suffering of those we love, is removed from us. And we have seen this very clearly in the injunctions that psy issues both to the distressed and to their families: something is not quite right; do not try to assist yourself or your loved ones; seek out and obey our 'advice'; do not question our authority, for you are powerless to act. As a recipe for the diminution of bodies' capacity to act, for the nullification of perseverance in being, this is surely as potent as one can get. So how might we alleviate suffering? At least as a start, by the repudiation of the mythology of psy, the forging of allegiances with those who would eschew coercion and control as forms of 'help', and via solidarity with those currently captivated by the nostrums of commercialised 'caring'.

With regard to the closely allied questions (also from our reader), 'If someone wanted advice on the best way to raise a family — where would they go? Would advice as we know it exist? These are questions that arise in the context of an NHS practitioner reading the book, one of our biggest markets', Spinozan answers are, again, direct. The sad but true answer is that, should Cartesian 'man' cease to exist, so would such markets. All psy-practitioners (be they NHS or private: British, Australian or American) would be out of a job.

Unemployed, they might look to their own affects, as a human body — which they could not deny that they are, or have. Advice, as such, would mean turning to bodies that necessarily love each other, as opposed to the current professional substitutes for compassion with all their inherent cruelties. If someone wanted advice on the best way to raise a family, they might then turn to those bodies that already constitute, for them, their family (whatever that might mean for them). As David Smail (1998) has elsewhere noted, 'taking care' may indeed offer an 'alternative' to therapy.

But we speculate. Things may well be otherwise. Psy-biz may continue to thrive, continue to leave its 'clients' beyond help. Pity.

References

Boyle, Mary (1990) *Schizophrenia: A Scientific Delusion?* London: Routledge
Button, Graham; Coulter, Jeff; Lee, John R.E. and Sharrock, Wes (1995) *Computers, Minds and Conduct*. Cambridge: Polity Press
Colors (2001/2002) Madness/Follia. *Colors, 47* (December/January)
Deleuze, Gilles (1988) *Spinoza: Practical Philosophy*. Trans. R. Hurley, San Francisco: City Lights Books
de Staël, Germaine (1987) [c.1810] Kant. In: *Major Writings of Germaine de Staël*. Trans. Vivian Folkenflik. New York: Columbia University Press, 302–14
Foucault, Michel (1970) *The Order of Things: An Archæology of the Human Sciences*. No translator named. London: Tavistock

Foucault, Michel (1977) *Discipline and Punish: The Birth of the Prison.* Trans. Alan Sheridan. London: Allen Lane

Foucault, Michel (1990) *The Care of the Self: The History of Sexuality, vol. 3.* Trans. Robert Hurley. London: Penguin

Gatens, Moira (1996) *Imaginary Bodies: Ethics, Power and Corporeality.* London: Routledge

Gaukroger, Stephen (1995) *Descartes: An Intellectual Biography.* Oxford: Clarendon Press

Howard, Andrew (2001) A New Kind of Dialogue. *Adbusters: A Journal of the Mental Environment,* 9(5) np

Hunter, Ian (1993) Setting Limits to Culture. In: Graeme Turner (ed.) *Nation, Culture, Text: Australian Cultural Studies.* London: Routledge, 140–63

Kant, Immanuel (1978) [1798] *Anthropology from a Pragmatic Point of View.* Trans. V.L. Dowdell. Carbondale: Southern Illinois University Press

Larkin, Phillip (1993) [1974] This Be The Verse. In *Phillip Larkin: Collected Poems.* Edited and with an introduction by Anthony Thwaite. New York: Farrar, Strauss and Giroux/Noonday Press

Masson, Jeffrey Moussaieff (1988) *Against Therapy: Emotional Tyranny and the Myth of Psychological Healing.* New York: Atheneum

Miller, Toby (1993) *The Well-Tempered Self: Citizenship, Culture and the Postmodern Subject.* Baltimore: The Johns Hopkins University Press

Schiller, Friedrich von (1967) *The Æsthetic Education of Man in a Series of Letters.* Trans. E.M. Wilkinson and C.A. Willoughby. Oxford: Oxford University Press

Scruton, Roger (1984) *A Short History of Modern Philosophy: From Descartes to Wittgenstein.* London: Routledge

Smail, David (1998) *Taking Care: An Alternative to Therapy.* London: Constable

Smail, David (1999) Psychotherapy, Society and the Individual. Paper presented to the 'Ways with Words' Festival of Literature. Dartington, 12 July. Also available at: (www.nottm.freeserve.co.uk/talk99.htm)

Spinoza, Benedict de (1996) *Ethics.* Trans. E. Curley. London: Penguin

Wittgenstein, Ludwig (1965) Wittgenstein's Lecture on Ethics. *Philosophical Review,* 74, 3–12

Index